The Quilted Clothing Collection

A Family Workshop Book
By Ed & Stevie Baldwin

Chilton Book Company
Radnor, Pennsylvania

Published in Radnor, Pa. by Chilton Book Company
Library of Congress Catalog Card Number: 83-43304
ISBN: 0-8019-7507-7
Manufactured in the United States of America

Created by The Family Workshop, Inc.
Editorial Director: Janet Weberling
Editors: Rhonda Mulberry, Mary Milander, Suzi West, Mike McUsic
Art Director: Dale Crain
Illustrator: Verna Stonecipher-Fuller
Production Artists: Wanda Young, Janice Harris Burstall,
Roberta Taff, Paula Kempe, Eddy Simpson
Typography: Deborah Gahm
Creative Director: April Bail
Project Designs: April Bail, Stevie Baldwin, Janice McKinney, Vickie Holder-Martin
Photography: Bill Welch

1 2 3 4 5 6 7 8 9 0 3 2 1 0 9 8 7 6 5 4

This book is dedicated to
Myrtle E. Stonecipher,
a super-mom and seamstress
who never ran low on fabric scraps or love.

Preface

Patchwork quilting is no longer a required living skill, as it was in the days when fabric was scarce and every little scrap counted. But even in our modern "throw-away society," the craft thrives. Why? Because there's absolutely nothing like it! And fortunately for modern followers of the art, sewing machines and many other conveniences have eliminated the most tedious, time-consuming aspects.

This book is a celebration of both old and new quilting designs and techniques. If you're an old-fashioned sort, you'll enjoy using those fabric scraps and remnants that have been stashed away for a rainy day. You may even take the time to quilt by hand. If you're more convenience minded, you'll enjoy the fact that most of the projects can be machine stitched in very little time at all.

Each of the project plans contained in this book includes a materials list, step-by-step instructions, scale or full-size patterns, and assembly diagrams. The Tips & Techniques section at the end of the book provides information on basic terms and procedures for both normal sewing and patchwork quilting. We recommend that you read it before beginning work. The section of full-color photographs is a real delight, and will help you envision your finished garments.

We would like to offer special thanks to the folks at Necchi Corporation, who provided a spanking-new sewing machine that we used to make the projects; to Jeffrey's of Village Square, a local firm that loaned us some wonderful antique dress forms; and to Vickie Holder-Martin, who designed and made the amazing patchwork puzzle jacket.

Happy quilting!

Contents

Drop-Waist Dress 1
Acute Caftan 10
Beach Cover-Up & Tote 16
Gown & Robe 25
Winter Ensemble 41
Tiny Tot's Sunsuit & Hat 50
Appliqued Jacket & Vest 57
Pinafore & Bonnet 66
Christmas Vest 75
Take-Me-Home Ensemble 83
Summer Caftan 89
Puzzle Jacket 96
Tips & Techniques 125

Please read Tips & Techniques before beginning work.

Drop-Waist Dress

There's nothing that's quite as easy to wear, or as attractive a style to any figure, as a drop-waist dress. Popular demand probably is why the sultans of fashion keep bringing them back. Our version features a Seminole patchwork front accent, with ribbon trim at the front and sleeves. The assembly is very easy.

Materials

Patchwork fabrics: a 1½ x 45-inch strip of each of four different fabrics, and a 3 x 45-inch strip of each of two different fabrics (We used lightweight cotton fabrics in peach calico, light peach, violet, and beige calico for the narrower strips; and in Kelly green and purple for the wider strips.)

⅜-inch-wide satin ribbon: 1 yard each of two different colors, and 2 yards each of two additional colors (We used 1 yard each of violet and peach, and 2 yards each of Kelly green and purple.)

3 yards of 44- or 45-inch-wide fabric for the dress (We used a lightweight, ivory-colored cotton.)

⅛ yard of 36-inch-wide lightweight lining fabric

Thread to match the dress fabric and the ribbon colors

Assembling the Patchwork

1. This is a typical Seminole patchwork assembly. Begin by sewing together the six patchwork fabric strips, side by side, as shown in **Figure A**. The seams should be ⅜ inch wide, and the wider strips should go on the outside, as shown. (Refer to the instructions for Seminole patchwork in the Tips & Techniques section of this book, if you're unclear on how to go about sewing together the strips.) We have indicated the arrangement of fabrics that we used. Press all of the seam allowances in one direction.

Figure A

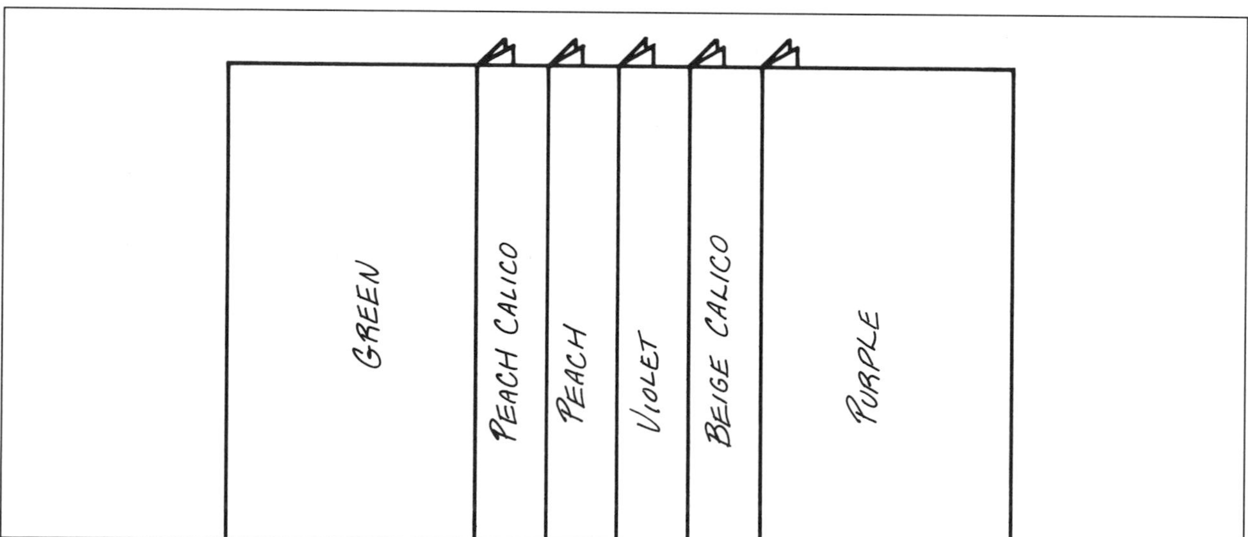

2. Cut across the assembled strips at 1½-inch intervals, as shown in **Figure B**, to create the Seminole strips. You should be able to get thirty Seminole strips from the assembly.

3. Stitch together the Seminole strips side by side, offsetting each row by one patchwork square, as shown in **Figure C**. These seams should also be ⅜ inch wide. Keep the color progression the same in each row, as shown. (We have used abbreviations for the colors, i.e., G = green, PC = peach calico, Pe = peach, etc..) Press all of the seam allowances in one direction.

4. Place the assembled patchwork wrong side up on a flat surface. Cut a 2¾ x 36-inch strip of lining fabric and place it on top of the patchwork, adjusting it so that the long zigzag edges of the patchwork extend equally beyond each side of the lining strip. Trim the side edges of the patchwork, so that each extends ⅜ inch beyond the side edge of the lining strip.

5. Press a ⅜-inch-wide allowance to the wrong side of the patchwork along each side edge. Pin the patchwork to the lining strip, placing the wrong side of the patchwork against the lining fabric, and aligning the long side edges. Stitch through all layers, ¼ inch from each long edge.

Cutting the Dress Pieces

1. A diagram of the Dress Front and Back pattern is

Figure B

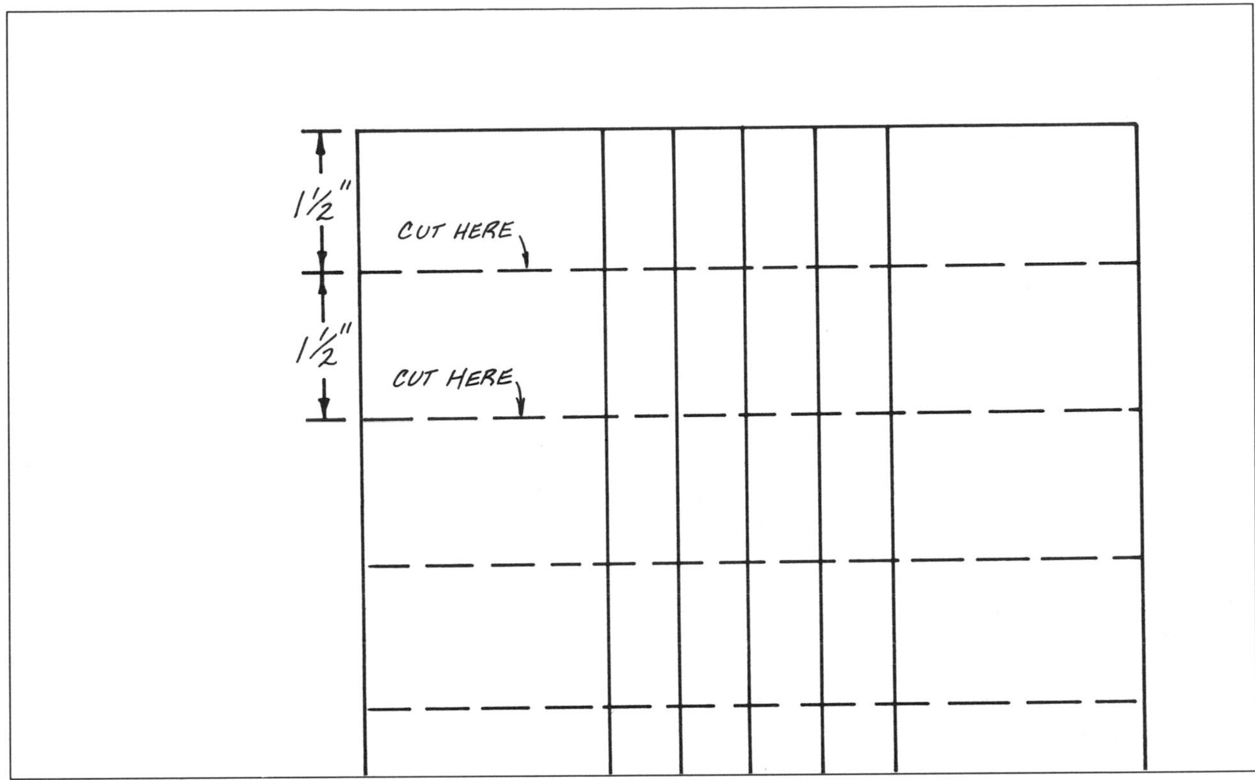

Figure C

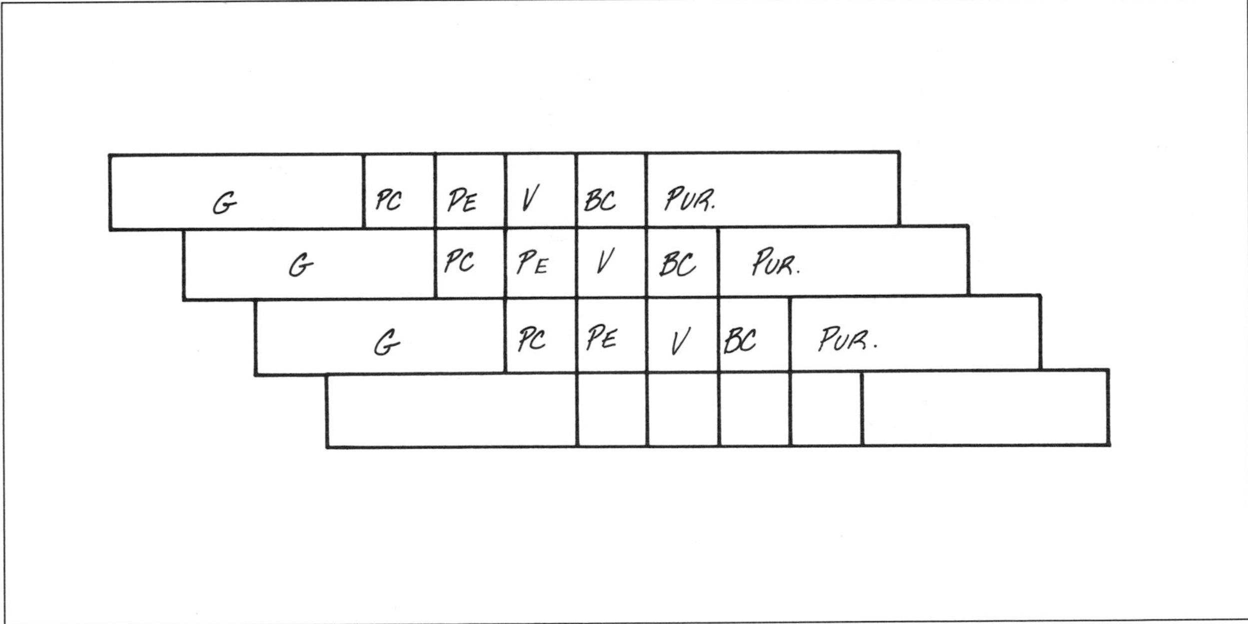

Figure D

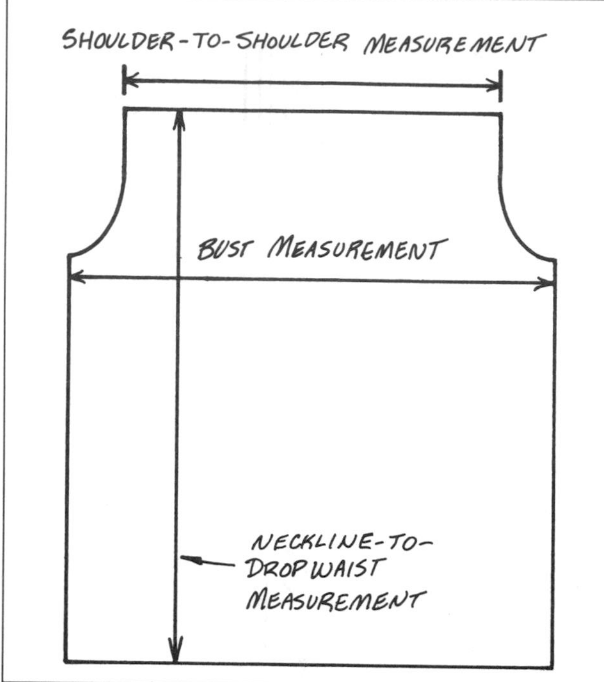

Figure E

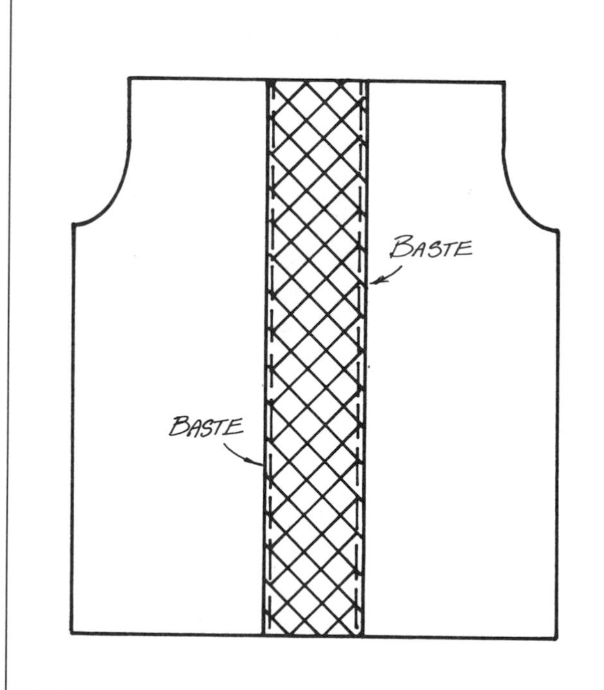

provided in **Figure D**. As you can see, it's quite simple. Make a full-size paper pattern, referring to the Tips & Techniques section of this book if you need help determining the armhole curves. The width of the pattern is the same from below the armholes to the lower edge, but if your hip measurement is larger than your bust measurement, you'll need to make the pattern wider at the bottom. Note that the lower edge should fall where you want the drop-waist line to be, which normally is a few inches below one's hips. Don't forget to add a ½-inch seam allowance to each edge of the pattern. (**Note:** The pattern is symetrical from side to side, so you can make a left- or right-half pattern and place the vertical center line on a fold of doubled fabric when you cut the pieces.)

2. Make a full-size Sleeve pattern, referring to Tips & Techniques for a basic shape and instructions. We made the sleeves rather puffy, which requires a sharp curve at the upper edge of the pattern, as indicated in the Tips. The sleeve should be about 2 inches shorter than elbow length. The lower edge of the sleeve should be about twice as long as a measurement taken around your arm, 2 inches above the elbow, because it will be gathered and attached to a border. Be sure to add a ½-inch seam allowance to each edge of the pattern.

3. A gathered flounce is sewn to the lower edge of the dress, and a lower border is sewn to the bottom of the flounce, to achieve the total desired length of the dress. You will need to cut two rectangular Flounce pieces, each the same size. To determine the dimensions of the Flounce pieces, fill in the blanks below.

a. desired length (neck to hem) = ____ inches
b. step a minus length of Dress pattern = ____ inches
c. step b minus 2 inches = ____ inches

The answer you arrived at in step c will be the width of each Flounce piece. To determine the length, first measure the width of the Dress Front pattern at the lower edge. (If you made a half pattern, be sure to double the width for this measurement.) Multiply this measurement by 2½, and you have the length of each Flounce piece – they must be quite long, to allow for the gathers. Fill in the blanks on the next page, for reference when you cut the pieces.

Flounce pieces:

Width = ____ inches
Length = ____ inches

4. There will be two rectangular Lower Border pieces. Each Lower Border piece should be 5 inches wide. The length must be the same as the length of each Flounce piece. Fill in the blanks below, for reference when you cut the pieces.

Lower Border pieces:

Width = 5 inches
Length = ____ inches

5. The neckline is a boatneck design, so the upper edges of the front and back dress pieces are finished with straight, rectangular Neckline Border pieces. The front and back Neckline Border pieces are identical. Each should be 4¼ inches wide. The length must be the same as the width of the Dress Front pattern, measured along the upper edge. (Double the width, if you made a half pattern.) Fill in the blanks below:

Neckline Border pieces:

Width = 4¼ inches
Length = ____ inches

6. The lower edge of each sleeve is bordered as well. Each Sleeve Border piece should be 4½ inches wide. The length is determined by the measurement around your arm, 2 inches above the elbow. Measure your arm, and add 2 inches for "breathing room" and seam allowances. Fill in the blanks below:

Sleeve Border pieces:

Width = 4½ inches
Length = ____ inches

7. You now have all the patterns and dimensions you need. Cut the pieces as listed below, from the fabric you have chosen for the dress:

Front/Back – cut two, using pattern
Sleeve – cut two, using pattern
Flounce – cut two, (dimensions from step 3)
Lower Border – cut two, (dimensions from step 4)
Neckline Border – cut two, (dimensions from step 5)
Sleeve Border – cut two, (dimensions from step 6)

Figure F

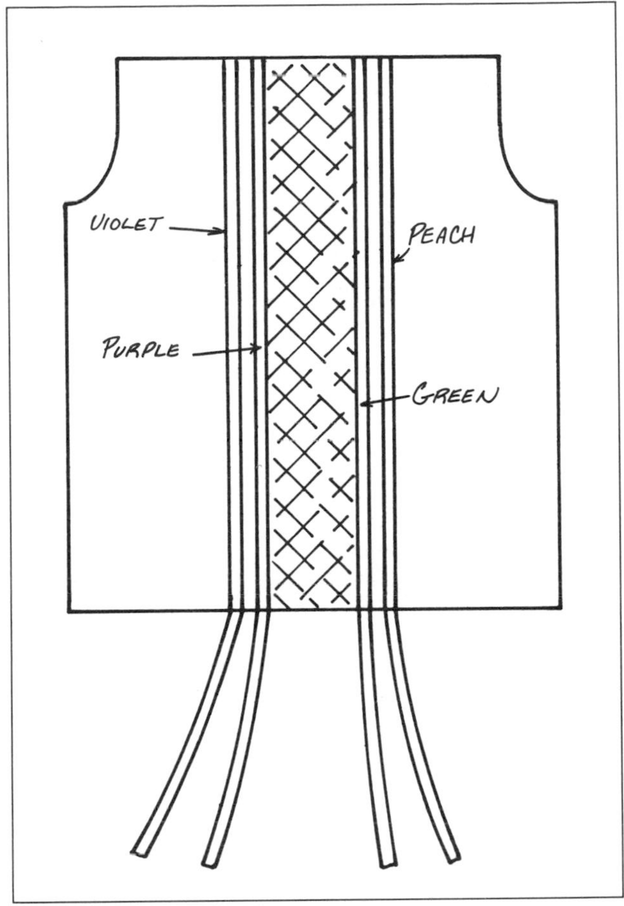

Attaching the Trim

1. Place the Dress Front piece right side up on a flat surface. Place the lined patchwork on top, right side up, along the vertical center line of the Dress Front (**Figure E**). Trim the ends of the patchwork and lining even with the upper and lower edges of the Dress piece, and pin the patchwork in place. Baste close to each edge of the patchwork.

2. For the ribbon trim, use the two 1-yard lengths of ribbon, and a 1-yard length cut from each of the two longer ribbons. The ribbons are sewn to the Dress Front piece as shown in **Figure F**. Place one ribbon (we used green) on top of the patchwork, so that the outer edge of the ribbon lies just outside one edge of the patchwork. The upper end of the ribbon should be even with

Figure G

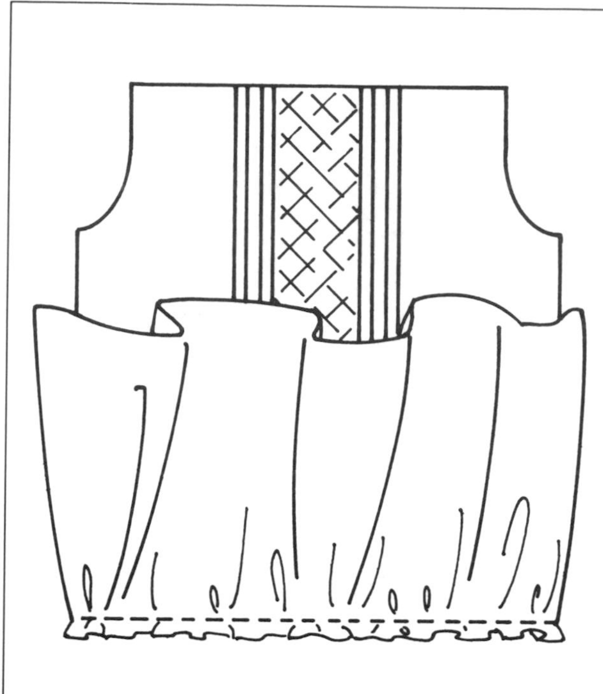

Figure H

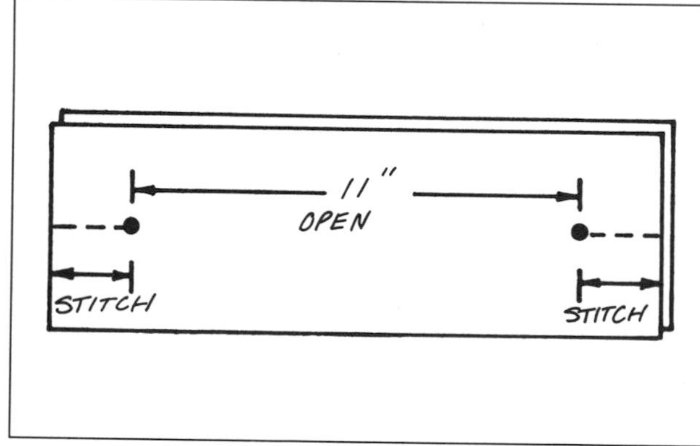

the upper edges of the patchwork and the Dress piece. The lower end of the ribbon will extend well past the lower edge of the Dress piece, but do not cut it off. Topstitch the ribbon in place close to each long edge and the upper end. Topstitch across the ribbon ¾ inch above the lower edge of the patchwork. Pull the lower end of the ribbon up onto the patchwork, and pin it there temporarily to keep it out of the way.

3. Pin a second ribbon (we used peach) to the Dress Front piece, about ½ inch from the first one, as shown in **Figure F**. Topstitch as you did for the first ribbon.

4. Topstitch a third ribbon (we used purple) to the patchwork and Dress piece as you did the first ribbon, covering the remaining long edge of the patchwork, as shown. Topstitch the fourth ribbon (violet) to the Dress piece, ½ inch from the third ribbon, as shown. Pin the lower ends of all ribbons to the patchwork.

Assembling the Dress

1. Gather one long edge of each Flounce piece, between the seam allowances at the ends, so that the gathered edge is the same length as the lower edge of the Dress Front piece. (See Tips & Techniques if you do not know how to make gathers.) Adjust the gathers evenly and baste them in place.

2. One Flounce piece is sewn to the lower edge of the Dress Front, as shown in **Figure G**. Pin the Flounce piece to the Dress Front piece, placing right sides together and aligning the gathered edge of the Flounce with the lower edge of the Dress Front. Be sure that the ribbons are out of the way of the seam line, and stitch the seam as shown. Press the seam allowances toward the Dress piece.

3. Pin and then stitch the remaining gathered Flounce piece to the lower edge of the Dress Back piece in the same manner.

4. The Neckline Border pieces are first stitched together to form the neck opening, and are then attached to the front and back dress assemblies. Pin the two Neckline Border pieces right sides together. Run a short line of straight machine stitches along the lengthwise center line, from each end toward the center as shown in **Figure H**. The stitching lines should be of equal lengths, and the unstitched space between them should be about 11 inches – long enough to accommodate your head, as shown.

5. Fold one of the Neckline Border pieces in half lengthwise, placing wrong sides together. Pin together the two long edges of this piece. Do the same with the other Neckline Border piece. The resulting assembly should look like the one shown in **Figure I**. Baste ⅜ inch from each pair of aligned long edges. To reinforce

Figure I

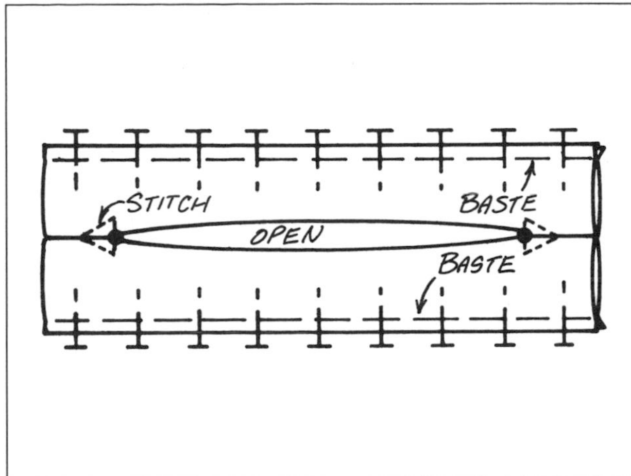

Figure J

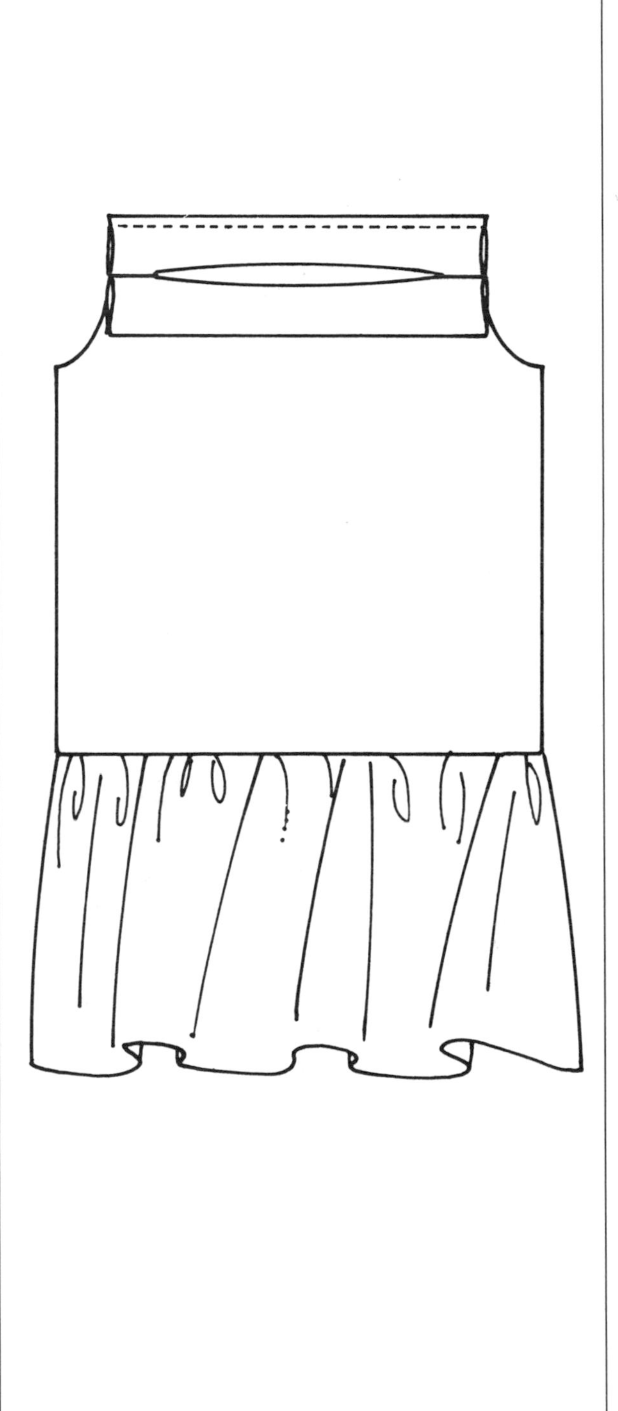

the ends of the neck opening, use a short straight machine setting and stitch in a triangular pattern at each end of the opening, as shown. Remove the pins and press the border assembly.

6. Place the dress back assembly right side up on a flat surface. Place the neckline border assembly on top, aligning one basted edge of the border assembly with the upper edge of the dress. Pin and then stitch the seam, as shown in **Figure J**. Press all seam allowances toward the border assembly. Follow the same procedures to stitch the opposite basted edge of the border assembly to the upper edge of the dress front assembly. Be sure that you place the same side of the border assembly against the right side of the dress front as you did against the right side of the dress back.

Adding the Sleeves

1. Gather the curved upper edge of one Sleeve piece, so that it will fit the armhole edge of the dress. Adjust the gathers evenly.

2. Pin and then stitch the gathered Sleeve piece to the dress assembly, placing right sides together and aligning the gathered edge of the Sleeve with the armhole edge on one side of the dress (**Figure K**). Press the seam allowances toward the dress.

3. Repeat the procedures in steps 1 and 2 to gather the second Sleeve piece and stitch it to the armhole opening at the other side of the dress assembly.

Figure K

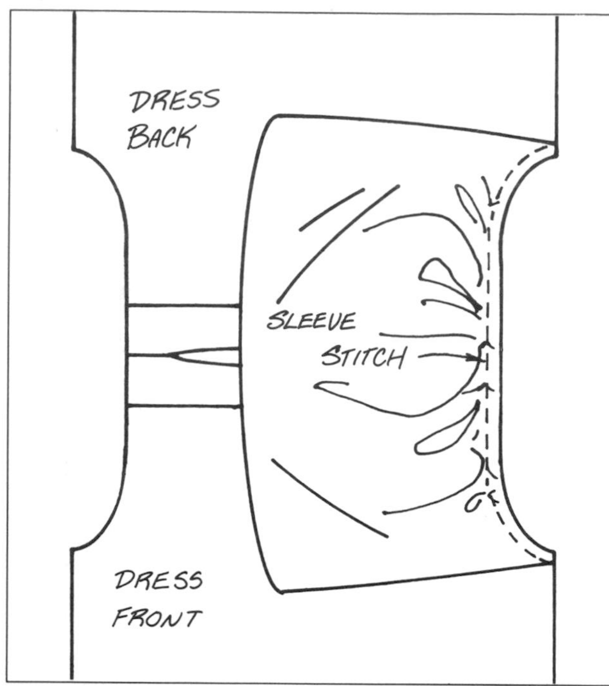

Figure L

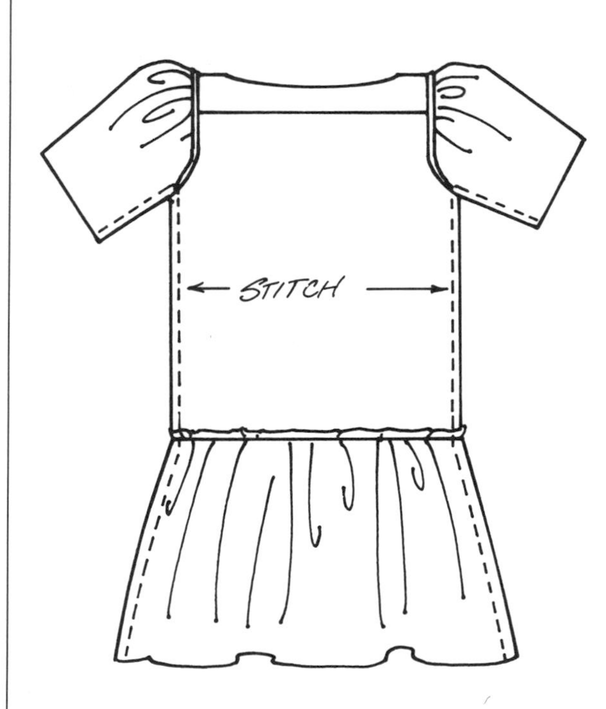

Figure M

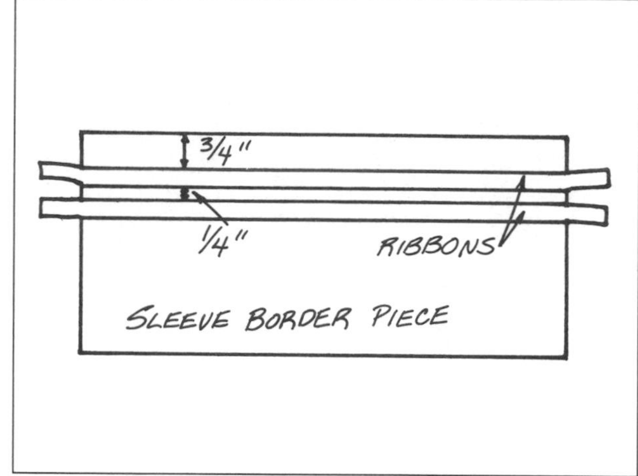

Figure N

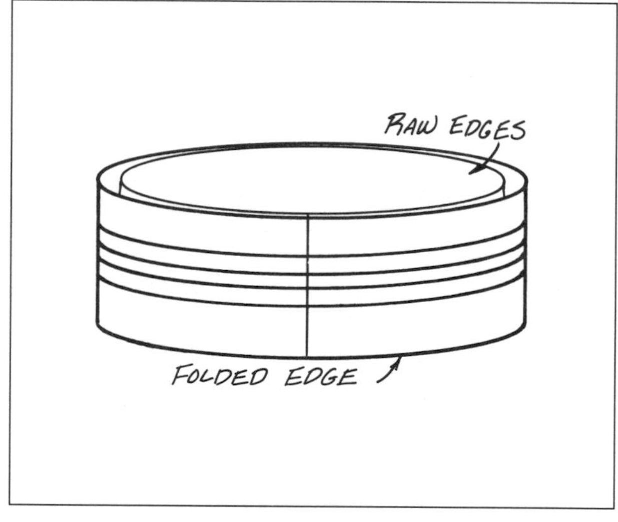

4. Fold the dress front and back sections right sides together, and stitch the underarm and side seam on each side, as shown in **Figure L**. Press the seams open.

5. We added ribbon trim to each sleeve border. You should have two lengths of ribbon left over. Cut each length in half to form two shorter pieces. Use one of each color for each sleeve border.

6. Place one length of ribbon lengthwise along the right side of one Sleeve Border piece, ¾ inch from one long edge as shown in **Figure M**. Cut off the ends of the ribbon even with the ends of the border piece. Stitch the ribbon in place, close to each long edge.

Stitch a second ribbon to the same Sleeve Border piece as shown, 1/4 inch from the first one.

7. Fold the border assembly in half widthwise, placing right sides together, and stitch the seam across the aligned ends. Press the seam open. You should now have a small cylinder.

8. Fold this cylinder in half, placing wrong sides together, so that you have a double-layered cylinder only half as wide as before, with the two long raw edges aligned (**Figure N**). Baste close to the aligned raw edges, all the way around the cylinder. Turn the cylinder so that the ribbons are on the inside.

9. Turn the dress right side out. Gather the lower edge of one sleeve, so that a measurement taken around the end of the sleeve is the same as the measurement around the basted edge of the border cylinder. Adjust the gathers evenly, and slip the border assembly up over the end of the sleeve. The raw edges of the border assembly should be even with the lower raw edge of the sleeve, and the folded edge of the border assembly should extend up toward the top of the sleeve. Rotate the border around the sleeve until the existing underarm and border seams are aligned. Stitch the seam around the border and sleeve as shown in **Figure O**. Turn the border assembly downward, and press the seam allowances toward the border.

10. Repeat the procedures in steps 6 through 9 to make a second border assembly and attach it to the other dress sleeve.

Figure O

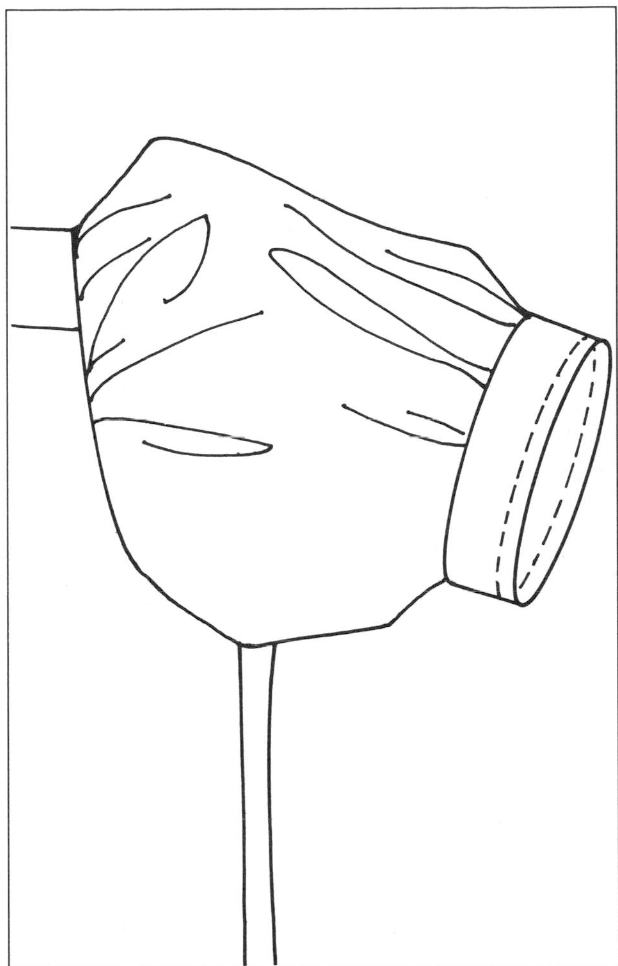

Adding the Lower Border

1. Piece together the two Lower Border pieces end to end. (See Tips & Techniques if you're not certain how to go about this.) Fold the resulting long strip in half widthwise, placing right sides together, and stitch the seam across the aligned ends. You should now have a very large cylinder.

2. Fold the cylinder in half, placing wrong sides together as you did the sleeve borders. You should now have a double-layered cylinder only half as wide as before, with the long raw edges aligned. Baste close to the long raw edges, all the way around the cylinder.

3. Slip the border assembly up over the lower edge of the flounce, so that the raw edges of the border are aligned with the lower raw edge of the flounce. The folded edge of the border should extend up toward the top of the flounce. Rotate the border so that the seams are aligned with the flounce side seams, and then stitch the seam all the way around the border and flounce. Turn the border downward, and press the seam allowances toward the dress.

Finishing Touch

Remove the pins that are holding the lower ends of the dress-front ribbons. Tie a half-knot in each ribbon, at the level of the dress-to-flounce seam. Cut the lower end of each ribbon at an angle, and tie a half-knot near the end.

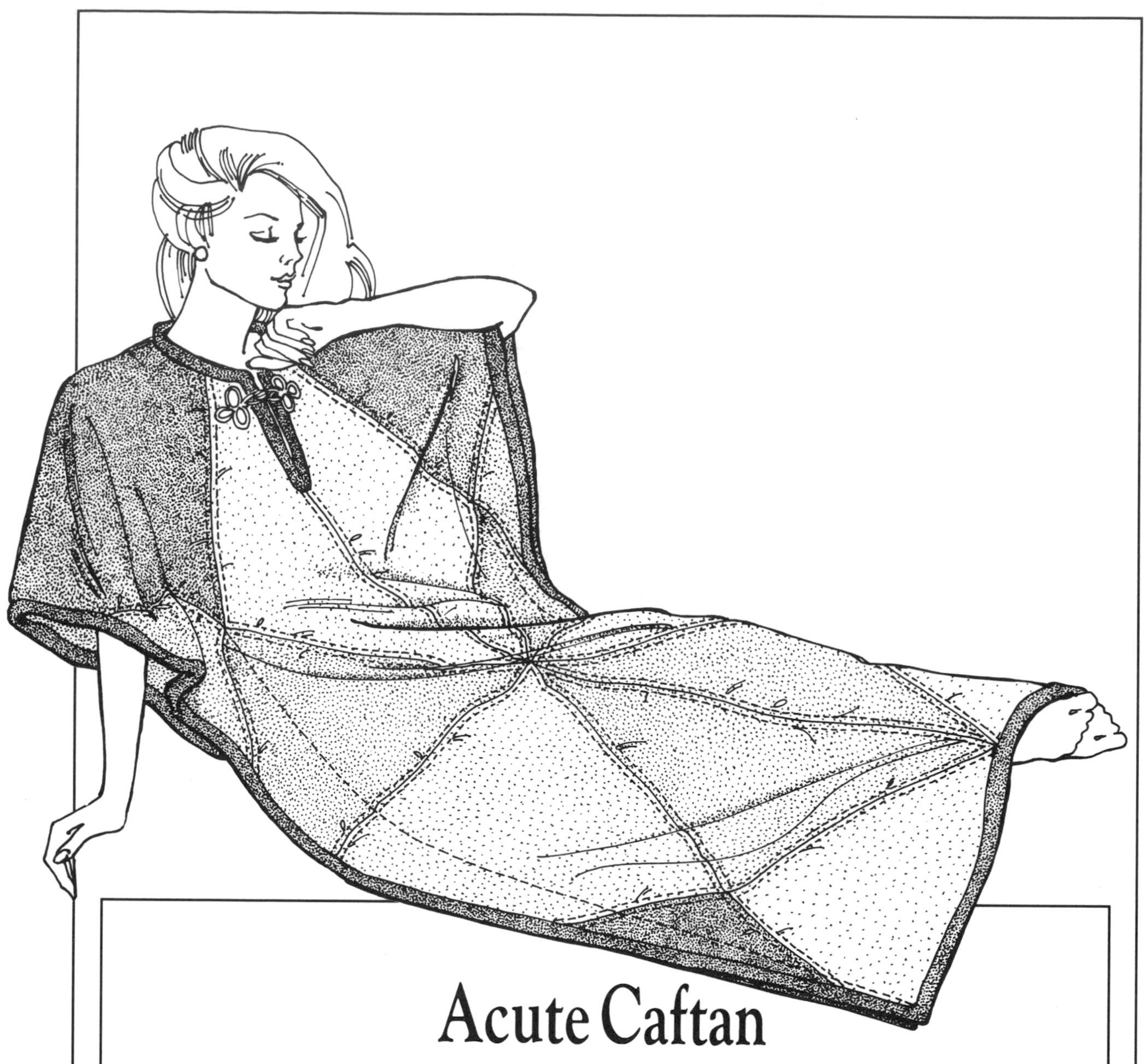

Acute Caftan

Pardon our pun, but we just had to name this attractive caftan after the acute triangles that make up the patchwork. (Remember your plane geometry?) Mathematics aside, the caftan requires only one pattern piece, and can be assembled in a single, pleasurable afternoon. One size fits all.

1 square = 1 inch **Figure A**

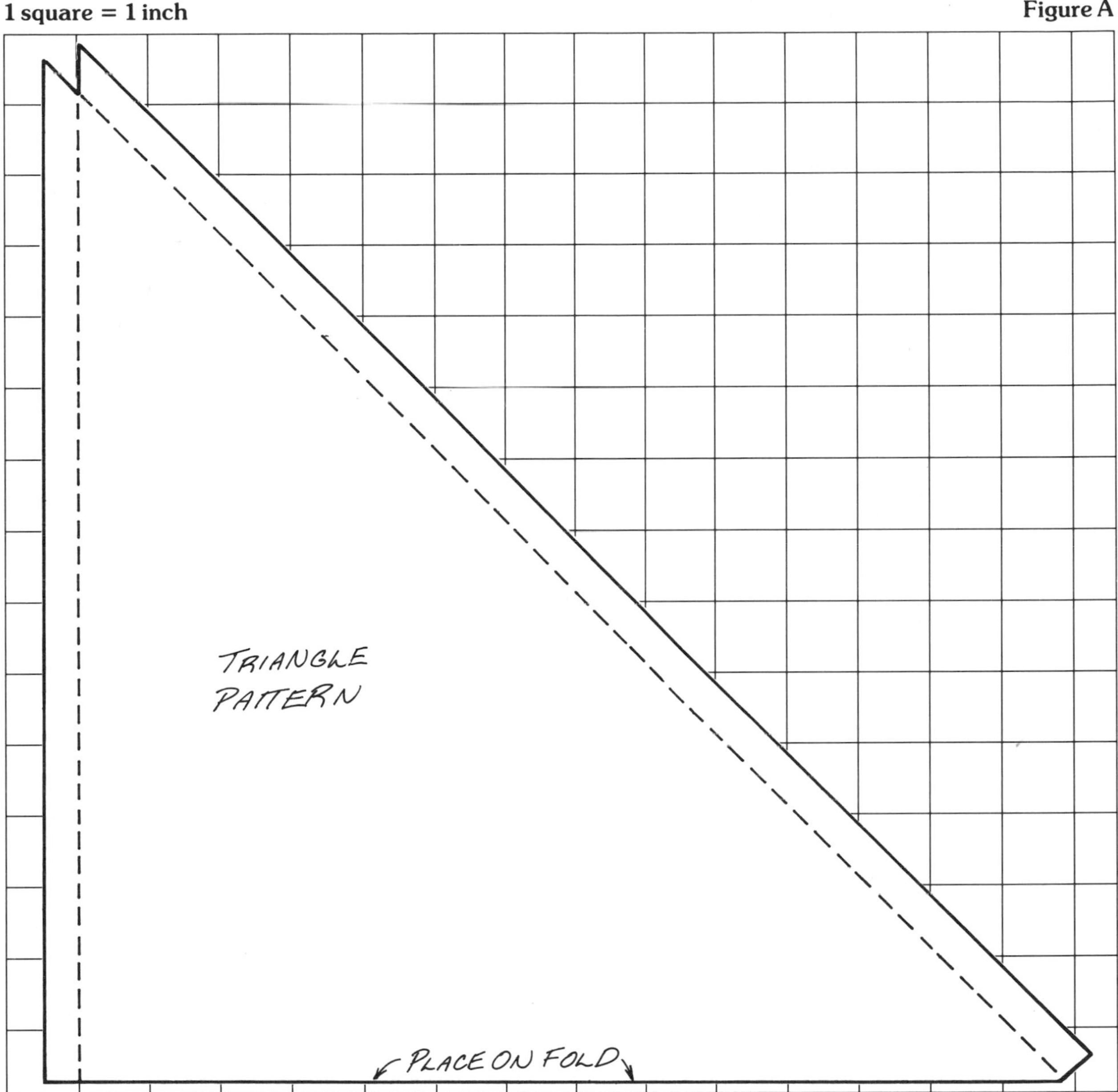

Materials

8 yards of 45-inch-wide polished cotton fabric for the patchwork triangles (We used 2 yards each of navy blue, sky blue, light gray, and fuchsia.)
3½ yards of 45-inch-wide contrasting polished cotton fabric for the lining (We used violet.)
3½ yards of lightweight quilt batting
10 yards of wide blanket binding (We used navy blue.)
1½ yards of seam binding tape (We used navy blue.)
One frog closure
Thread to coordinate with the fabrics

Figure B

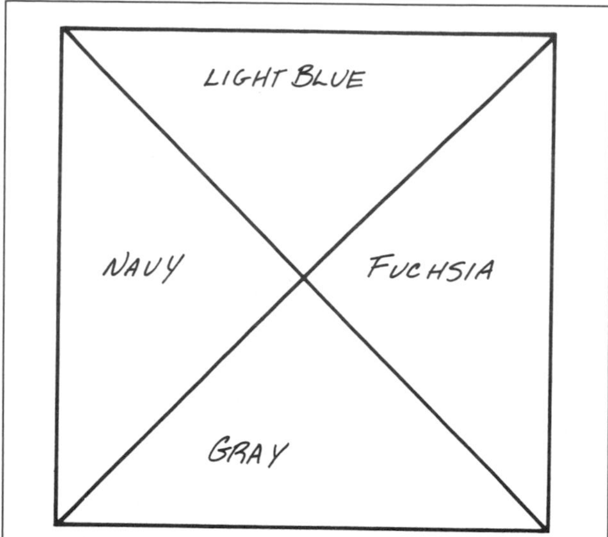

Figure C

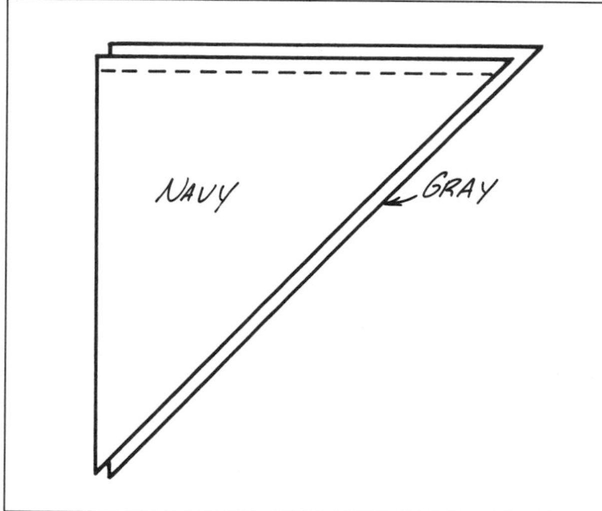

Assembling the Patchwork

Note: All seams are ½-inch wide unless otherwise specified in the instructions.

1. The patchwork is assembled in groups of squares, each formed by four triangles. A scale drawing for the triangle pattern is provided in **Figure A**. Enlarge the drawing to make a full-size pattern, and use it to cut eight pieces from each of the four colors of fabric.

Figure D

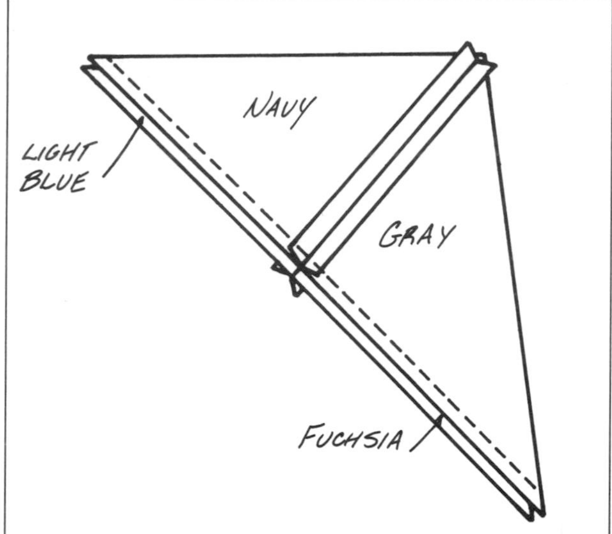

2. One complete square is shown in **Figure B**. To make this square, place a gray and a navy triangle right sides together and stitch the seam along one short edge (**Figure C**). Press the seam open. Stitch together a fuchsia and a light blue triangle in the same manner.

3. Place the two halves of the square right sides together, and stitch the seam along the long edge (**Figure D**). Press the seam open.

4. Make three additional squares, each identical to the first one, in the same manner. We'll call these the "first squares."

5. Make four additional squares in the same manner, changing the color arrangement as shown in **Figure E**. We'll call these the "second squares."

6. You may want to enlist the aid of the local puzzle-cube expert for this step. The patchwork squares are stitched together to form two larger squares, and then the larger squares are stitched together to form a single large rectangle, two squares wide and four squares long. One of the large squares is shown in **Figure F**. Arrange two of the first squares and two of the second squares as shown, before you start stitching them together. You will have to rotate two of the squares to get the colors in the correct positions. When you have achieved the proper arrangement, pin the two lower squares right sides together and stitch the seam along the fuchsia triangles. Press the seam open. Stitch together the two upper squares in the same manner, along the gray triangles. Now place the two rows right sides together, and stitch the seam along the long horizontal center edge. The resulting large square should look exactly like the one in **Figure F**.

7. Assemble the four remaining squares to form an identical large square.

8. Place the two large squares right sides together and stitch the seam along the navy triangles (**Figure G**).

Quilting

1. Place the lining fabric wrong side up on a flat surface. Cut a matching piece of quilt batting and place it on top of the lining fabric. Place the assembled patchwork right side up on top of the stack, and pin all three layers together.

2. Baste the layers together from the center to each corner, from the center to the middle of each edge, and close to each outer edge. Trim the batting and lining layers even with the patchwork.

Figure E

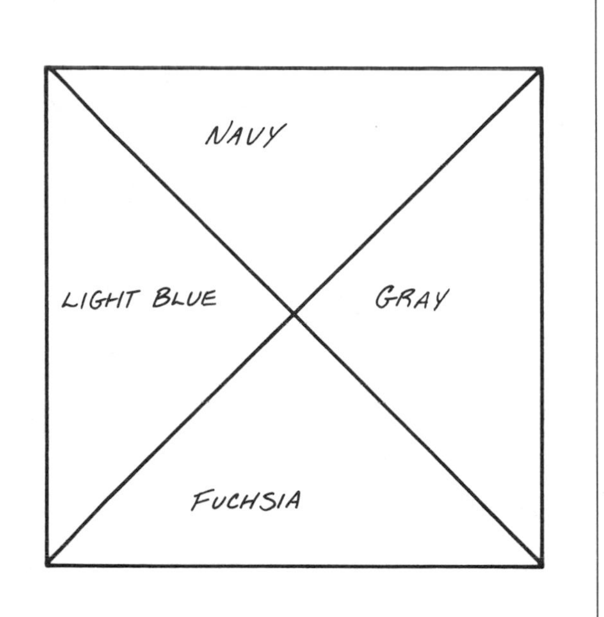

Figure F

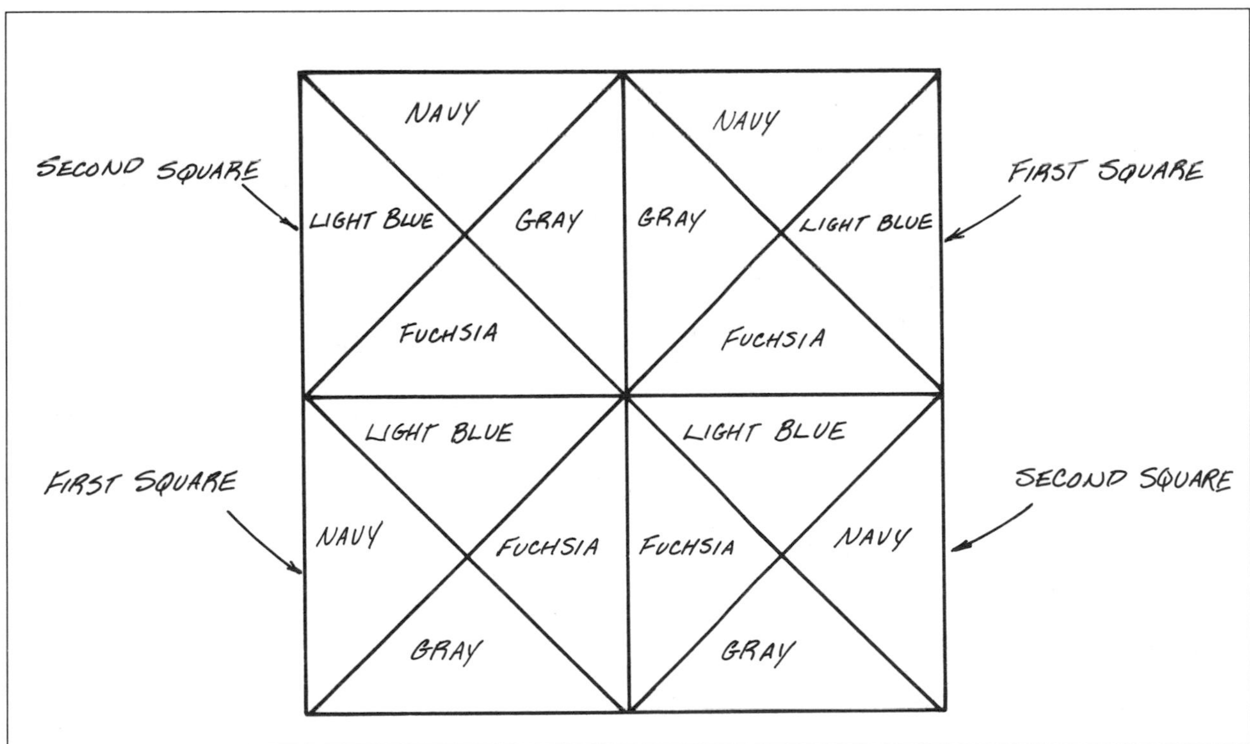

Figure G

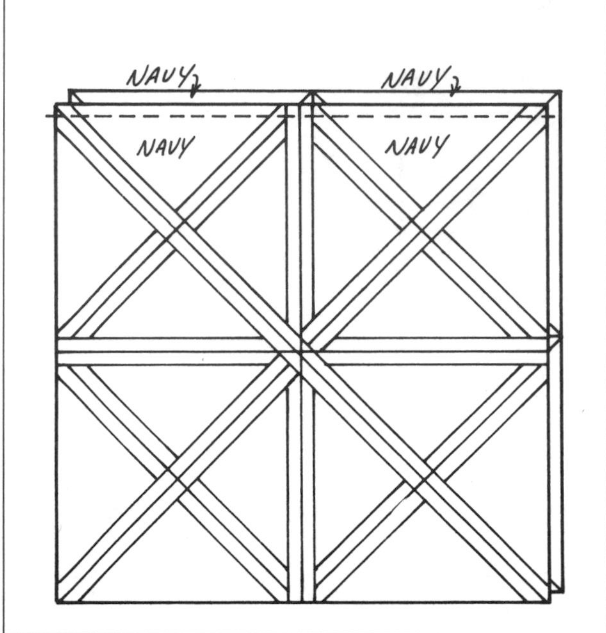

Figure H

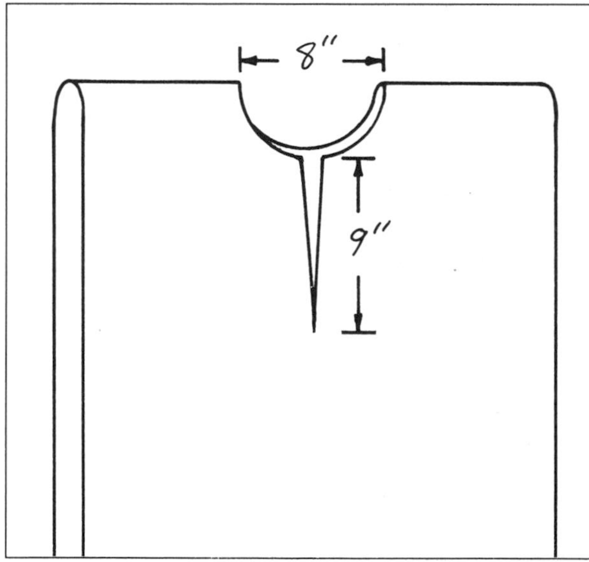

3. To quilt, stitch by hand or machine through all thicknesses, ½ inch from each existing seam, along all edges of each triangle. When you have finished, remove the basting from the center of the assembly, but do not remove the basting near the outer edges.

Figure I

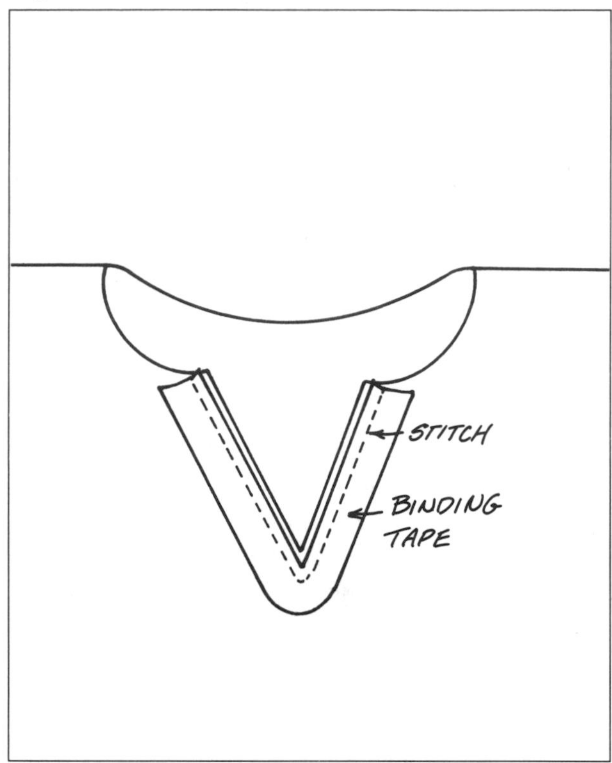

Finishing

1. To create the neck opening, fold the caftan in half widthwise along the center patchwork seam, placing wrong sides together. Cut an 8-inch-diameter semi-circle from the center, as shown in **Figure H**. To create the front opening, cut a 9-inch-long slit along the vertical center front seam, from the neck opening downward, as shown.

2. Cut one 20-inch length and one 26-inch length of seam binding tape. Press each length open. Use the shorter strip to bind the edges of the front slit. (Refer to **Figure I** for the preliminary step, and proceed as specified in the Tips & Techniques section of this book for encasing raw edges with binding tape.) Trim the ends of the strip even with the neck edge.

3. Use the longer strip to bind the neck edge of the caftan, leaving equal extensions of the strip at each front corner of the neck opening. Finish the ends of this strip as specified in Tips & Techniques.

Figure J

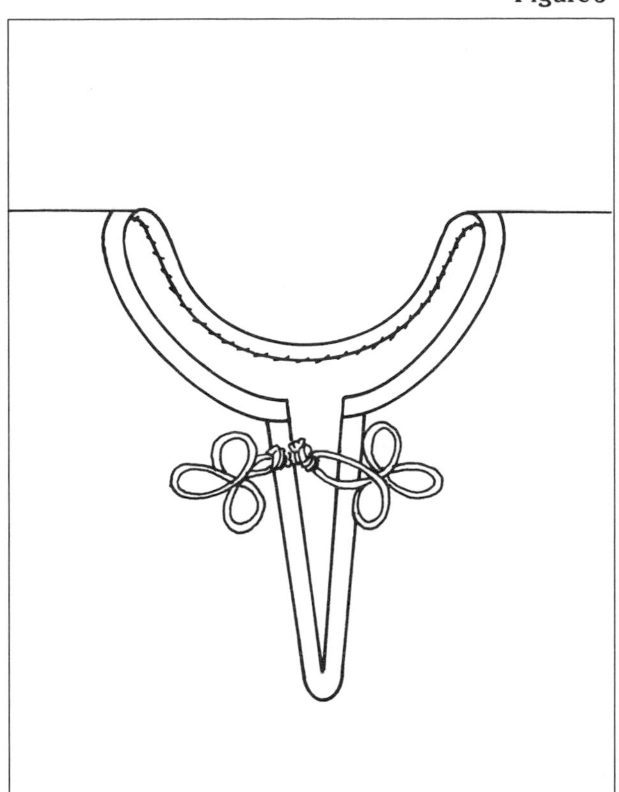

Figure K

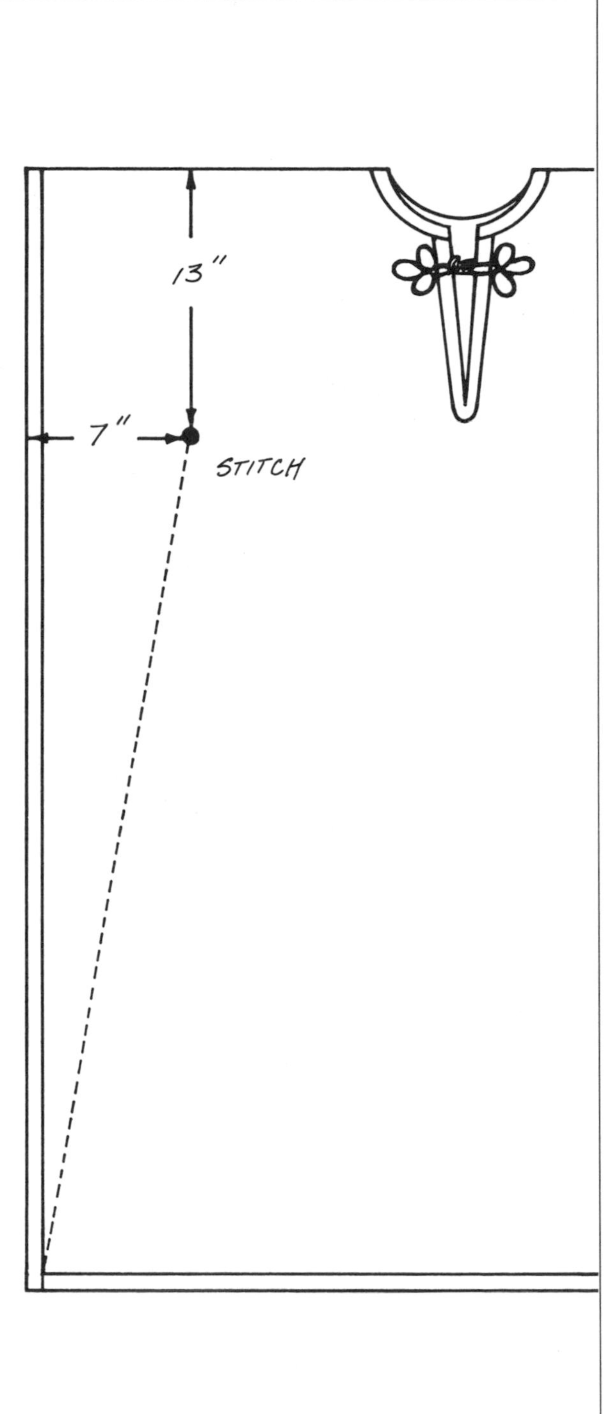

4. Stitch the frog closure to the top of the neck opening as shown in **Figure J**.

5. Use the blanket binding to encase all outer edges of the caftan, following the same procedures as you did to bind the slit and neck edges. Bind the two short edges first, and trim the ends of these binding strips even with the side edges of the caftan. Bind the two long side edges next, finishing the ends of these strips in the same manner as you did the ends of the neck binding strip.

6. All that's left to do is to stitch the side seams. Fold the caftan in half widthwise, placing wrong sides together. Measure 13 inches down from the shoulder fold, and 7 inches in from one side edge, as shown in **Figure K**, and mark this point. Topstitch through all thicknesses, from the marked point down to the lower corner on that side. Stitch the other side seam in the same manner, and then crawl inside your acute caftan for a nice, long snooze.

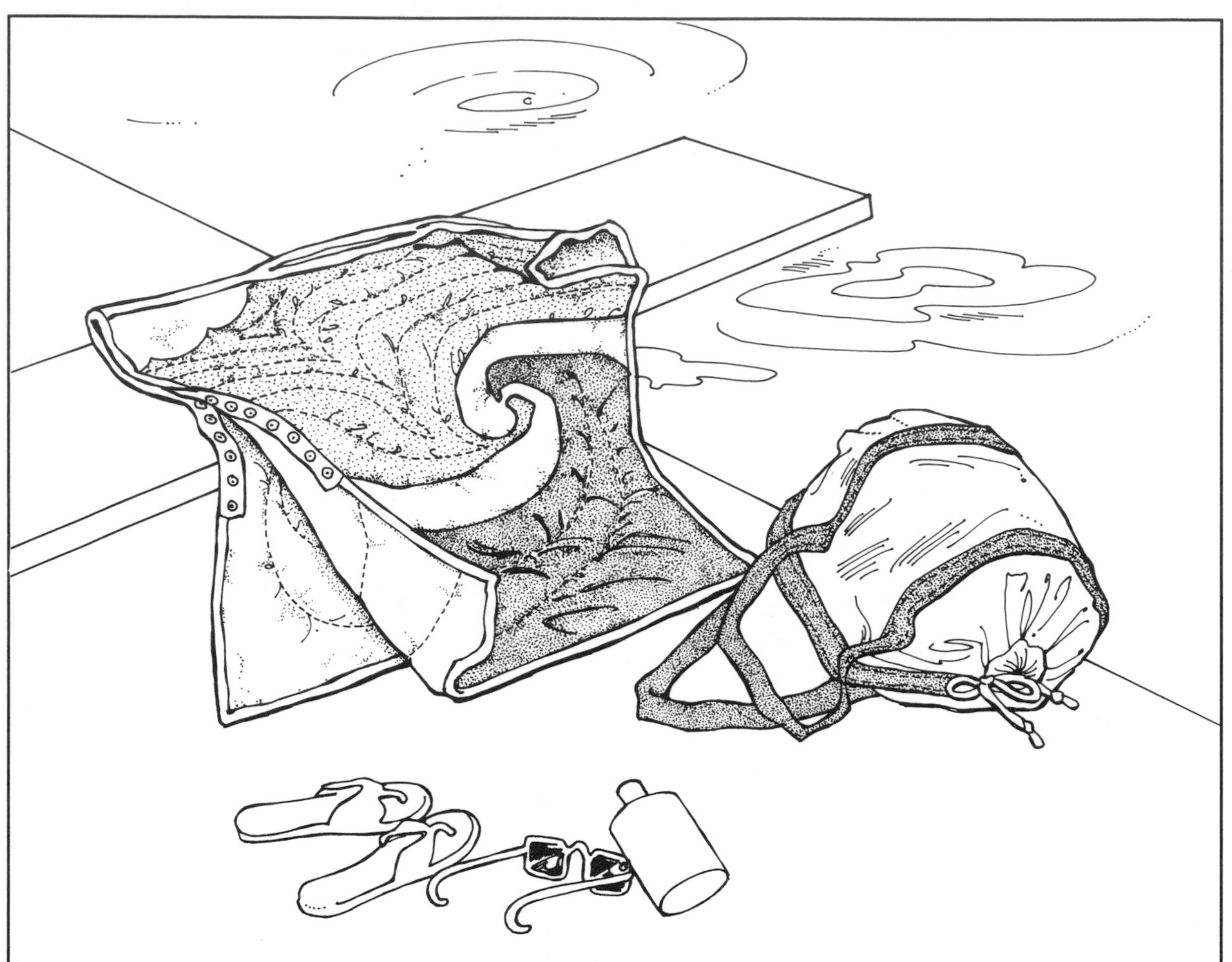

Beach Cover-Up & Tote

If the beach or pool ranks high on your summer agenda, you'll love this dreamy cover-up and convenient tote! Both are easy to make from lightweight terry. The quilted cover-up features colorful wave contours that evoke images of the sea and sky, and side closures that allow you to spread it flat for use as a beach towel.

Materials

Note: We have specified the colors of terry cloth that we used for this project. If you wish to use others, simply purchase the specified amount of each substitute color. We used lightweight nylon terry, because it makes a very lightweight garment and feels so nice next to the skin. You may prefer to use cotton terry, which is more absorbent but also is heavier and not as soft.

4½ yards of 36-inch-wide white terry cloth
1½ yards of 36-inch-wide aqua terry cloth
2 yards of 36-inch-wide dark blue terry cloth
1¾ yards of white heavy-duty snap tape or nylon fastener tape
1¾ yards of ⅜-inch-diameter white nylon cord
Two 34 x 36-inch pieces of fleece batting
Regular sewing thread to match the fabrics, or you can do all the stitching using white thread

THE COVER-UP

Cutting the Pieces

1. Cut two rectangles from the aqua-colored terry, each 24 x 34 inches.

2. Cut the pieces listed below from white terry. A cutting diagram is provided in **Figure A**.

Tote – 26 x 36 inches, cut one
Backing – 34 x 36 inches, cut two
Large White Wave – 15 x 34 inches, cut two
Binding Strips – 2 x 37 inches, cut four
Binding Strips – 2 x 34 inches, cut four
Triangular White Wave – 9 x 12 inches, cut two

3. Cut the pieces listed below from dark blue terry. A cutting diagram is provided in **Figure B**.

Strap – 4 x 68 inches, cut two
Dark Blue Wave – 20 x 34 inches, cut two
Side Trim – 4 x 39 inches, cut two
End Trim – 4 x 26 inches, cut two

4. Scale drawings for the wave contour patterns are provided in **Figure C**. Enlarge the drawings to make full-size patterns.

5. Place one of the terry Large White Wave pieces

Figure A

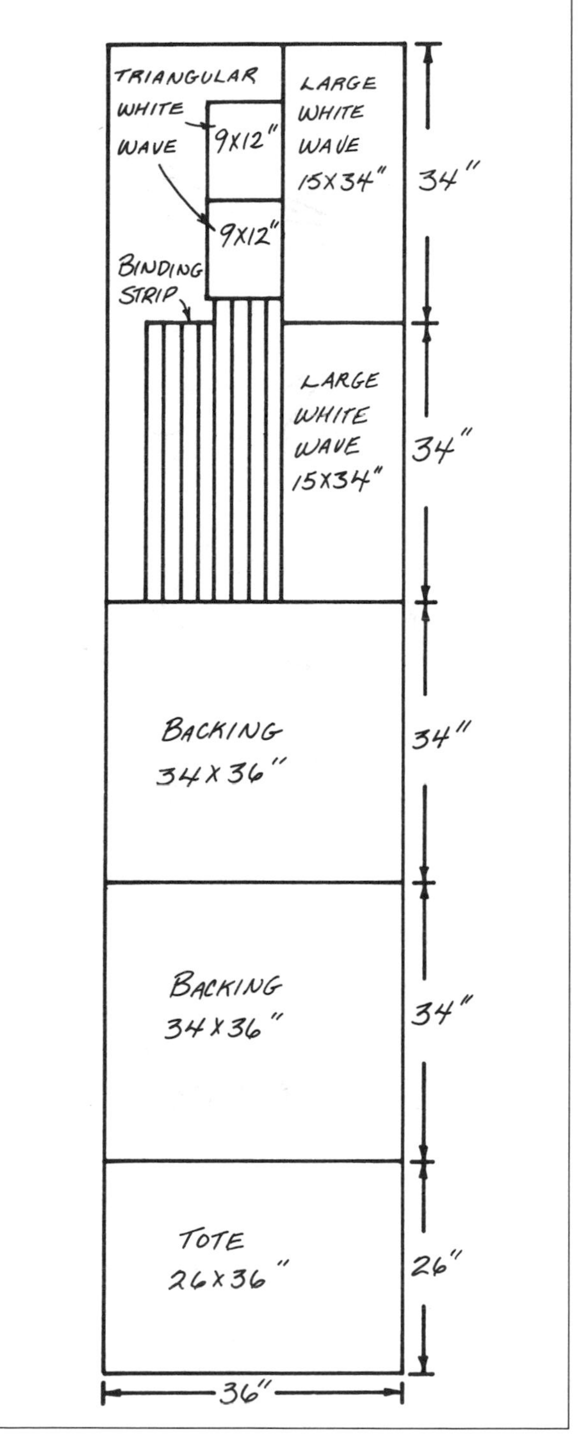

Figure B

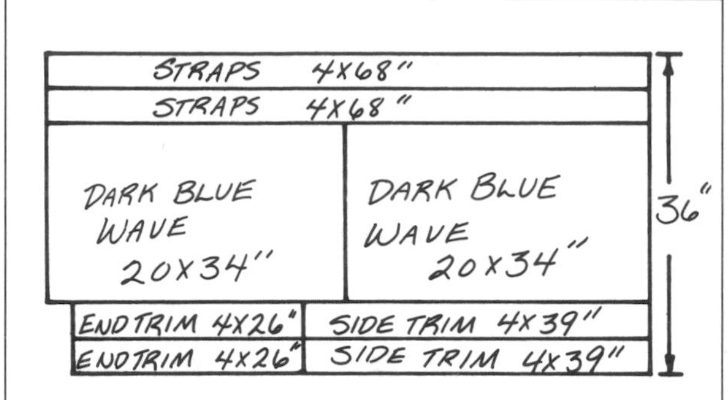

right side up on a flat surface. Pin the Large White Wave contour pattern on top, placing it close to one long edge as shown in **Figure D**. Cut the fabric along the wave contour.

6. Repeat the procedures in step 5 to contour the remaining terry Large White Wave piece.

7. Follow the same procedures to cut a contour along one long edge of each terry Dark Blue Wave piece, using the pattern for the Dark Blue Wave contour.

8. Use the pattern for the Triangular White Wave to contour the two terry Triangular White Wave pieces that you cut in step 2.

Figure C

1 square = 1 inch

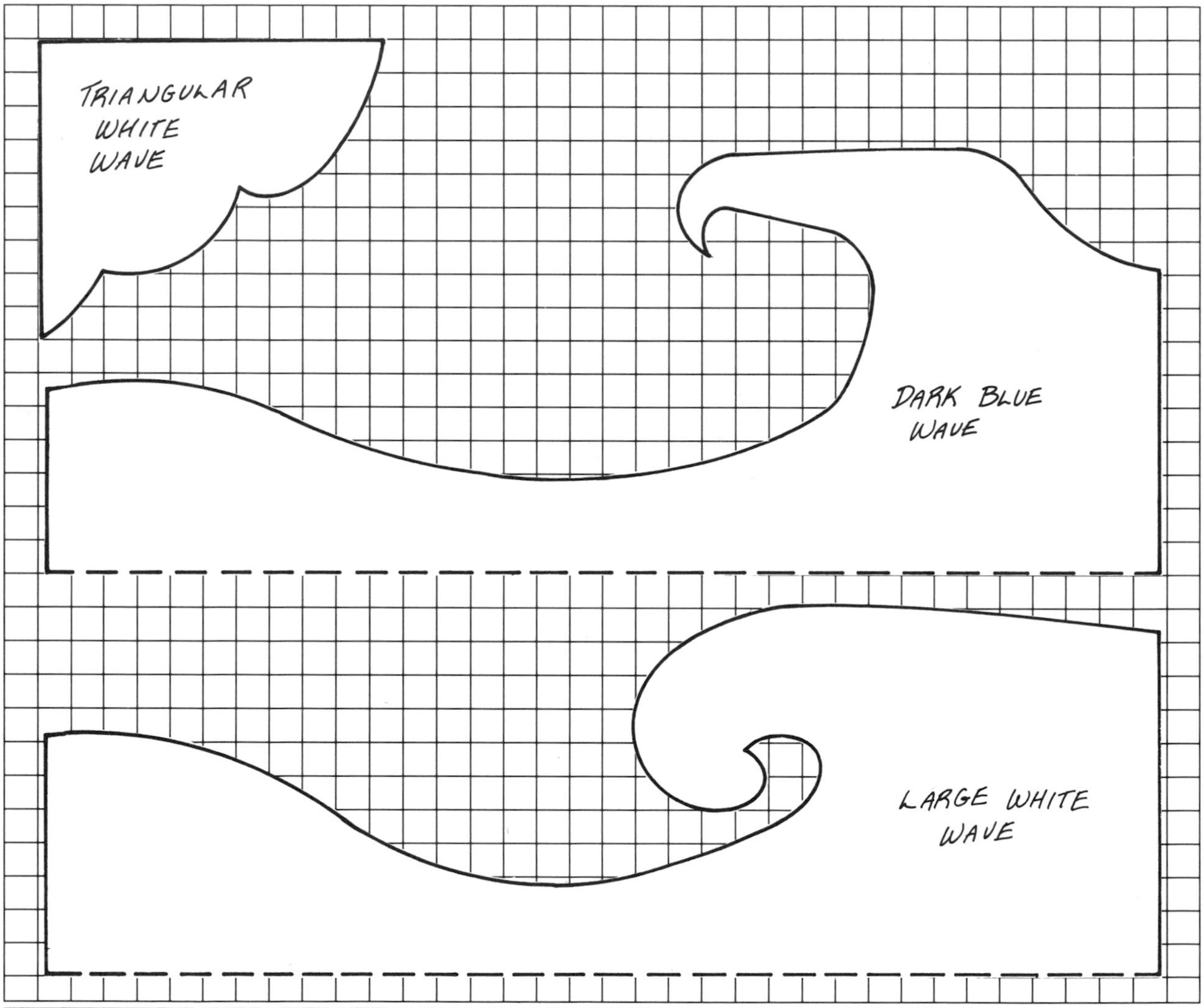

TRIANGULAR WHITE WAVE

DARK BLUE WAVE

LARGE WHITE WAVE

Figure D

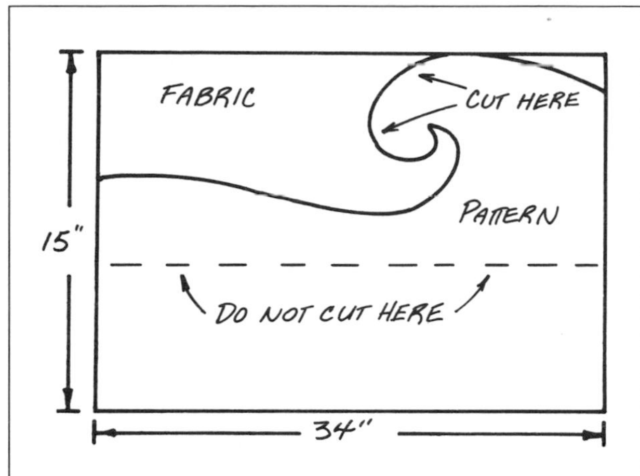

Figure E

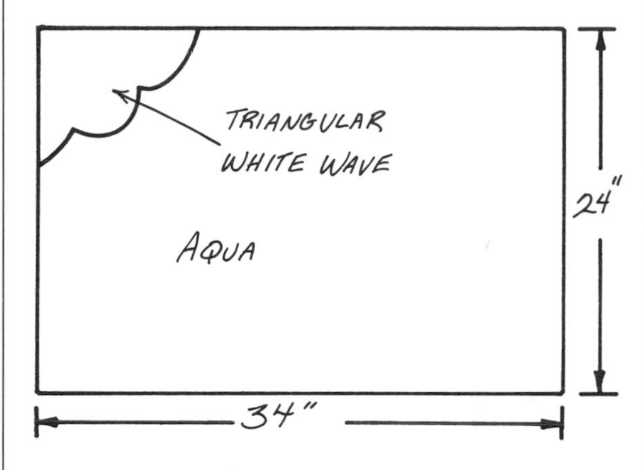

Figure F

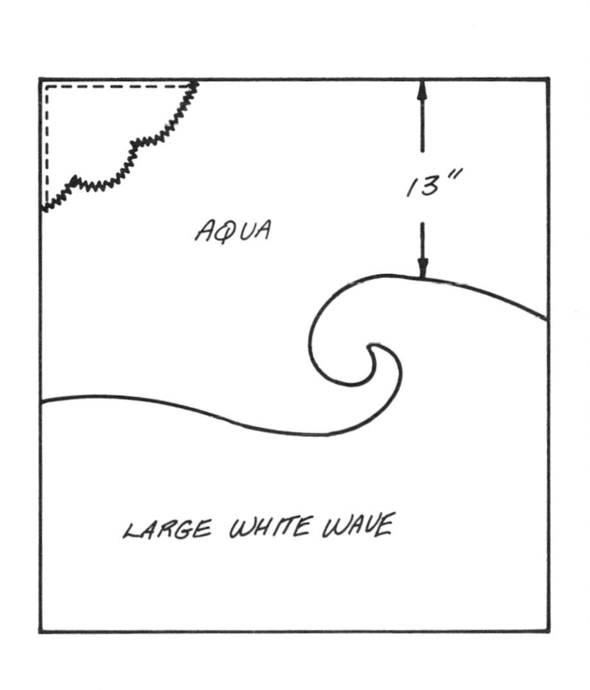

Assembly

The front and back sections of the beach cover-up are identical. For each section, the patchwork outer layer is assembled first, and then it is quilted to the backing layer. When the edges have been bound, the front and back sections are sewn together along the shoulders, and the side closures are added.

1. To begin, take one of the aqua-colored terry rectangles that you cut in step 1 above, and place it right side up on a flat surface. Pin one of the Triangular White Wave pieces right side up on top, aligning the square corner with one upper corner of the aqua rectangle as shown in **Figure E**. Be sure you have the aqua rectangle turned the right way, as shown. Baste the two pieces together, working from the center of the triangular piece outward toward each corner. Baste close to all edges as well. Use a closely-spaced zigzag machine setting to stitch over the contoured edge of the triangular piece.

2. Place the assembly from step 1 right side up on a flat surface, and pin one of the Large White Wave pieces on top, right side up, as shown in **Figure F**. Adjust the White Wave piece so that the contoured edge is close to the lower edge of the aqua piece. There should be about 13 inches between the upper edge of the aqua rectangle and the uppermost edge of the White Wave close to the right-hand side, as shown. Baste the two layers together so they will remain nice and flat, and then zigzag stitch along the entire contoured edge of the White Wave piece. Turn the assembly wrong side up, and trim away the portion of the aqua terry cloth that extends below the zigzagged edge of the Large White Wave.

Figure G

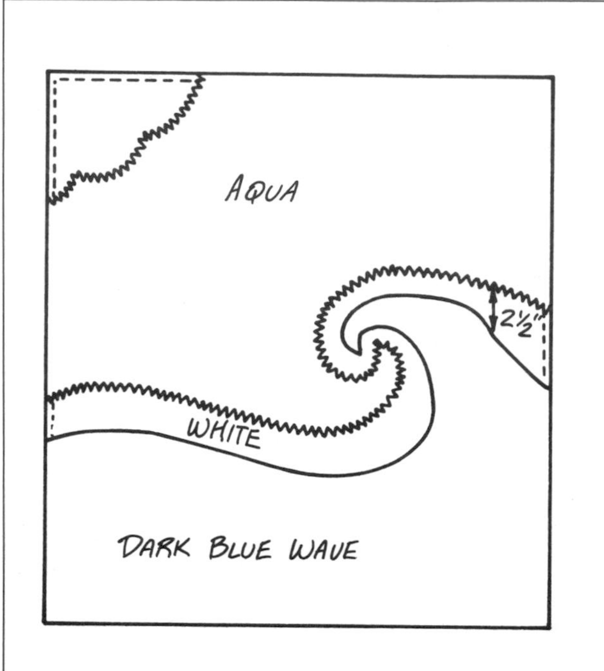

Figure H

3. Turn the assembly right side up and pin one of the contoured Dark Blue Wave pieces on top, right side up, as shown in **Figure G**. Adjust it as shown, allowing approximately 2½ inches between the uppermost edge of the White Wave piece and the uppermost edge of the Dark Blue Wave piece, close to the right-hand side. Baste the two layers together and then zigzag along the contoured edge of the Dark Blue Wave piece. Turn the assembly wrong side up and trim away the portion of the White Wave piece that extends below the zigzagged edge of the Dark Blue Wave. Remove all remaining basting stitches from the assembly.

4. You have now completed the outer patchwork layer of one cover-up section. To finish the section, first place one of the white terry Backing pieces wrong side up on a flat surface. Place one of the batting rectangles on top, and place the assembled outer layer on top of the batting, right side up. Align the three layers as evenly as possible, smooth them out, and pin them together. Baste the layers together, starting at the center and working out toward each corner. Then run additional lines of basting stitches in vertical rows, all the way across the assembly.

5. You can do the quilting by hand or by machine, whichever is your preference. We used the machine and stitched horizontally across the assembly, following the wave contours. The pattern of quilting stitches is indicated by dotted lines in **Figure H**.

6. We contoured the side edges of the section, to make it more attractive than a simple rectangle. A cutting diagram is provided in **Figure I**, and a scale drawing for the upper contour is provided in **Figure J**. Enlarge the drawing, and use the full-size pattern as a guide to contour the side edges of the quilted assembly as shown in **Figure I**. Trim the upper and lower edges, if necessary, to even up the layers of batting and terry cloth. Baste all layers together close to each edge.

7. Use one of the shorter white terry Binding Strips to encase the lower edge of the quilted section. (Instructions are provided in Tips & Techniques.) Trim the ends of the Binding Strip even with the side edges of the cover-up.

8. Use one of the longer Binding Strips to encase one side edge of the cover-up section. Trim this strip even

Figure I

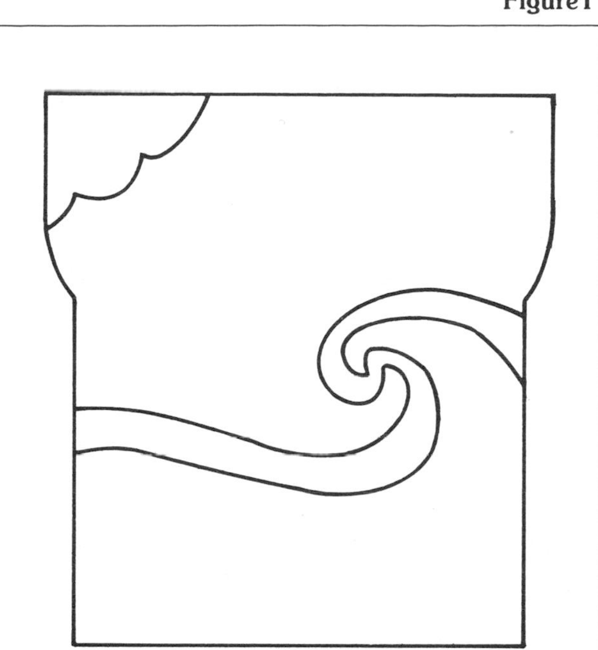

1 square = 1 inch

Figure J

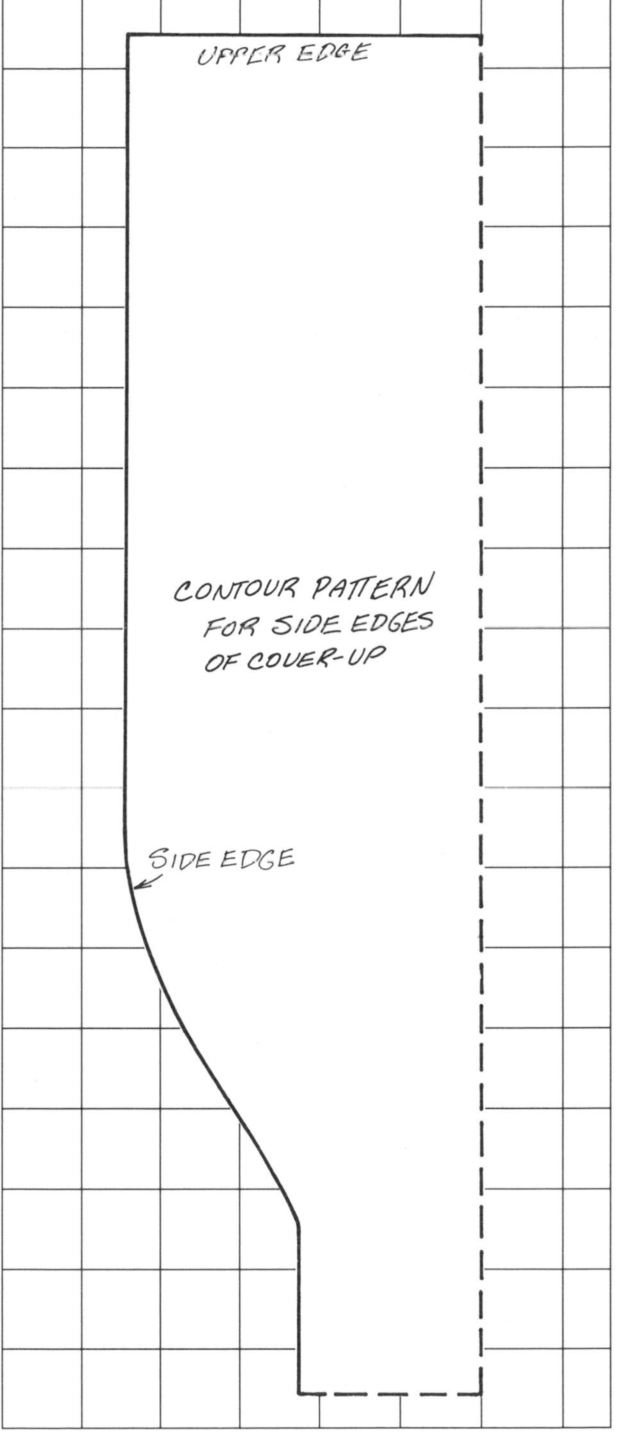

with the upper edge of the cover-up, but finish the lower end as specified in Tips & Techniques. Use another of the longer Binding Strips to encase the other side edge in the same manner.

9. To encase the upper edge of the cover-up, use one of the shorter Binding Strips. Finish both ends of this strip. Remove all basting stitches from the finished cover-up section.

10. Repeat all of the procedures in steps 1 through 9 to make an identical cover-up section.

Finishing

1. Place the two completed cover-up sections wrong sides together, aligning the upper edges. Whipstitch the bound upper edges together, leaving an 11-inch-long neck opening at the center.

2. Turn the cover-up inside out, so that the sections are right sides together. Whipstitch the upper edges together in the same manner as you did in step 1. This will provide extra strength along the shoulders.

3. We used snap tape along the sides of the cover-up, but you may prefer nylon fastening tape. Either way,

Figure K

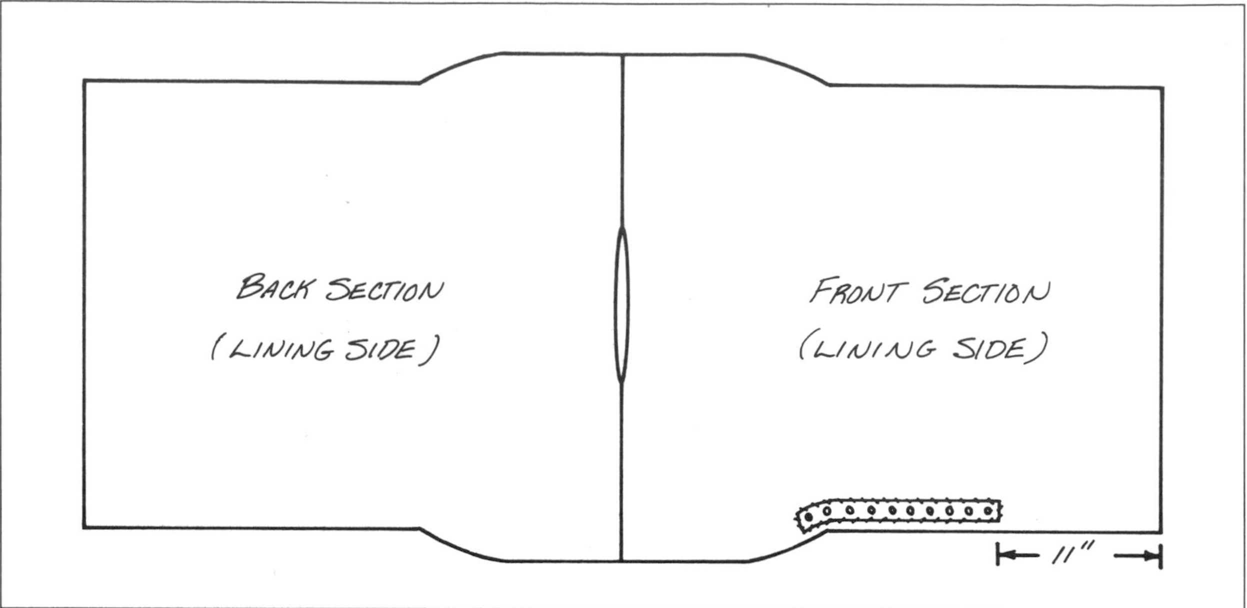

Figure L

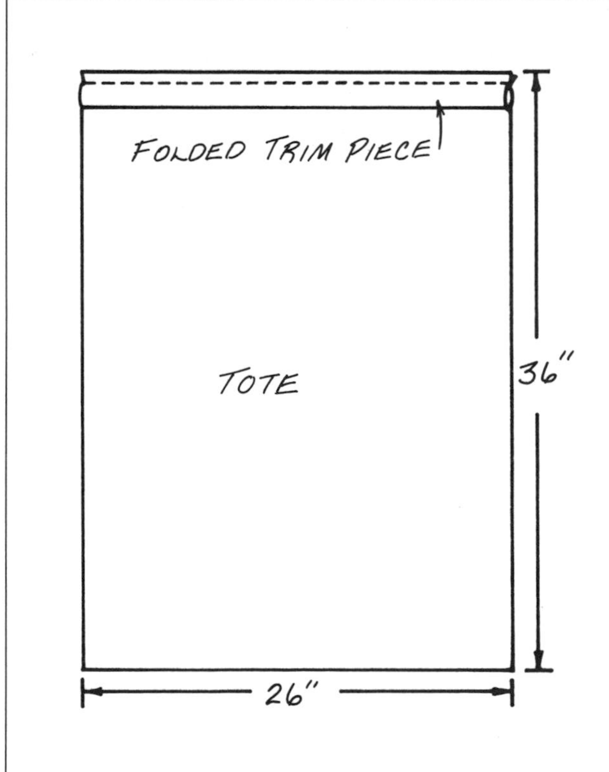

the fastening material will hold the sides together when the cover-up is worn as a garment, but it will allow you to open the cover-up and use it as a beach towel if you like. Cut one 14-inch length of snap tape or fastening tape, and separate the halves. Pin one piece to the lining side of the front cover-up section, close to one side edge, placing the lower end about 11 inches from the lower edge of the cover-up as shown in **Figure K**. If you are using snap tape, turn under the raw ends of the tape before you stitch it in place. Whipstitch along each edge and end of the tape to secure it in place, but be careful that the stitches do not go all the way through to the right side of the cover-up. Stitch the matching half of the length of fastening tape to the lining side of the back cover-up section in the same manner.

4. Cut another 14-inch length of fastening tape and stitch the halves to the lining side of the cover-up, close to the opposite side edges, in the same manner.

THE TOTE

Note: All seams are ½-inch wide, unless otherwise specified in the instructions.

The beach tote is basically just a rectangle of white terry with dark blue trim and straps. The trim piece

Figure M

along each side forms a casing for nylon cord, which is used to gather and close the side. The trim piece along each end is primarily for reinforcement, and fastening tape is used to create the closure. The straps extend all the way around the tote bag for extra strength. You already have cut the pieces for the tote, so we'll start right in on the assembly.

Attaching the Trim

1. Fold one of the dark blue End Trim pieces in half lengthwise, placing wrong sides together, and press.

2. Place the white Tote piece right side up on a flat surface, and place the pressed End Trim piece on top as shown in **Figure L**. The two aligned long raw edges of the Trim piece should be even with one short edge of the Tote piece as shown. Stitch the seam, trim the seam allowances to 1/4 inch, and use a zigzag setting to finish the raw edges of the seam allowances. Press the Trim upward.

3. Repeat the procedures in steps 1 and 2 to attach the remaining End Trim piece to the opposite end of the Tote piece.

Figure N

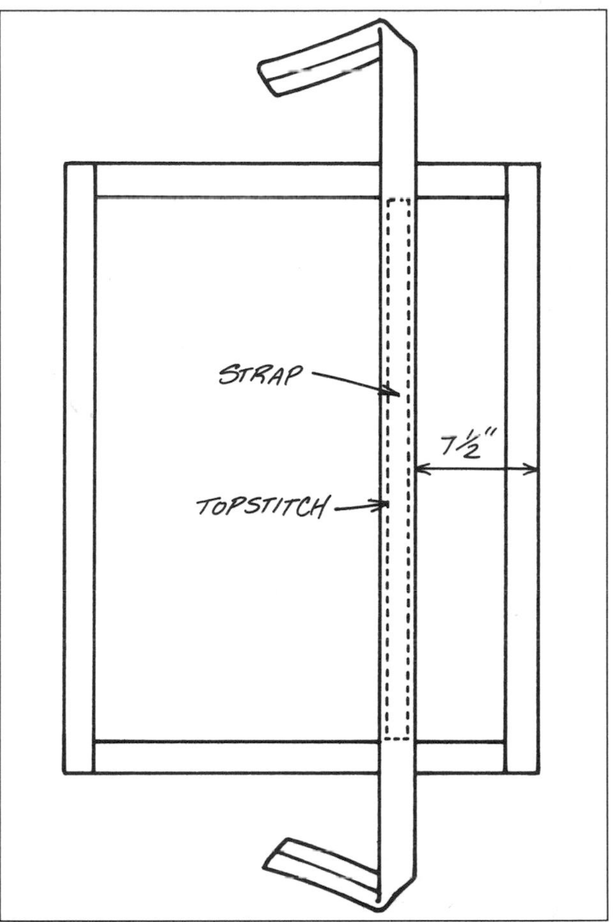

4. To prepare one of the Side Trim pieces, first press the seam allowance to the wrong side of the fabric along each short end of the Side Trim piece. Fold the Trim piece in half lengthwise, placing wrong sides together, and press. Stitch this Trim piece along one long edge of the Tote piece in the same manner as you did the End Trim pieces. The Side Trim piece should just fit along the side of the Tote piece, extending over the End Trim pieces as well. Trim the seam allowances and zigzag the raw edges as you did before. Leave the ends of the Side Trim piece open, so that it can be used as a casing.

5. Repeat the procedures in step 4 to finish the opposite long edge of the Tote piece, using the remaining Side Trim piece.

Figure O

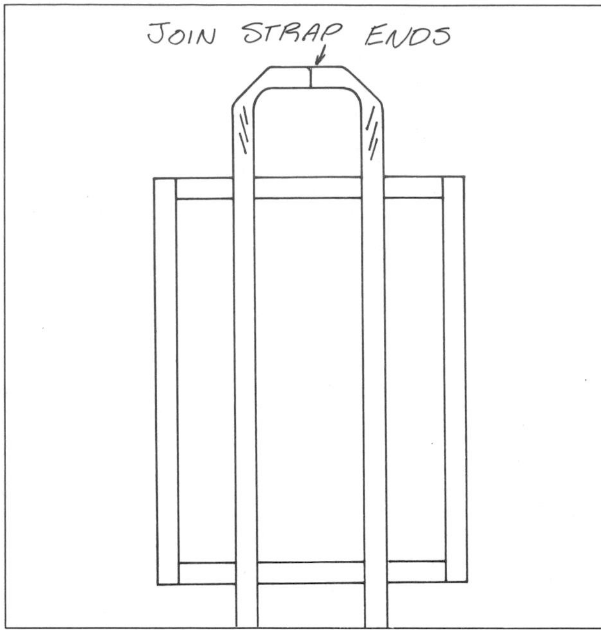

Figure P

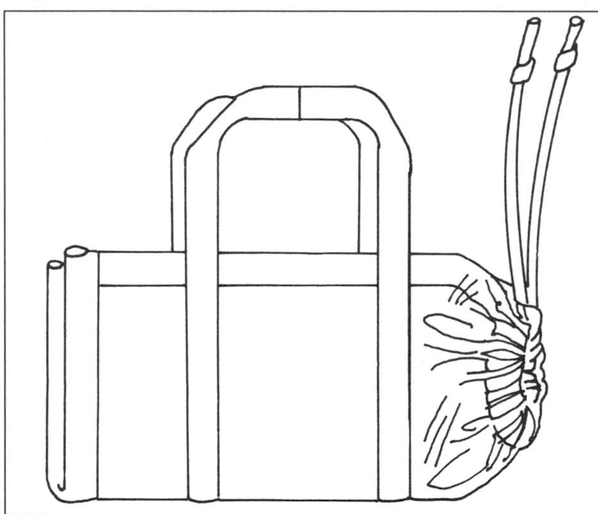

6. Cut a 25-inch length of fastening tape and separate the halves. If you are using snap tape, turn the raw ends of each piece to the wrong side and press. Place the tote assembly wrong side up on a flat surface, and place one of the fastener halves right side up along the trim at one end of the tote (**Figure M**). We stitched the tape in place by machine, along each edge and end. Stitch the matching half of the fastener tape to the end trim at the opposite end of the tote in the same manner.

Adding the Straps

1. Fold one dark blue Strap piece in half lengthwise, placing right sides together. Stitch the seam along the long edge, leaving the two short ends open and unstitched. Turn the strap right side out and press it flat.

2. Repeat the procedures in step 1 to prepare the remaining dark blue Strap piece.

3. Place the tote assembly right side up on a flat surface. Place one of the stitched straps on top lengthwise as shown in **Figure N**, 7½ inches from one side edge of the tote. Adjust the strap so that it extends equally beyond each end of the tote, and pin it in place. Topstitch ¼ inch from each long edge of the strap, between the end trims, as shown.

4. Repeat the procedures in step 3 to attach the remaining stitched strap to the tote, 7½ inches from the opposite side edge.

5. The two separate strap ends are now joined at each end of the tote. First, press a ½-inch-wide allowance to the inside of one strap, at one end of the tote. Take the unpressed end of the other strap, at the same end of the tote, and insert it inside the pressed strap about 1 inch (**Figure O**). Whipstitch or machine stitch the strap ends together.

6. Repeat the procedures in step 5 to join the ends of the two straps at the opposite end of the tote.

Finishing

1. Cut the nylon cord in half so that you have two equal lengths.

2. Tie a knot at each end of one cord, and thread the cord through the casing formed by the side trim on one side of the tote. When you have threaded it through, pull up on both ends of the cord and push the tote fabric toward the center to gather it tightly and close the end of the bag (**Figure P**). Tie the ends of the cord together in a square knot, and then a bow.

3. Repeat the procedures in step 2 to gather the opposite side of the tote, using the remaining length of nylon cord.

4. Fill the tote with beach paraphernalia, snap it closed, and you're ready for summer!

Gown & Robe

This lovely ensemble, with quilted patchwork accents, is perfect for all but the coldest winter spells. The full gown is made of lightweight cotton, and is gathered around front and back yokes, with tie straps so it will fit any figure. The front yoke consists of triangular quilted patchwork pieces. We made the robe from warm, soft fleece, with quilted patchwork pocket and sleeve accents to match the gown yoke.

Materials

3 yards of 44- or 45-inch-wide lightweight cotton or cotton blend fabric in a solid color, for the gown (We used light blue.)
5 yards of 44- or 45-inch-wide fleece fabric in a solid color, for the robe (We used dark blue.)
Patchwork fabrics: We used four different coordinating fabrics, all lightweight cotton blends, for the patchwork and trim pieces. In order to make the instructions easier to read and follow, we have numbered the fabrics. You'll need 2 yards of fabric #1 (we used a dark blue flowered print); 1 yard of fabric #2 (we used a light blue pin-dot fabric); ½ yard of fabric #3 (we used a dusky blue flowered print); and ½ yard of fabric #4 (we used a red pin-dot fabric that matched the red flowers in one of the other fabrics).
4 yards of ⅛-inch-diameter piping cord
14 x 18-inch piece of the lightest-weight quilt batting
Sewing threads to match the fabrics, or choose one coordinating color of thread to use throughout
Dressmaker's pattern paper

CUTTING THE PIECES

Instructions are provided in this section for cutting the pieces for both the gown and robe. We suggest that you label the pieces as you cut them, to prevent confusion later on.

1. The body of the gown consists of two large rectangles. Open out the 3-yard length of gown fabric, and cut it in half widthwise so that you have two identical rectangles, each 44 or 45 inches wide and 1½ yards long. Fold both of the rectangles in half lengthwise, and stack them so that the long folded edges are aligned.

2. A scale drawing for the Gown Top Contour pattern is provided in **Figure A**. Enlarge the drawing to make a full-size pattern.

3. Place the pattern on top of the stacked Gown pieces as shown in **Figure B**. The center front edge of the pattern, which specifies "place on fold," should be aligned with the folded edges of the two Gown pieces. The shoulder edge of the pattern should be even with the aligned top raw edges of the Gown pieces. (It doesn't matter if the pattern edge designated as the

Figure A **1 square = 1 inch**

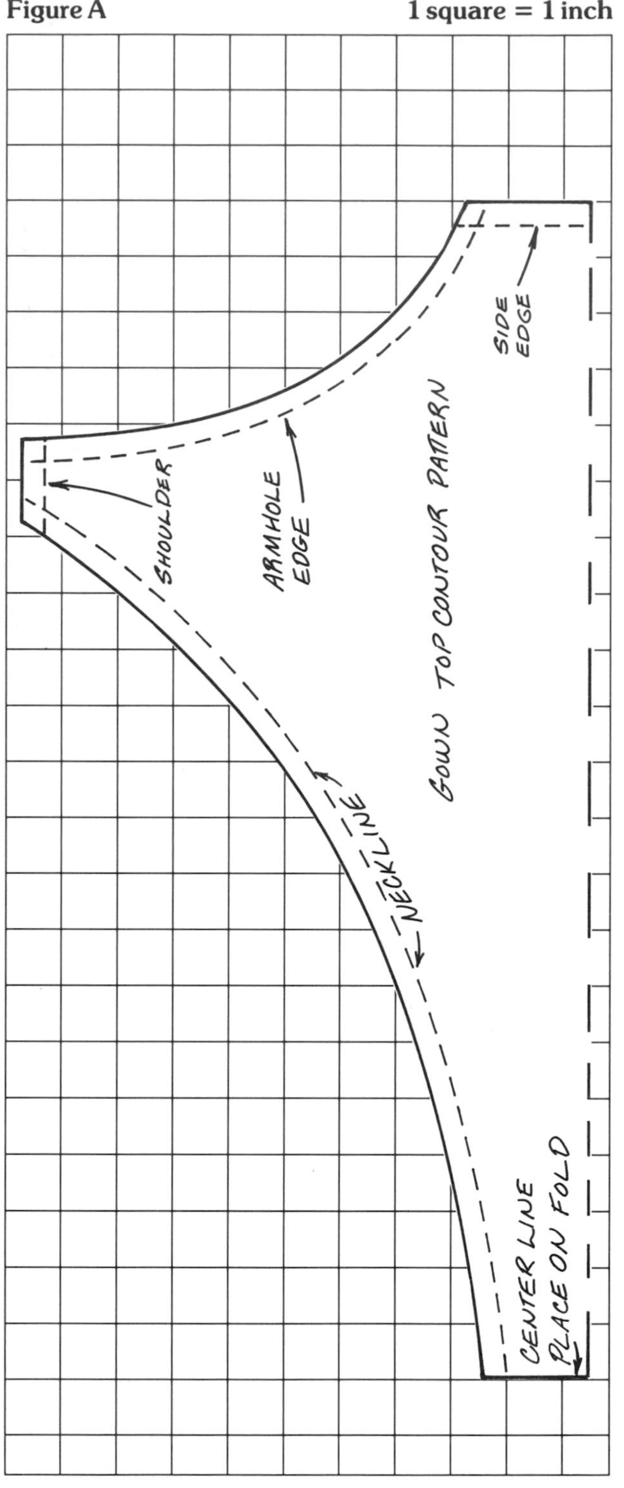

Figure B

"side" reaches all the way to the unfolded long side edges of the fabric layers.) Cut through all layers of fabric along *only* the curved neckline and armhole edges of the pattern. Do not cut the fabric along any of the other edges. When unfolded, the two Gown pieces should now look like the one shown in **Figure C**.

4. Scale drawings for the Robe Front and Robe Back are provided in **Figure D**. Enlarge the drawings to

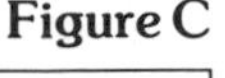
Figure C

make full-size patterns. The resulting patterns will be medium (36-38) size. It may be necessary to alter the patterns to fit, but this will not be a very complicated task since the shoulders and length are the only places where fit will make a difference. The shoulder seam on each Robe pattern should be about 3 inches longer than your shoulder measurement, as that's how the robe is designed. The patterns should be 2 to 3 inches longer than the desired finished length of the robe. Alter both the Robe Front and Back patterns in the same manner. (See Tips & Techniques, if necessary, for instructions on altering patterns.)

5. A scale drawing of the Robe Sleeve is provided in **Figure E**. Enlarge the drawing to make a full-size pattern. Measure the length of the full-size Sleeve pattern, from the shoulder seam line down to the lower edge. Measure your own arm, from 3 inches below your shoulder down to the desired finished length of the sleeve. (The lower edge of the sleeve will be bound, so there's no need to add a hem allowance to the length of the pattern.) Add 2 inches to the desired length of

Figure D

1 square = 2 inches

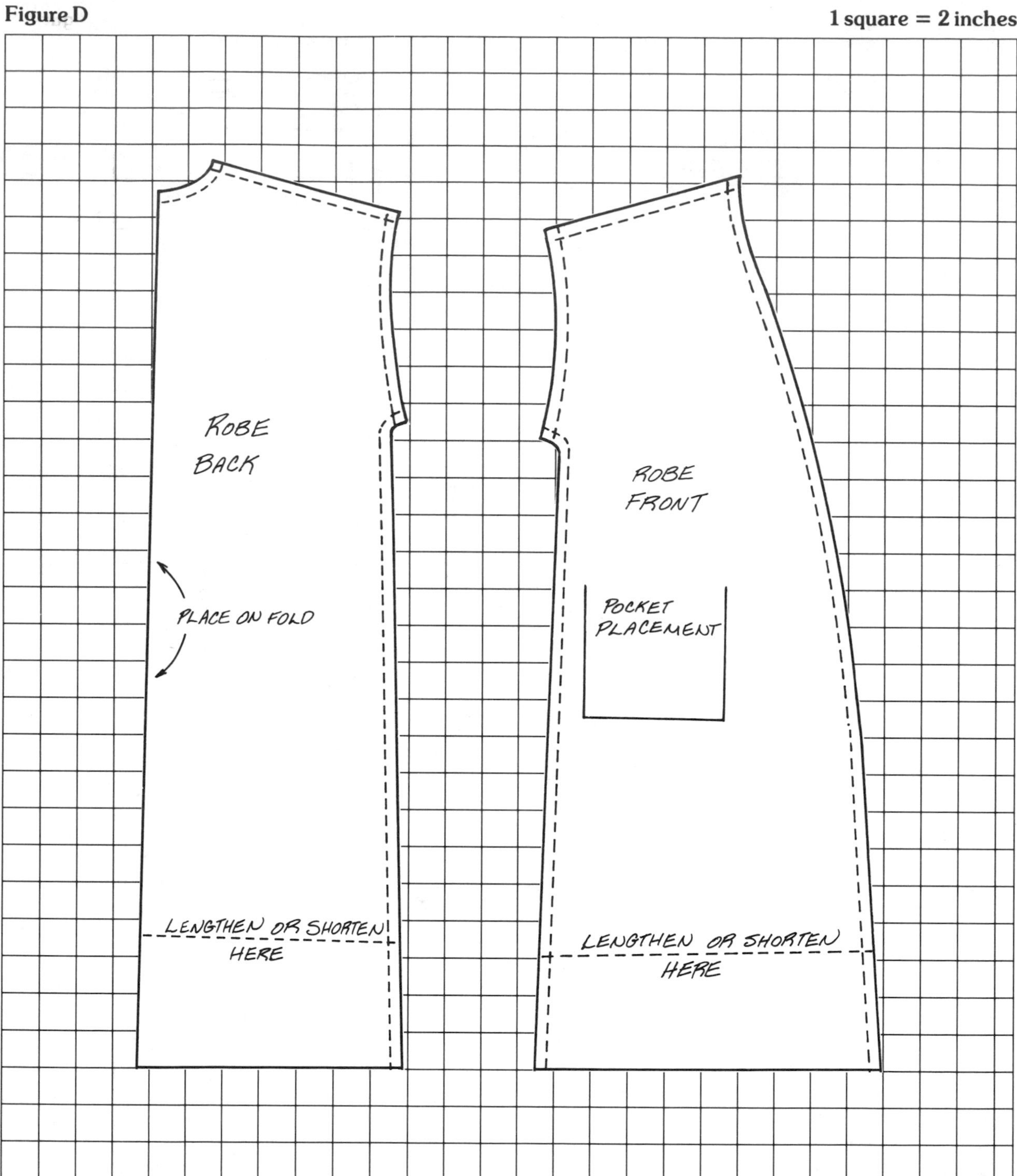

1 square = 2 inches

Figure E

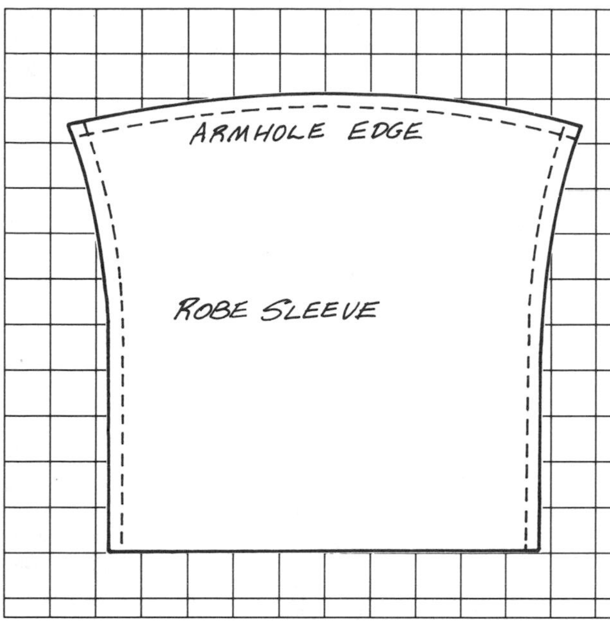

Figure F

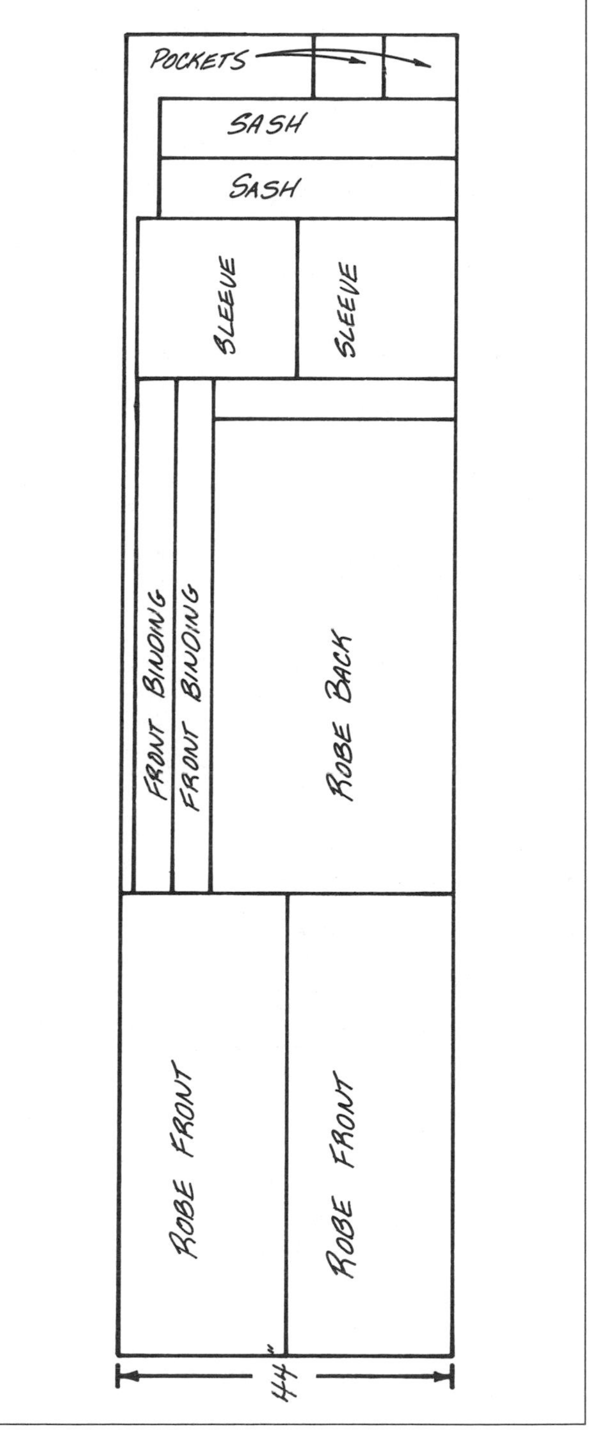

the sleeve, which will be taken up by the creation of the sleeve cap. If the measured length of the sleeve pattern is longer or shorter than your arm measurement plus 2 inches, alter the pattern to fit.

6. Cut the pieces listed below from the fleece robe fabric. A general cutting diagram is provided in **Figure F**. (**Note**: To cut the two Robe Front pieces, fold the fabric and cut both at once, so the resulting pieces are mirror images of one another.)

Robe Front – cut two, using pattern
Robe Back – cut one, place pattern on fold
Sash – 8 x 39 inches, cut two
Sleeve – cut two, using pattern
Pocket – 8½ x 9½ inches, cut two
Front Binding – 5 x 68 inches, cut two

(**Note:** If you altered the length of the Robe Front and Back patterns, add or subtract an equal number of inches from the length of each Front Binding piece.)

7. The remaining pieces you will have to cut are mostly patchwork and trim pieces. Begin by cutting a 2 x 24-inch Front Yoke Binding Strip, along the bias, from fabric #1. (See Tips & Techniques for instructions on cutting bias strips.)

Figure G **1 square = 1 inch**

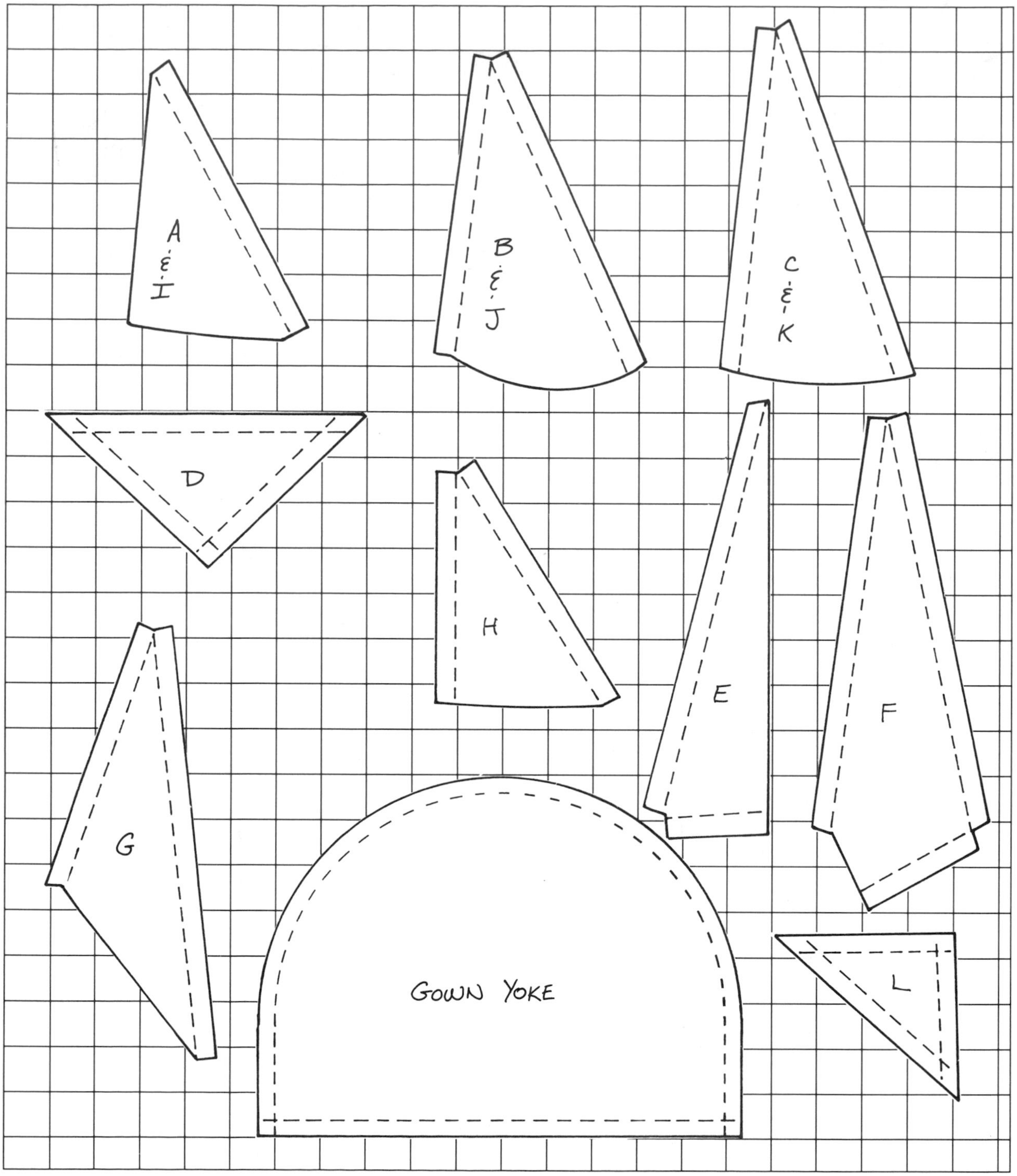

8. Cut a 20-inch square from fabric #2. From this square, cut seven bias strips, each 1½ inches wide, and of the following lengths: one 26 inches, two 24 inches, two 22 inches, and two 19 inches. Label each strip as a Piping Strip.

9. Scale drawings for all of the patchwork pieces and for the Gown Yoke are provided in **Figure G**. Enlarge the drawings to make full-size patterns, and cut the pieces as listed below, from the specified fabrics. Label each piece for easy identification. The patchwork pieces should be labeled by letter and fabric number; for example, a Patchwork Piece A that is cut from fabric #3 should be labeled "3A." (**Note**: When you are instructed to cut two of a patchwork piece, fold the fabric and cut both at once, so that the resulting pieces are mirror images of one another. When you are instructed to cut only one of a patchwork piece, use the pattern right side up unless the instruction specifies "upside down." In that case, use the pattern upside down.)

From Fabric #1:

- Patchwork Piece B – cut one, upside down
- Patchwork Piece C – cut one
- Patchwork Piece G – cut two
- Patchwork Piece H – cut two
- Patchwork Piece K – cut two
- Gown Yoke – cut one, using pattern provided
- Pocket Binding – 3 x 10½ inches, cut eight
- Bottom Gown Binding – 2 x 36 inches, cut two
  2 x 17 inches, cut one
- Yoke Top Binding – 2 x 13 inches, cut two
- Armhole Binding – 2 x 12 inches, cut four
- Straps – 3 x 14 inches, cut four

From Fabric #2:

- Patchwork Piece D – cut one
- Patchwork Piece E – cut two
- Patchwork Piece G – cut two
- Patchwork Piece L – cut two
- Gown Yoke – cut one, using pattern provided
- Sleeve Binding – 2 x 20 inches, cut two

From Fabric #3:

- Patchwork Piece A – cut two
- Patchwork Piece E – cut two
- Patchwork Piece F – cut two
- Patchwork Piece I – cut two

Figure H

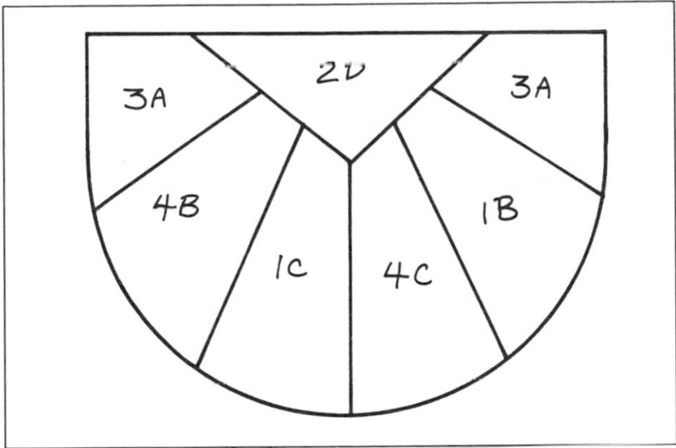

Figure I

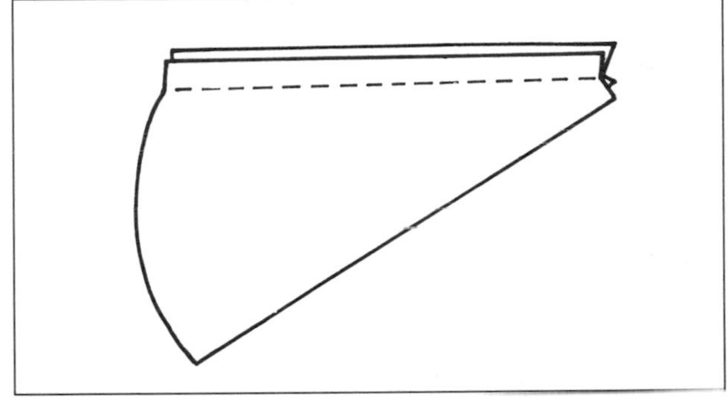

From Fabric #4:

- Patchwork Piece B – cut one
- Patchwork Piece C – cut one, upside down
- Patchwork Piece F – cut two
- Patchwork Piece H – cut two
- Patchwork Piece J – cut two

THE GOWN

Making the Patchwork Yoke

Note: All seams are ½-inch wide, unless otherwise specified in the instructions.

1. The assembled patchwork yoke is shown in **Figure H**. To begin, place a 3A piece right side up on a flat surface. Place a 4B piece right side down on top, aligning the two edges that are the same length. Stitch the seam as shown in **Figure I**, and press the seam open. Trim the ends of the seam allowances if they extend beyond the ends of the patchwork pieces.

Figure J

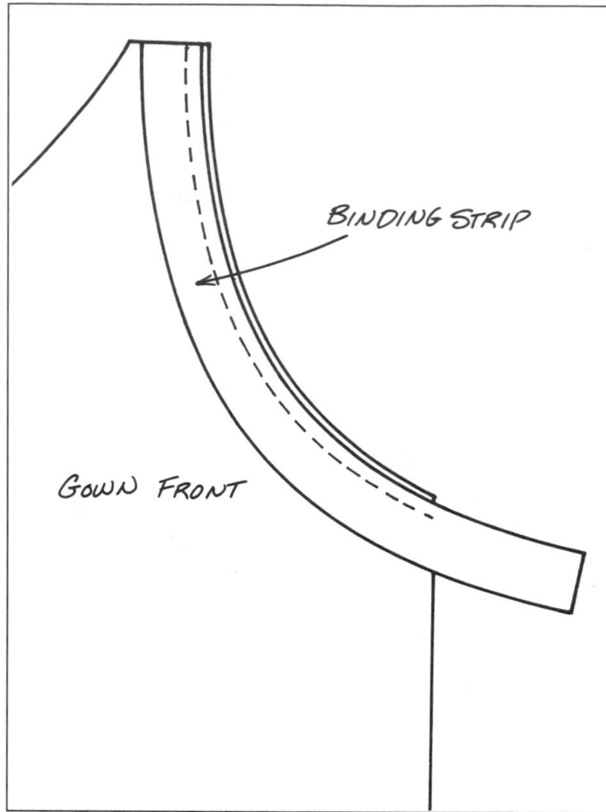

2. Place the assembly from step 1 right side up on a flat surface, and place a 1C piece right side down on top, aligning the equal edges of the 1C and 4B pieces. Stitch the seam and press open. This completes the left-hand side of the yoke, as shown in **Figure H**.

3. Repeat the procedures in steps 1 and 2 to stitch together the three patchwork pieces (3A, 1B, and 4C) that form the right-hand side of the yoke.

4. Place the two yoke sections right sides together, aligning the free long edges of pieces 1C and 4C, stitch the seam, and press it open.

5. To prepare the 2D piece, press the seam allowance to the wrong side of the fabric along the two lower edges. Pin the pressed 2D piece to the assembled patchwork, placing it as shown in **Figure H** so that the unpressed upper raw edge is even with the upper raw edges of the patchwork pieces. Baste close to the pressed lower edges of the 2D piece.

6. Use the Yoke pattern to cut a piece of quilt batting. Place the fabric #2 Yoke piece wrong side up on a flat surface, and place the batting Yoke piece on top. Place the patchwork yoke right side up on top of the batting, smooth out the layers so that they are flat and even, and pin all layers together. Baste the layers together from the center outward, running several lines of basting stitches so that the layers are secure. In addition, baste all layers together close to each raw outer edge.

7. You can quilt by hand or machine. We used the machine, and stitched in the ditch along each of the existing seam lines. We also stitched close to the pressed edges of the 2D piece. When you have completed the quilting, remove all basting stitches from the center portion of the yoke, but not the basting stitches close to the raw outer edges.

8. Use the fabric #1 Front Yoke Binding Strip to encase the long curved edge of the yoke. (See Tips & Techniques for instructions on encasing a raw edge with a binding strip.) Trim the ends of the Strip even with the upper edge of the yoke.

9. Use one of the fabric #1 Yoke Top Binding Strips to bind the upper edge of the yoke. Finish both ends of this strip.

Assembling the Gown Front

1. Begin by binding the armhole edges of one Gown piece, using two of the fabric #1 Armhole Binding Strips. Choose one of the Gown pieces as the front, and place it right side up on a flat surface. Place one of the Armhole Binding Strips right side down on top, aligning one long edge of the Strip with one armhole edge of the Gown piece. The upper end of the Strip should be even with the shoulder edge of the Gown, and the lower end of the strip should extend past the side edge of the Gown by several inches. Stitch the seam as shown in **Figure J**. Complete the binding procedures as for any other assembly. Do not trim the extending lower end of the strip.

2. Repeat the procedures in step 1 to bind the other armhole edge of the same Gown piece, using a second Armhole Binding Strip.

3. The Gown Front piece is gathered and stitched to the patchwork yoke. (See Tips & Techniques if you do

Figure K

Figure L

Figure M

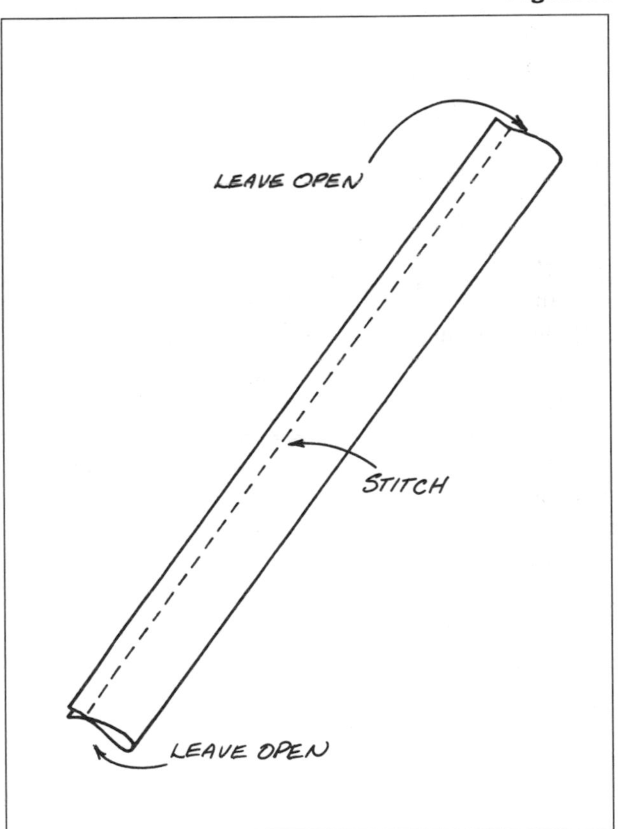

not know how to form gathers.) Gather the curved neckline edge as shown in **Figure K**, and adjust the gathers evenly until the edge is just slightly shorter than the curved edge of the patchwork yoke. Baste over the gathers to hold in them in place.

4. Place the gathered Gown Front right side up on a flat surface, and place the patchwork yoke right side up on top so that the curved edge overlaps the gathered Gown neckline edge by about 1 inch. Pin the two pieces together along the curved edge, and then topstitch through all thicknesses, close to the inner edge of the yoke binding (**Figure L**).

5. To make one strap, fold one of the fabric #1 Strap pieces in half lengthwise, placing right sides together. Stitch a straight seam along the long edge only, leaving both short ends open as shown in **Figure M**. Press the seam open and turn the strap right side out. Adjust the strap so that the seam line runs along the center of one side, and press. Press the seam allowances to the inside at one open end, and whipstitch or topstitch the end closed. At the opposite end, turn the allowances to the inside at an angle (**Figure N**), and whipstitch or topstitch the end closed.

6. Repeat the procedures in step 5 to make three additional straps, using the three remaining Strap pieces.

Figure N

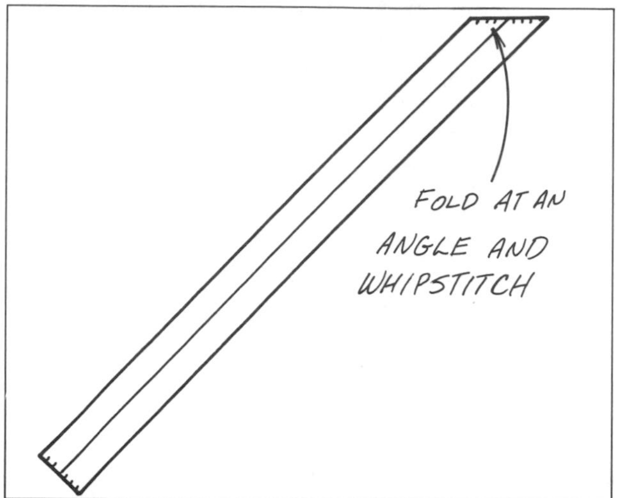

7. Place the straight end of one assembled strap underneath one upper corner of the front gown-and-yoke assembly, overlapping the edges by about 1 inch as shown in **Figure O**. The right side of the strap (the side opposite the one with the centered seam line) should face the wrong side of the gown-and-yoke assembly. Topstitch through all thicknesses, in a square pattern as shown, to secure the strap in place. Stitch a second strap to the opposite upper corner of the gown-and-yoke assembly in the same manner.

Assembling the Gown Back

1. Bind the armhole edges of the Back Gown piece as you did the Front Gown piece, using the two remaining Armhole Binding Strips.

2. Bind the straight upper edge of the fabric #1 Gown Yoke piece, using the remaining fabric #1 Yoke Top Binding Strip. Trim the ends of the Binding Strip even with the side edges of the Yoke piece.

3. Gather the curved neckline edge of the Back Gown piece as you did the Front Gown. Pin the fabric #1 Yoke piece and the Back Gown piece right sides together, aligning the gathered neckline edge of the Gown piece with the curved edge of the Yoke piece. Stitch the seam, turn the yoke upward, and press the seam allowances toward the yoke.

4. Topstitch a strap to each upper corner of the back gown-and-yoke assembly.

Figure O

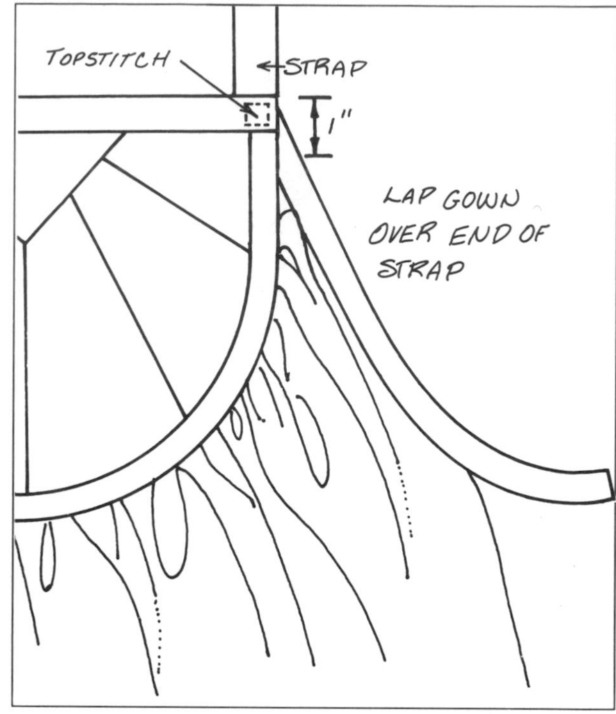

Final Assembly

1. Place the gown front and back assemblies right sides together and stitch the seam along each side as shown in **Figure P**. Press the seams open.

2. At the top of one side seam, on the wrong side, fold the ends of the two armhole binding strips into a neat triangle as shown in **Figure Q**. Overlap the ends, and turn the raw edges under. Topstitch through all thicknesses, following the triangular shape. Finish the ends of the armhole binding strips on the opposite side of the gown in the same manner.

3. Try on the gown, tying the free ends of the straps together in a bow over each shoulder. Adjust the straps until the gown feels comfortable and looks right. You may wish to take a couple of tacking stitches through each bow, since you can pull the gown on and off over your head. That way, you won't have to tie and untie the straps each time. The lower edge of the gown will be bound with fabric #1 strips, so simply mark and then cut off the lower edge of the gown at the desired length, all the way around.

Figure P

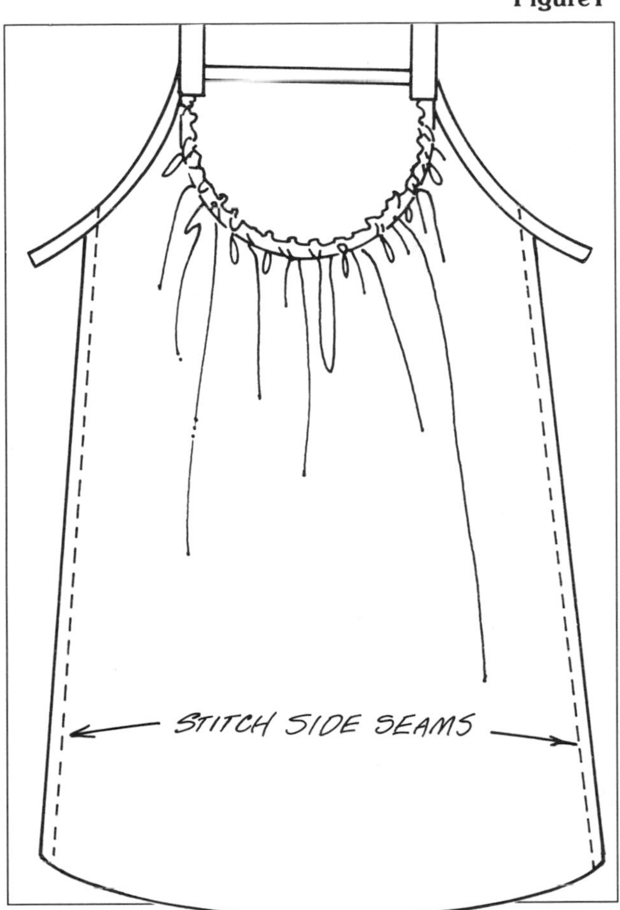

4. Piece together the three fabric #1 Bottom Gown Binding Strips end to end (see Tips & Techniques for piecing instructions). Use the long binding strip to encase the lower edge of the gown. Overlap the ends of the strip where they meet, cut one end so that it overlaps the other by about 1 inch, and turn the raw end under before making the final stitches.

THE ROBE

Assembling the Sleeve Patchwork

1. Each sleeve has a patchwork trim section at the lower end. The two patchwork sections are mirror images of each other. Both are shown in **Figure R**. It will be less confusing if you will lay out the pieces that form each separate section before you begin stitching.

Figure Q

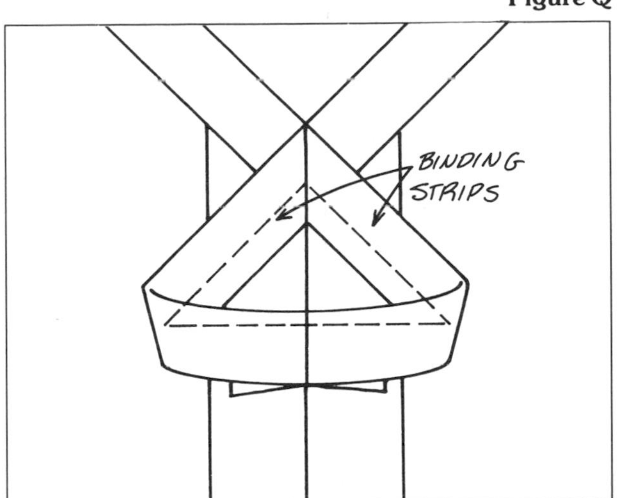

Figure R

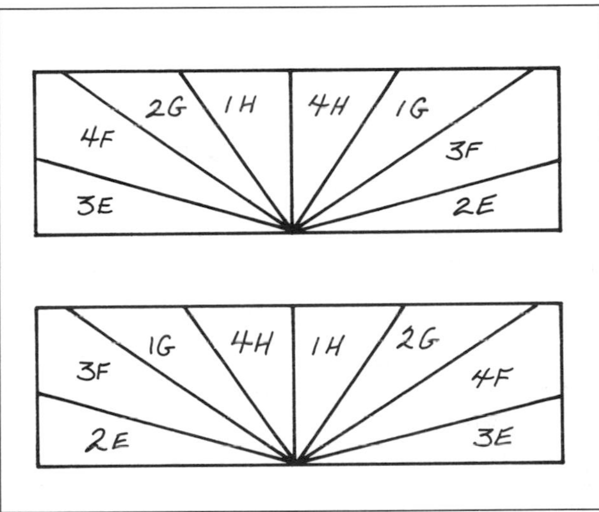

2. To assemble the two patchwork sleeve sections, follow the same procedures as you did to assemble the patchwork gown yoke. Refer to **Figure R** for the proper arrangement of the various pieces.

3. Fold one of the patchwork trim sections in half widthwise, placing right sides together. Stitch the seam across the ends. Press the seam open and turn the section right side out. It should now be a cylinder, with both ends open. Press the seam allowance to the wrong side all the way around each raw edge. Finish the other patchwork section in the same manner.

Figure S

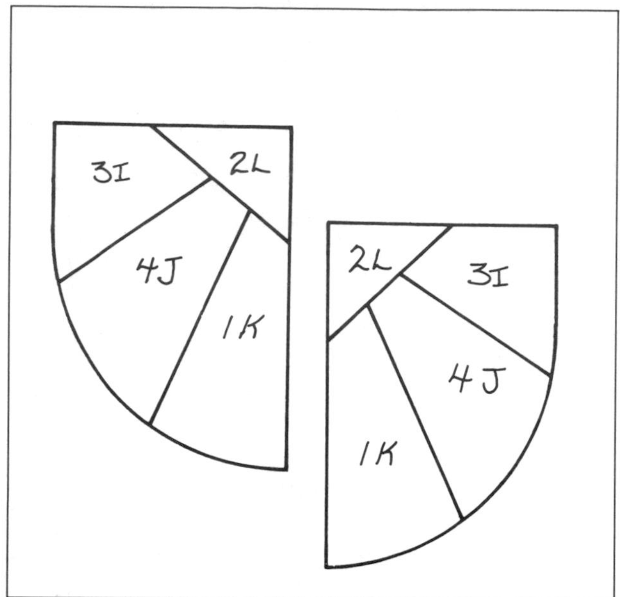

Assembling the Pockets

1. Each pocket has a patchwork trim section. The two pocket trim sections are mirror images of each other. Both sections are shown in **Figure S**. Lay out the pieces for each section before you begin work.

2. Begin by stitching together the I, J, and K pieces for one pocket section. Press the seam allowance to the wrong side of the L piece, along one edge only, and baste it to the I-J-K assembly as shown.

3. Press the seam allowance to the wrong side of the assembled trim section along the long curved edge only. It may be necessary to clip the allowance in a few places to make it lie flat.

4. Assemble the mirror-image pocket trim section in the same manner.

5. Place one of the fleece Pocket pieces right side up on a flat surface. Place one of the patchwork trim sections right side up on top, aligning the square corner of the trim section with one upper corner of the Pocket piece as shown in **Figure T**. Pin the layers together, and then run several lines of basting stitches through both layers to secure them while you quilt. Baste the layers together close to each outer edge as well, and neatly whipstitch the curved edge of the trim to the Pocket.

Figure T

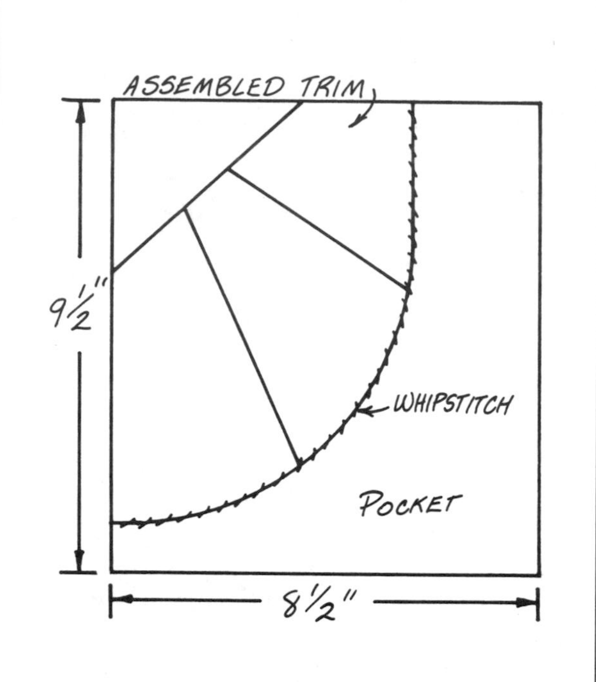

Figure U

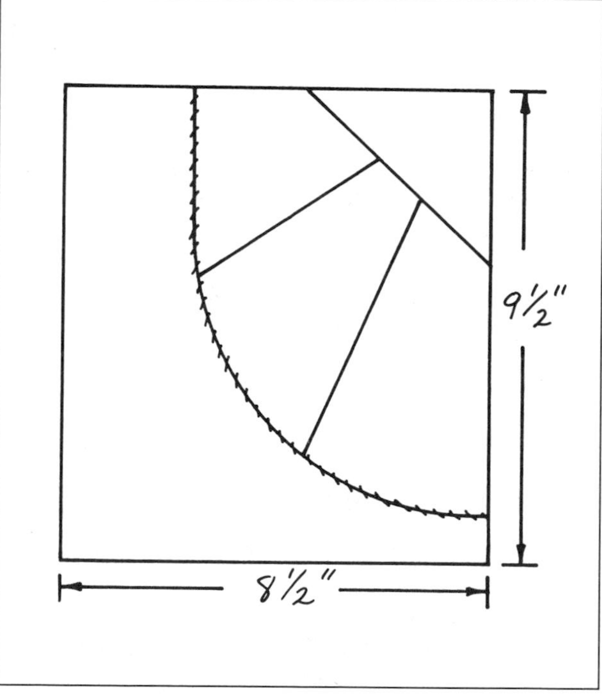

Figure V

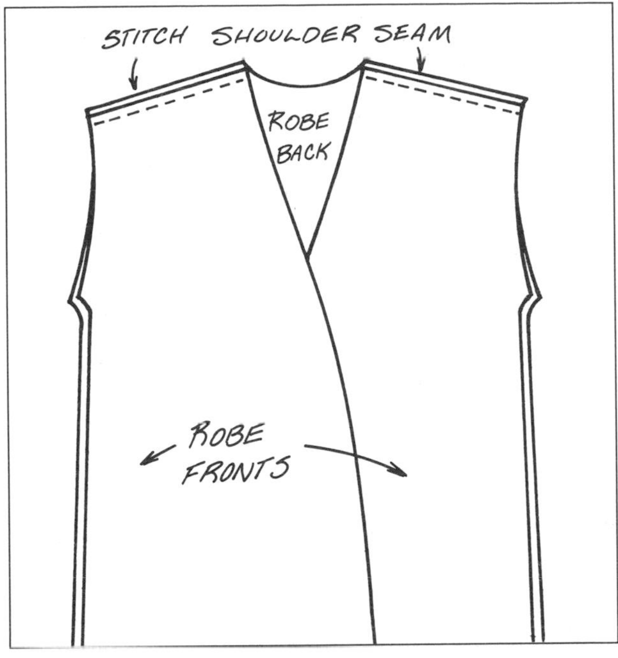

Figure W

6. You can quilt by hand or machine. We used the same technique as we did for the gown yoke, quilting by machine along each existing seam line and close to the pressed edge of the L piece. When you have completed the quilting, remove all basting stitches from the center of the assembly, but do not remove the basting that holds the outer edges together.

7. Repeat the procedures in steps 5 and 6 to baste, whipstitch, and quilt the second pocket trim section to the remaining Pocket as shown in **Figure U**.

8. To bind the edges of one pocket, use four of the fabric #1 Pocket Binding Strips. Bind the upper edge of the pocket, and cut off the ends of the Strip even with the side edges of the pocket. Bind the lower edge, using a second Strip, in the same manner. Use an additional Strip to bind each side edge, finishing both ends of each of these Strips.

9. Use the four remaining Pocket Binding Strips to encase the edges of the other pocket.

Assembling the Robe

1. Pin an assembled pocket to one of the Robe Front pieces, placing the wrong side of the pocket against the right side of the Robe Front piece. (Pocket placement lines are provided on the scale drawing for the Robe Front pattern.) Hold the Robe Front piece against your body to make sure the pocket is at a comfortable height for you, and adjust the placement if necessary. Topstitch close to the inner edge of the binding strip, along each side and the lower edge. Do not stitch across the upper edge.

2. Stitch the remaining pocket to the other Front Robe piece in the same manner.

3. Place the Back Robe piece right side up on a flat surface. Place the two Robe Front pieces right sides down on top, aligning the shoulder edges on each side. (Be sure the Front Robe pieces are turned the right way, with the center front edge at the center.) Stitch the shoulder seam on each side as shown in **Figure V**. Press the seams open.

4. Open out the robe sections, and place the assembly right side up on a flat surface. Place one of the Sleeve pieces right side down on top, aligning the armhole edge of the sleeve with the armhole edge of the robe on one side. Stitch the seam along the aligned armhole edges as shown in **Figure W**. Press the seam allowances toward the sleeve. Follow the same procedures to stitch the remaining Sleeve piece to the armhole edge on the opposite side of the robe.

Figure X

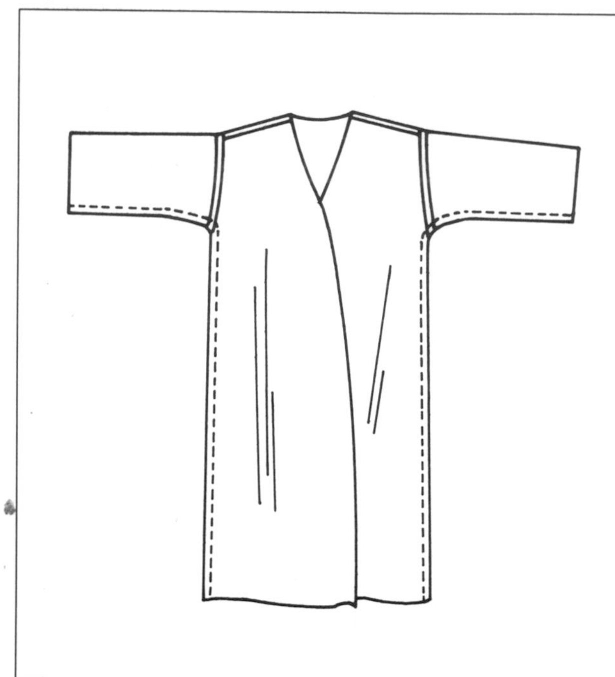

Figure Y

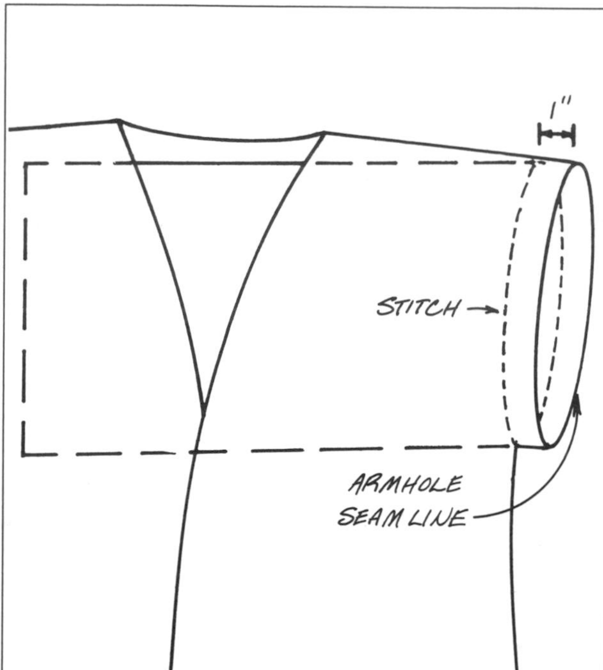

5. Fold the entire robe assembly right sides together and stitch a continuous underarm and side seam on each side, as shown in **Figure X**. Press the seams open.

6. Turn the robe right side out. To create the sleeve cap on one side, turn the sleeve inside out, tucking it inside the robe. Pin the sleeve and robe wrong sides together all the way around the armhole, and topstitch through both thicknesses, 1 inch from the armhole seamline, all the way around (**Figure Y**). Pull the sleeve out of the robe. Repeat these procedures to create a sleeve cap on the other sleeve.

7. To finish the lower edge of one sleeve, first slip one of the patchwork sleeve trim assemblies over the end of the sleeve, placing the wrong side of the trim assembly against the right side of the sleeve. The lower pressed edge of the trim should be ½ inch above the lower raw edge of the sleeve. If the trim is too large or too small for the sleeve, adjust the sleeve seam or the trim end seam so that the two fit together nicely. Remove the trim from the sleeve temporarily. Fit the remaining sleeve trim assembly to the other sleeve in the same manner.

8. Use one of the fabric #2 Sleeve Binding Strips to bind the lower edge of one sleeve, overlapping the ends and turning them under. Use the remaining Sleeve Binding Strip to encase the lower edge of the other sleeve in the same manner.

9. Replace the patchwork trim around one sleeve, adjusting it so that the lower pressed edge of the trim lies along the inner edge of the binding strip. Rotate the trim around the sleeve until the end seam is aligned with the underarm seam on the sleeve. Pin the trim in place and whipstitch around the pressed upper and lower edges to secure the trim. Repeat these procedures to attach the remaining sleeve trim section to the other sleeve.

Adding the Front Binding

1. We added piping to the front binding seam. To create the corded piping, first piece together all of the fabric #2 Piping Strips, end to end. Use the resulting long strip to encase the piping cord. (See Tips & Techniques for instructions on piecing strips and making corded piping).

Figure Z

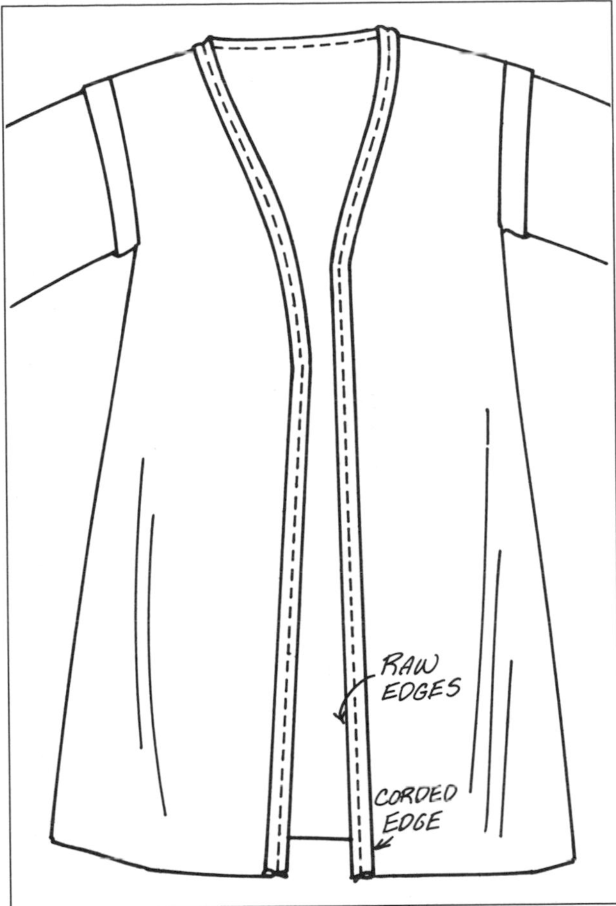

Figure AA

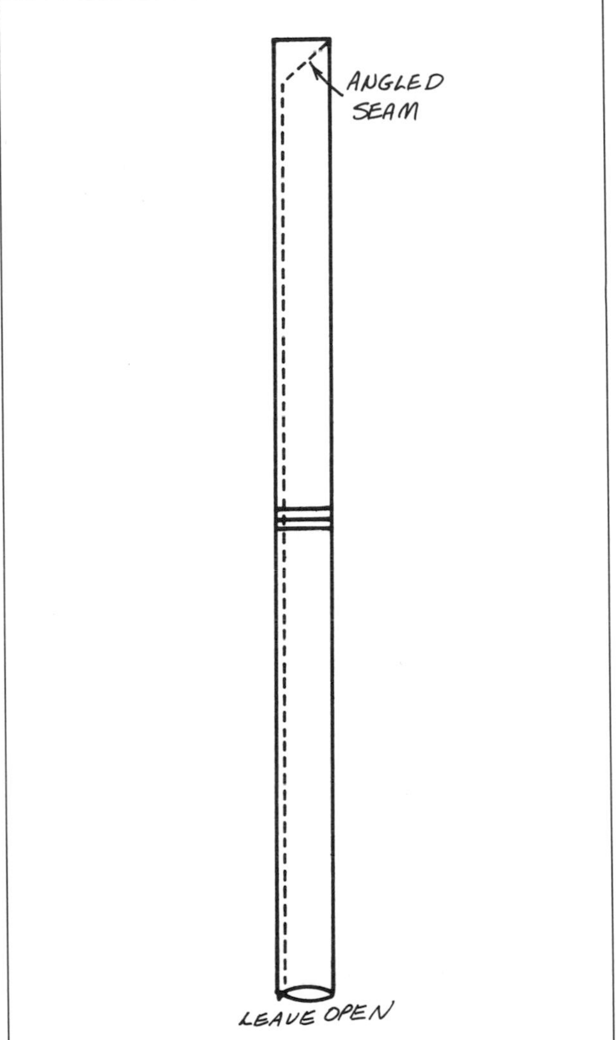

2. Pin the assembled piping to the right side of the robe, along the front raw edge as shown in **Figure Z**. First, find the center of the piping, and place it at the center of the robe back neck edge. Work from this point along the edge in each direction, down to the lower front corner on each side. The aligned raw edges of the piping strip should be even with the raw edge of the robe, and the corded edge of the piping should extend toward the robe as shown. Baste the piping in place.

3. Piece together the two fleece Front Binding Strips, end to end.

4. Pin the assembled long Front Binding Strip to the robe as you did the piping. The Strip and robe fabrics should be right sides together, and the piping will be sandwiched between. One long edge of the Strip should be even with the aligned raw edges of the robe and piping. Begin as you did for the piping, placing the seam that joins the two Front Binding Strips at the center back neck edge of the robe, and work downward in each direction. Cut off the ends of the piping and Binding Strip if they extend below the lower edge of the robe. Now stitch all layers together, using a zipper foot attachment so that the stitching line will be as close as possible to the cord inside the piping, on the side closest to the aligned raw edges.

Figure BB

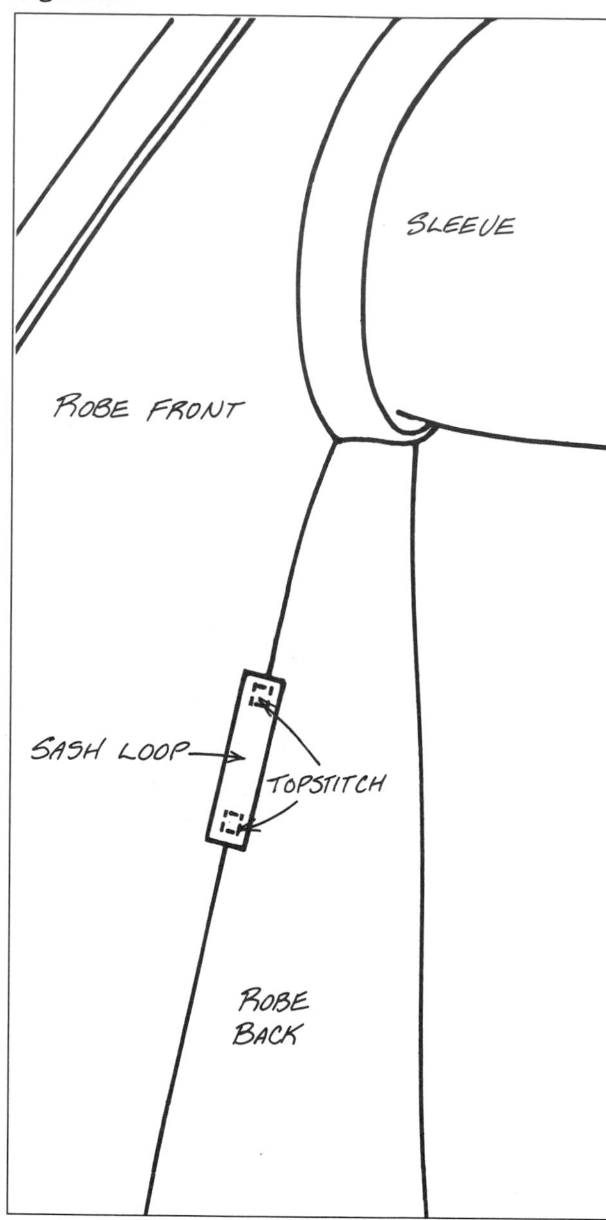

5. Turn the Binding Strip outward and press all seam allowances toward the Strip. Turn and press the seam allowance to the wrong side of the Strip along the free long edge. Fold the Strip in half lengthwise, placing wrong sides together, and whipstitch the pressed edge of the Strip to the wrong side of the robe.

6. Try on the robe and mark the desired hemline. Press a ½-inch-wide allowance to the wrong side of the fabric around the lower edge of the robe, and machine stitch. Turn the hem along the marked length, and stitch the hem.

Making the Sash

1. To begin, piece together the two fleece Sash pieces, end to end.

2. Fold the Sash in half lengthwise, placing right sides together. Stitch the seam along the long edge, and then angle the seam across one short end as shown in **Figure AA**. Leave the opposite short end open and unstitched. Trim the seam allowance ½ inch from the angled end seam, clip the corners, and turn the sash right side out.

3. Press the sash flat, with the long seam line running along one edge. Press the seam allowances to the inside at the open end, turning them at an angle so both ends look alike. Whipstitch the opening edges together.

4. Topstitch ½ inch from each edge of the sash. In addition, topstitch along the center line of the sash.

5. To make sash loops for the robe, cut two Loop pieces from leftover fleece fabric, each 1¾ inches wide and 2½ inches long.

6. Fold one of the Loop pieces in half lengthwise, placing right sides together. Stitch the seam along the long edge and across one short end. Leave the other end open and unstitched. Trim the seam allowances to ¼ inch. Turn the loop right side out and press a ¼-inch-wide seam allowance to the inside at the open end. Whipstitch the opening edges together. Repeat these procedures, using the remaining Loop piece.

7. Try on the robe again, and wrap the sash around your waist at a comfortable level. Mark the level of the top of the sash on each side seam of the robe.

8. Pin one of the assembled loops to the right side of the robe, lengthwise along one side seam. The top of the loop should be about ¼ inch above the top-of-sash mark that you made in step 6. Topstitch the loop to the robe at the upper and lower ends, stitching in a ¼-inch-square pattern as shown in **Figure BB**. Topstitch the remaining loop to the opposite side of the robe in the same manner.

Winter Ensemble

Don't be left out in the cold! You can hold Jack Frost at bay with this warm and comfy winter ensemble – matching vest, tam, and mittens. Easy to wear and even easier to assemble, all of the items are fully lined. The quilted designs are a variation on candlewicking, with graceful, machine-stitched stem-and-leaf patterns, and French knot accents.

Figure A

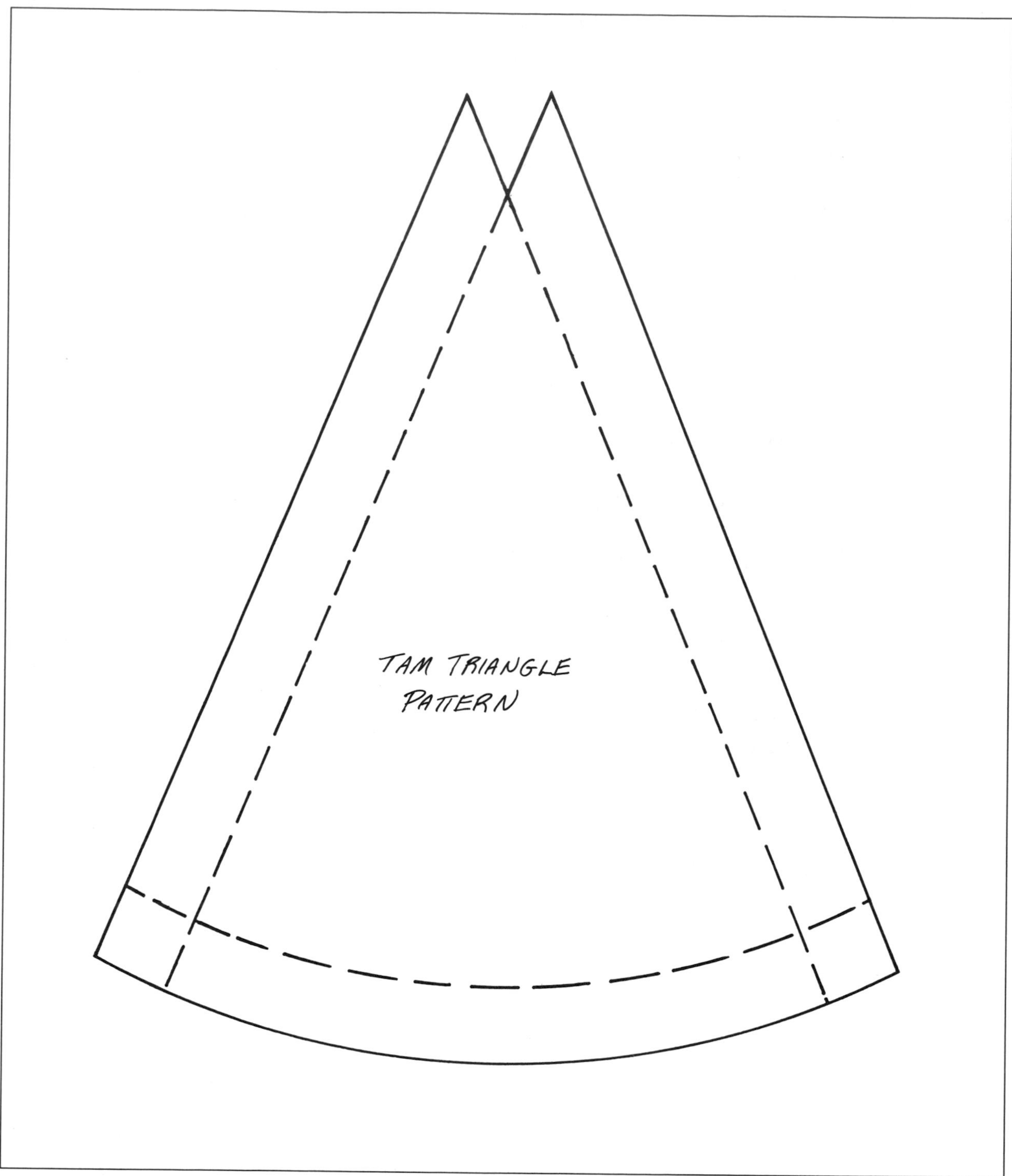

Materials

2 yards of 36-inch-wide fabric for the outer vest, tam, and mitten pieces (We used a dusky fuchsia nylon suede cloth.)

1 yard of 36-inch-wide fabric for the tam and mitten linings (We used a dusky purple nylon suede cloth.)

1 yard of 44- or 45-inch-wide fabric for the vest lining (We used a calico print that picked up the colors of the solid suede cloth fabrics. If you prefer to use the same fabric for all of the linings, you'll need 1½ yards of 36-inch-wide fabric for the vest lining, in addition to the 1 yard length for the tam and mittens.)

Lightweight batting: a 12-inch square for the tam, a 24 x 30-inch piece for the mittens, and a 34 x 45-inch piece for the vest

Embroidery floss in a color that coordinates with the outer and lining fabrics (we used a dusky pink), and an embroidery needle

Thread of the same color as the fabric for the outer pieces, but in a darker hue

A 1½-inch-diameter pompon for the tam, in the same color as the thread

A fabric-marking pen with water-soluble ink

Cutting The Pieces

1. To make patterns for the Vest Front and Back pieces, refer to the Tips & Techniques section of this book for a general shape and instructions. You can choose the style you like. We made our vest with rounded lower corners at the center front.

2. The tam consists of two basic pieces: the Crown and the Rim. The outer-layer Crown is composed of eight triangles that are sewn together to form a large circle. A full-size pattern for the Tam Triangle is provided in **Figure A**. Trace the pattern, and in addition, make a full-size circular pattern for the Crown, 11¼ inches in diameter. (Refer to Tips & Techniques if you do not know how to make a circular pattern.) The diameter measurement provided includes a ½-inch-wide seam allowance all the way around the outer edge.

3. The pattern for the Rim is a circle, 11¼ inches in diameter, with a 5¾-inch-diameter circle cut from the center (**Figure B**). Make a full-size pattern for the Rim, as shown. The specified measurements include ½-inch seam allowances around the outer and inner edges.

Figure B

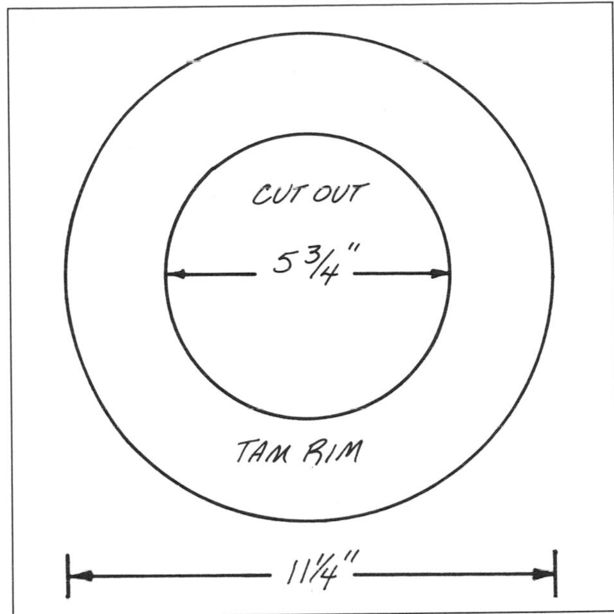

4. To make the Mitten pattern, place your hand on a piece of pattern paper, as shown in **Figure C**. Your fingers should be aligned, not spread apart, but not pressed tightly together either. Your thumb should extend outward at a natural and comfortable angle. Draw a dotted line, which will serve as the stitching line on the pattern, as shown. You should allow about ¾ inch between the stitching line and your hand around your aligned fingers, but only ½ inch between the stitching line and your thumb, as shown. Then draw a solid cutting line ⅝ inch outside the dotted stitching line, all the way around the contoured edge of the mitten shape. Make the total length of the pattern as long as you would like the mitten to be, plus a ½-inch seam allowance at the wrist end.

5. You now have the patterns that you need. Cut the pieces listed in this step from the specified fabrics:

Outer Fabric:

Vest Front – cut two (Either fold the fabric right sides together and cut both at once, or use the pattern right side up for the first piece, and right side down for the second. The resulting pieces should be mirror images of each other.)

Figure C

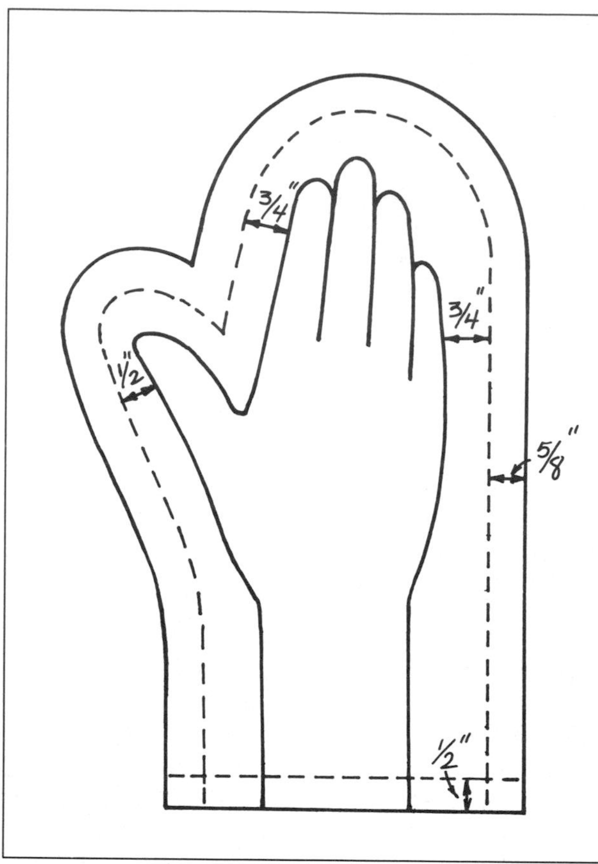

Vest Back – cut one
Patchwork Triangle – cut eight
Rim – cut one
Mitten – cut four (Two of these pieces should be mirror images of the other two.)

Lining Fabric:

Vest Front – cut two (mirror images of each other)
Vest Back – cut one
Crown – cut one
Rim – cut one
Mitten – cut four (two mirror images of the other two)

Batting:

Vest Front – cut two
Vest Back – cut one
Crown – cut one
Mitten – cut four

Making the Vest

1. Pin and then baste the batting vest pieces to the wrong sides of the matching outer vest pieces. The basting stitches should be placed close to all edges. For each Vest Front piece, run a few additional lines of basting stitches from the center out toward the edges.

2. The outer Vest Front pieces are embellished with decorative stitching before the vest is assembled. You may wish to substitute a design of your own creation, but we have provided a diagram in **Figure D** showing the design we used. Whether you wish to use ours or your own, we suggest that you first draw the full-size design directly on the Vest Front pattern. Be certain that you leave enough space between the outer limits of the design and the stitching lines of the pattern. When you are satisfied with the results, reproduce the design on each Vest Front piece, using a water-soluble fabric marking pen. This will provide a stitching guide, and prevent your having to rip out misplaced stitches on the fabric pieces. We used a straight, short, machine stitch for the stem-and-leaf lines, and French knots for the tiny flower buds. If you're not sure how to go about making French knots, please refer to the instructions provided in Tips & Techniques. When you have completed the decorative stitching, remove the basting from the center areas of the Vest Front pieces, but do not remove it from the edges.

3. Place the outer Vest Back and Front pieces right sides together, and stitch the shoulder and side seams on each side, as shown in **Figure E**. Press all seams open, and trim the seam allowances of the batting layers only, close to the seam lines.

4. Follow the procedures described in step 3 to assemble the lining Vest Back and Front pieces.

5. Leave the outer vest assembly wrong side out, and turn the lining assembly right side out. Place the lining inside the outer layer, so that the fabrics are right sides together. Pin the layers together all the way around the outer edge. Stitch the seam along the outer edges, as shown in **Figure F**, but leave an opening about 5 inches long at the center of the lower back edge. Clip the curves and trim the batting seam allowances. Turn the vest and lining layers right sides out through the opening, and press. Press the seam allowances to the

Figure D

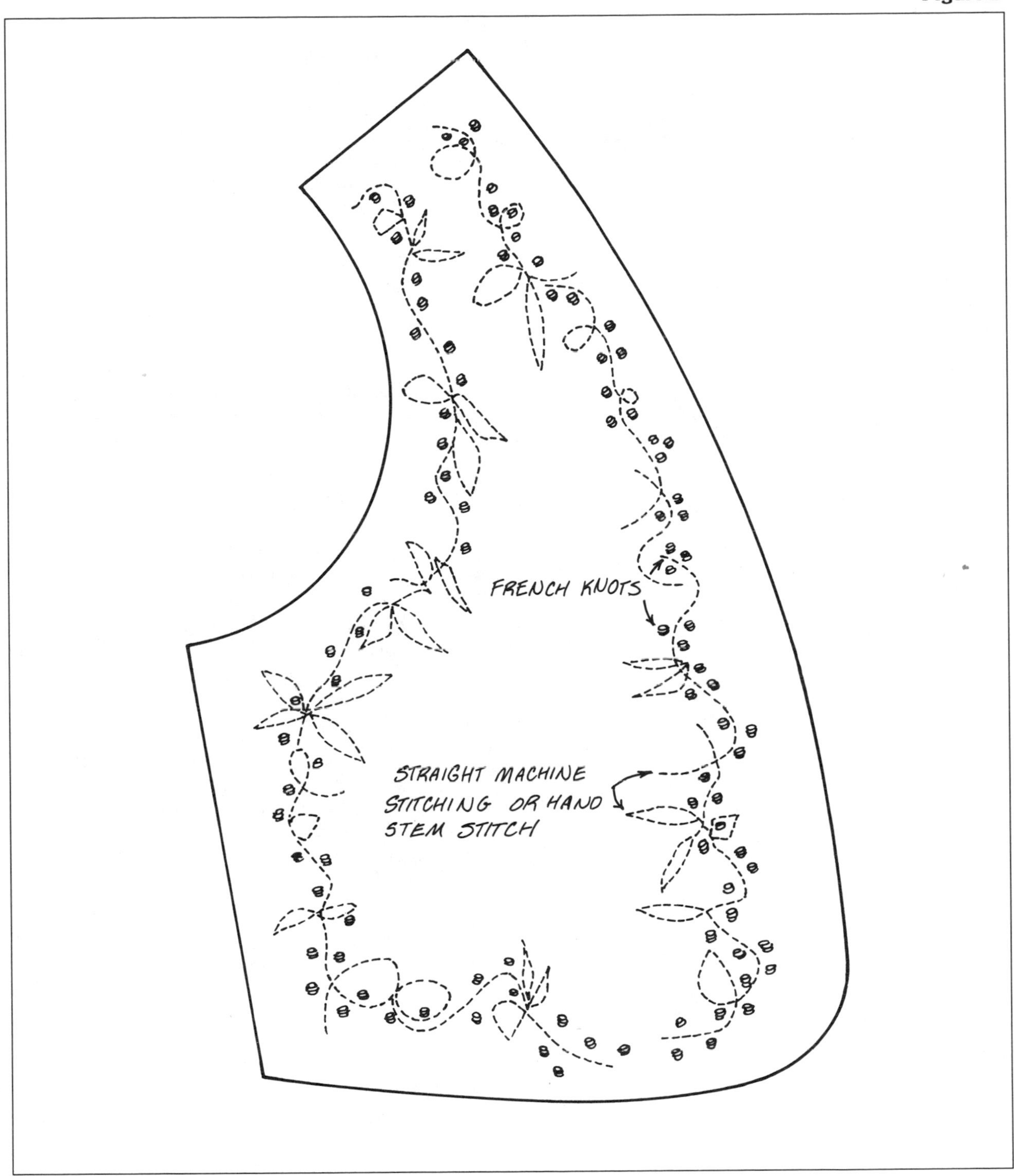
FRENCH KNOTS
STRAIGHT MACHINE
STITCHING OR HAND
STEM STITCH

Figure E

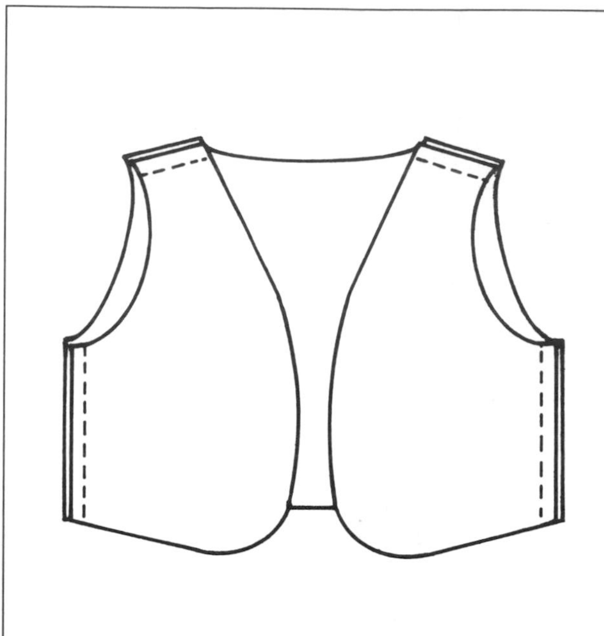

Figure F

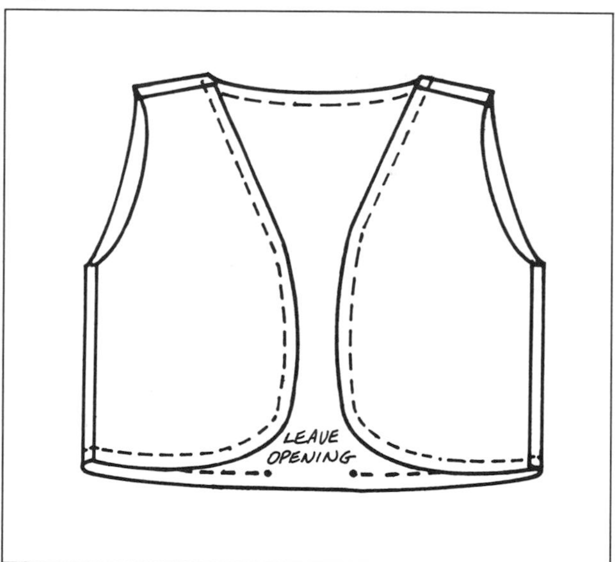

inside along the opening, and then whipstitch the opening edges together. Press the seam allowances to the inside around each armhole, clipping when necessary. Whipstitch the pressed lining and outer edges together around each armhole.

Making the Tam

1. Begin by assembling the Patchwork Triangles. Place two of the Triangles right sides together and stitch the seam along one long edge. Press the seam open.

2. Stitch a third Triangle to one free long edge of this assembly in the same manner.

3. Continue adding Triangles in the same manner, until all eight have been used. Fold the assembly in half, placing right sides together, and stitch the end Triangles together along the free long edges. Press all seams open. You should now have a large circle.

4. Place the Crown pattern on top of the triangle assembly, aligning the center of the pattern with the center of the assembled triangles, and trim the outer edge to match the pattern. Baste the batting Crown piece to the wrong side of the assembled patchwork, close to the outer edge and from the center outward.

5. We added the same decorative design to the assembled Crown as we did to the vest front. Proceed as you did for the vest, by drawing the design on the Crown pattern, and then reproducing it on the Crown assembly, using a water-soluble pen. Our version is shown in **Figure G**. Again, be sure to leave sufficient space between the outer limits of the design and the circular edge of the fabric. When you have completed the decorative stitching, remove the basting stitches from the center of the assembly.

6. Pin the outer-fabric Rim piece and the patchwork Crown assembly right sides together, and stitch the seam all the way round the aligned outer edges (**Figure H**). Clip the curve at evenly spaced intervals, and trim the seam allowance of the batting layer close to the seam line. Press the seam open. Leave the assembly turned wrong side out.

7. Pin the lining-fabric Rim and Crown pieces right sides together as you did the outer pieces in step 6. Stitch the seam along the outer edges, leaving a 3-inch opening. Clip the curve, press the seam open, and turn the lining assembly right side out.

8. Tuck the lining inside the outer assembly. If each was turned as specified in steps 6 and 7, the fabrics should now be right sides together. Pin the layers together around the inner Rim edges, stitch the seam as shown in **Figure I**, and clip the curves. Turn the tam and lining right sides out through the short opening that

Figure G

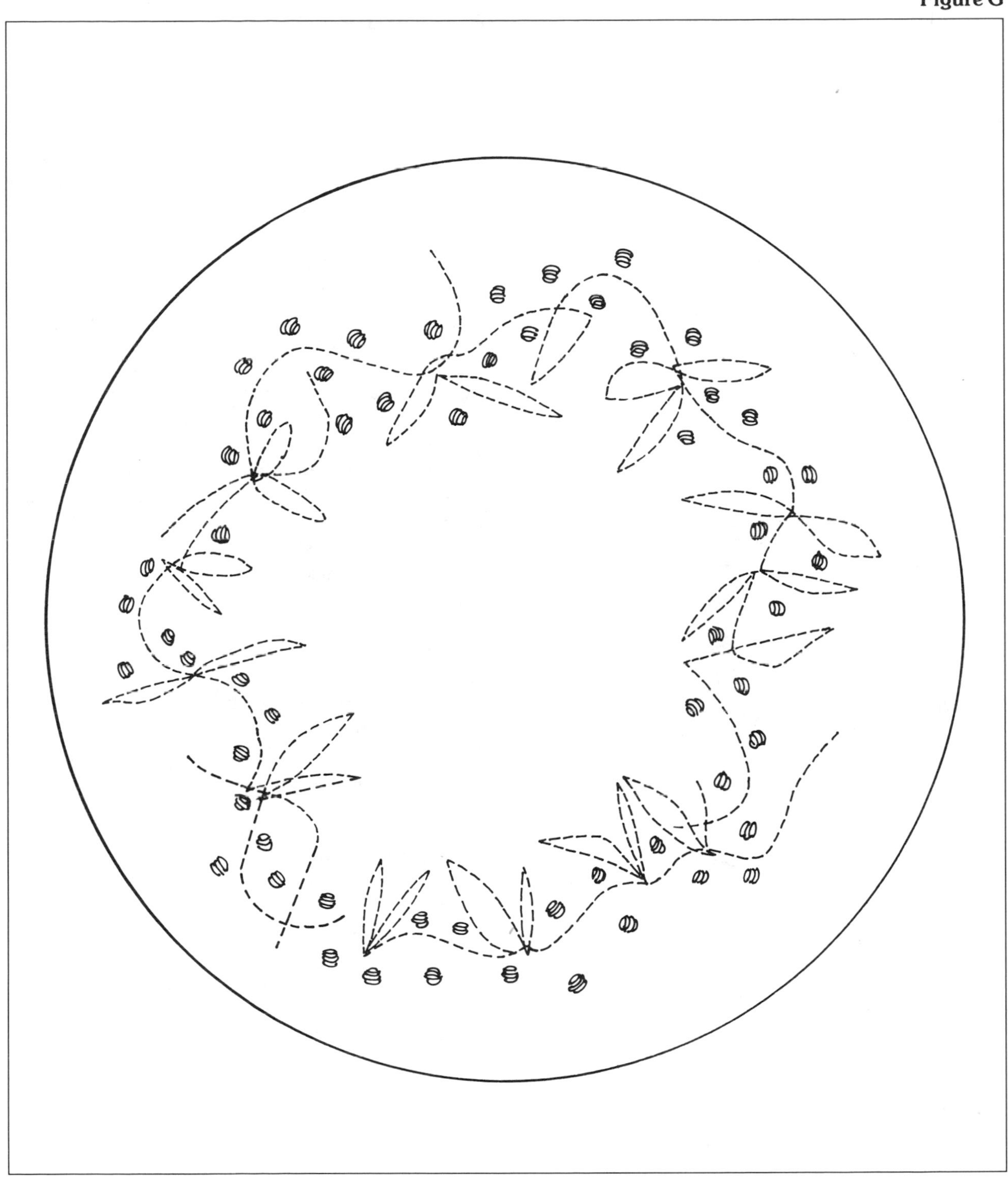

Figure H

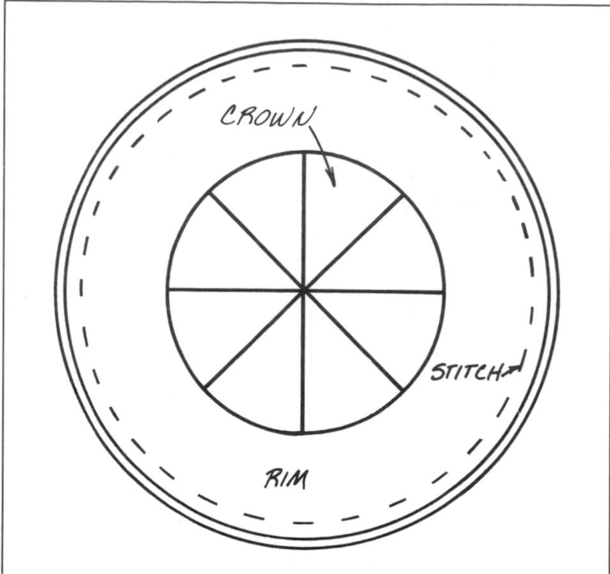

Figure I

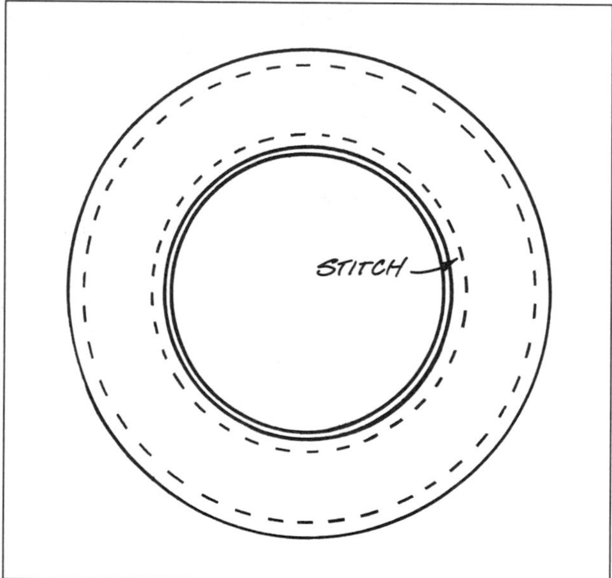

you left in the crown-to-rim seam of the lining layer. Press the seam allowances to the wrong side of the lining along the opening, and whipstitch the opening edges together. Tuck the lining inside the outer layer.

9. Stitch the pompon to the tam, placing it at the center of the outer layer.

Making the Mittens

1. Baste a batting Mitten piece to the wrong side of each outer-fabric Mitten piece, close to the outer edges. Choose one of these pieces for the back of each mitten (they must be mirror images of each other), and baste from the center out to the edges on each of these pieces. We'll call these the Mitten Backs, as they will cover the backs of your hands. We'll call the two remaining outer-fabric Mitten pieces the Mitten Fronts, as they will cover the palms of your hands.

2. We added the same decorative stitching to each Mitten Back. Our design is shown in **Figure J**. Proceed as you did for the previous bouts with decorative stitching (drawing and reproducing a full-size design, etc.), and when you have completed the stitching, remove the basting from the center area of each Mitten Back.

3. To assemble the outer layer of one mitten, choose one Mitten Back and one Mitten Front. Pin them right sides together along the long contoured edges, and stitch a ½-inch-wide seam as shown in **Figure K**. Even though the seam allowance on the pattern is ⅝ inch wide, the outer mitten should be stitched using a ½-inch allowance to allow extra room for the batting. Leave the straight wrist edge open, as shown. Trim the seam allowances of the batting layers only, close to the seam line. Clip the curves, and clip the seam allowances all the way to the stitching line at the corner where the thumb joins the finger portion of the mitten. We suggest that you stitch over the corner seam a couple of times, because it will have to withstand a lot of stress. Leave the outer mitten assembly turned wrong side out.

4. Pin two lining-fabric Mitten pieces right sides together. Stitch a ⅝-inch-wide seam along the long contoured edges, but leave a 3-inch opening opposite the thumb as shown in **Figure L**. Clip the seam allowances and reinforce the corner as you did in step 3. Stitch together the two remaining lining Mitten pieces in the same manner. Turn each lining mitten assembly right side out.

5. Stuff one of the lining mittens inside the assembled outer mitten, working the layers until they are perfectly aligned. The lining thumb should be inside the outer thumb, all fabric should be smooth and unwrinkled, and the wrist edges of the lining and outer layers should

Figure J

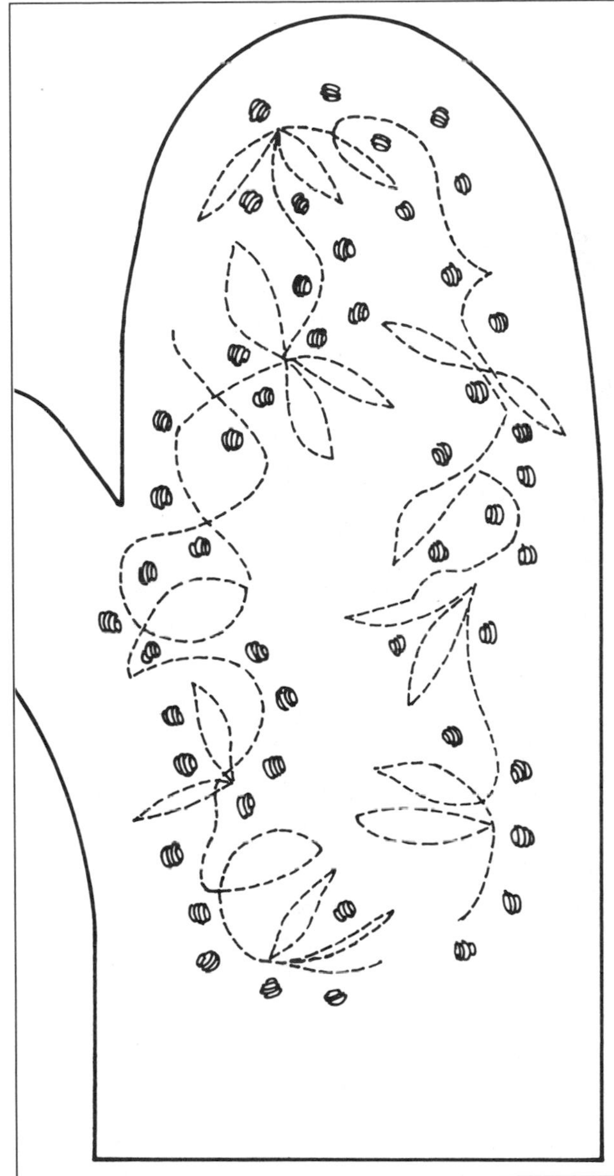

Figure K

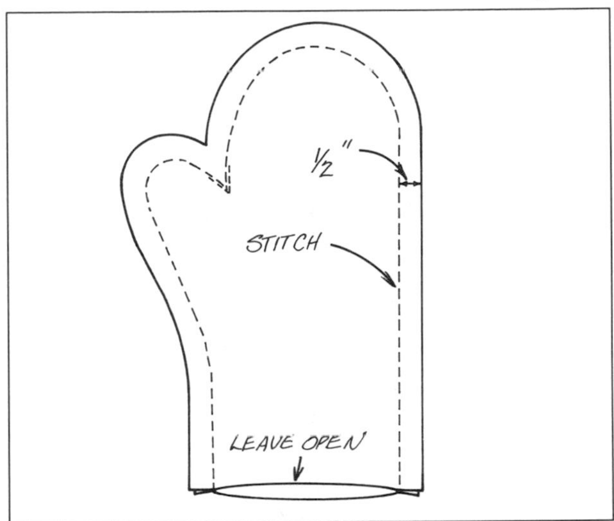

Figure L

be aligned. If you turned the assemblies as specified in steps 3 and 4, the fabrics should now be right sides together. Stitch the seam all the way around the aligned wrist edges.

6. Pull the lining layer out of the outer mitten, and turn the entire assembly inside out through the opening that you left in the lining side seam. Both the outer and lining layers should now be right side out. Press the seam allowances to the wrong side of the lining along the opening, and whipstitch the opening edges together. Tuck the lining back inside the outer mitten, and work the layers until they are aligned correctly. Press the wrist seam.

7. Repeat the procedures in step 3 to assemble a second outer mitten, using the remaining Front and Back Mitten pieces. Repeat the procedures in steps 5 and 6 to join the second outer mitten to the remaining lining assembly, and you're all set for a stylish winter!

Tiny Tot's Sunsuit & Hat

This wrap-around sunsuit is designed so that mom will have no trouble dressing and undressing the little one. The hat is made with an extra-wide brim that does a great job of shading Junior's face from the sun. Bias patchwork adorns both the hat brim and sunsuit bib. Rated very easy.

Materials

1⅛ yards of 44- or 45-inch-wide white fabric for the sunsuit and linings (We used lightweight cotton.)

Accent fabrics: We used lightweight cotton fabrics, all 36 inches wide, for the patchwork strips and a few additional pieces. We have numbered them for easier reading. You'll need ⅜ yard of fabric #1 (we used a medium blue fabric with white stripes); ⅛ yard of fabric #2 (tan fabric with red pin dots); and ¼ yard of fabric #3 (fire-engine red).

5 x 9-inch piece of medium-weight white iron-on backing fabric

Three white ½-inch-diameter buttons for the sunsuit and hat straps

Six decorative buttons for the sunsuit leg closures

White thread

Cutting the Pieces

Note: Label all of the pieces as you cut them, to prevent confusion later on.

1. A scale drawing of the Sunsuit Body pattern is provided in **Figure A**. Enlarge the drawing to make a full-size pattern.

2. Cut two Sunsuit Body pieces from the white fabric. In addition, cut a 6 x 18-inch Hat Lining piece from the same fabric.

3. Cut a 20-inch square from the remaining white fabric, using the selvage as one edge so that the piece is perfectly square. The pieces listed below should be cut on the bias, from this 20-inch square. (Refer to Tips & Techniques for instructions on cutting bias strips, if you're not certain how to go about it.)

Bib Top Border – cut one, 2½ x 8½ inches
Bib Side Border – cut two, each 2½ x 5 inches
Sunsuit Strap – cut two, each 3½ x 21 inches

4. Cut the pieces listed below from fabric #1. These are all straight pieces, and should not be cut on the bias.

Patchwork Strip – cut one, 5¾ x 33½ inches
Hat Brim – cut one, 3¾ x 18 inches
Inner Border – cut one, 1½ x 8½ inches
Hat Strap – cut one, 2½ x 12 inches

1 square = 2 inches **Figure A**

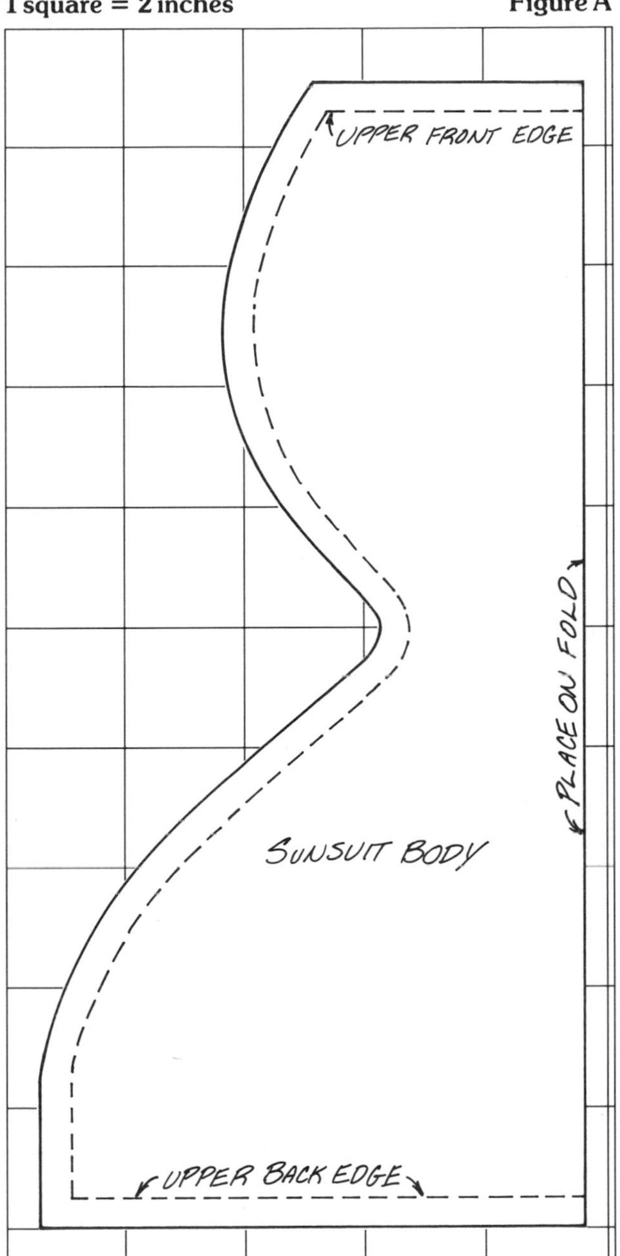

5. Cut a 2½ x 29½-inch straight Patchwork Strip from fabric #2.

6. Cut the straight pieces listed below from fabric #3.

Patchwork Strip – cut one, 3½ x 31½ inches
Hat Back – cut two, 3½ x 18 inches

Figure B

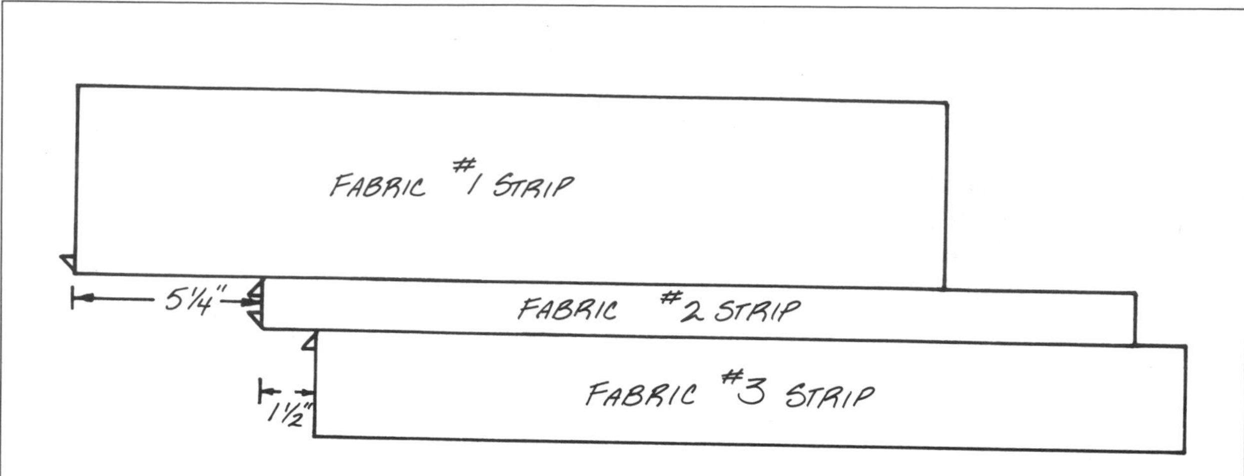

Figure C

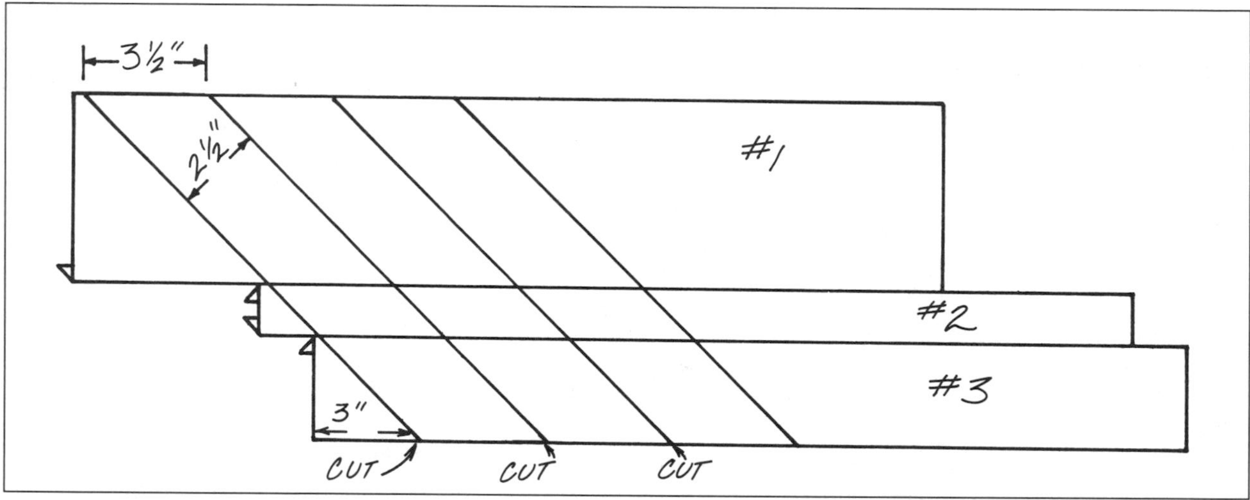

Assembling the Patchwork

This is a Seminole-style bias patchwork assembly. You may wish to read over the appropriate portions of the Tips & Techniques section of this book, for general instructions on how to go about the various assembly procedures. Specific instructions for this particular project are provided here. All seam allowances are ½ inch unless otherwise specified in the instructions.

1. To create the basic patchwork fabric, shown in **Figure B**, you'll need the fabric #1, #2, and #3 Patchwork Strips. Stitch together the #1 and #2 strips side by side, offsetting the ends by 5¼ inches as shown. Stitch the #3 strip to the free long edge of the #2 strip, offsetting the ends by 1½ inches in the same direction. Press the seams open.

2. Cut bias strips from the patchwork fabric as shown in **Figure C**. Each strip should be 2½ inches wide, measured perpendicularly across the diagonal cutting lines. If you measure straight across the upper edge of the top strip, the distance between cutting lines will be 3½ inches. You should be able to get eight complete bias strips from the assembled fabric.

Figure D

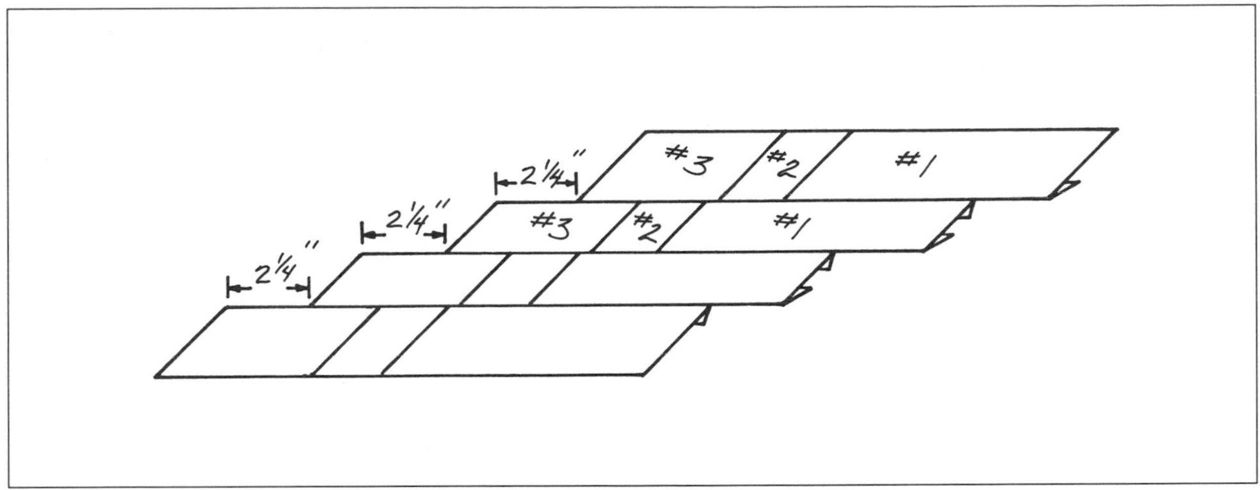

Figure E

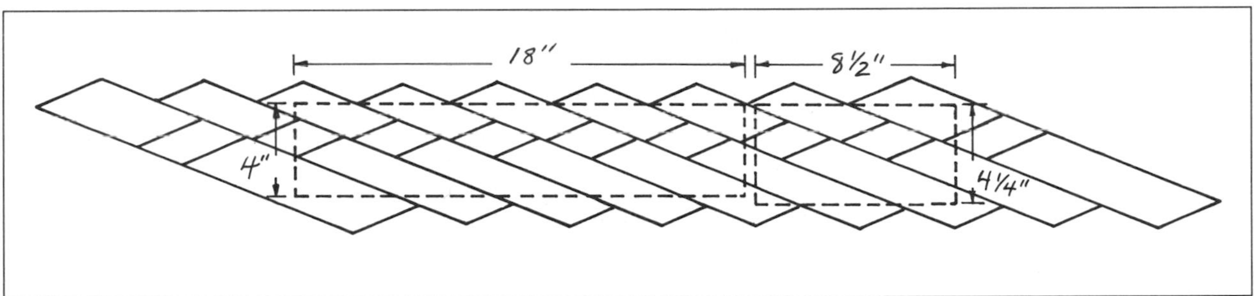

Figure F

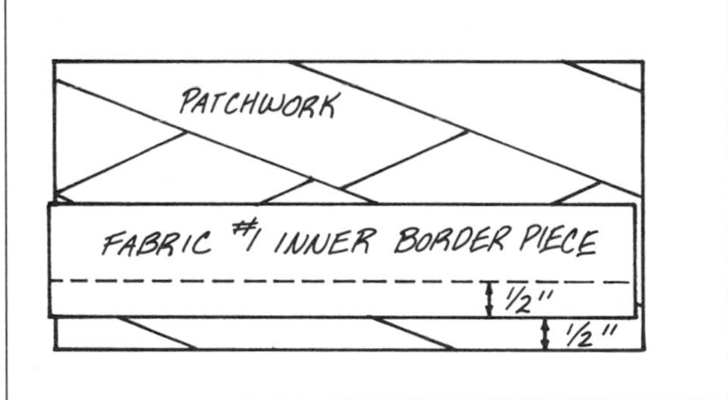

3. Now stitch together all of the bias strips,side by side, offsetting each successive strip by 2¼ inches in the same direction. **Figure D** shows several of the strips sewn together properly. Be sure that each one is turned the same way end for end, so the color progression remains the same throughout the assembly, as shown.

4. Cut from pattern or tracing paper a 4¼ x 8½-inch rectangular pattern for the sunsuit Bib Patchwork, and a 4 x 18-inch rectangular pattern for the Hat Patchwork. Place the patterns on top of the assembled patchwork as shown by the dotted lines in **Figure E**, and cut the two pieces.

Finishing the Bib Patchwork

1. Pin the fabric #1 Inner Border piece to the Bib Patchwork piece, placing right sides together and aligning one long edge of the Border piece ½ inch from the lower edge of the Patchwork piece. Stitch the seam ½ inch from the edge of the Border piece, as shown in **Figure F**. Turn the Border piece downward, so the fabric is right side up and forms a border along the bottom of the Patchwork piece. Press the Border piece flat, and baste it to the Patchwork piece close to the lower edge.

Figure G

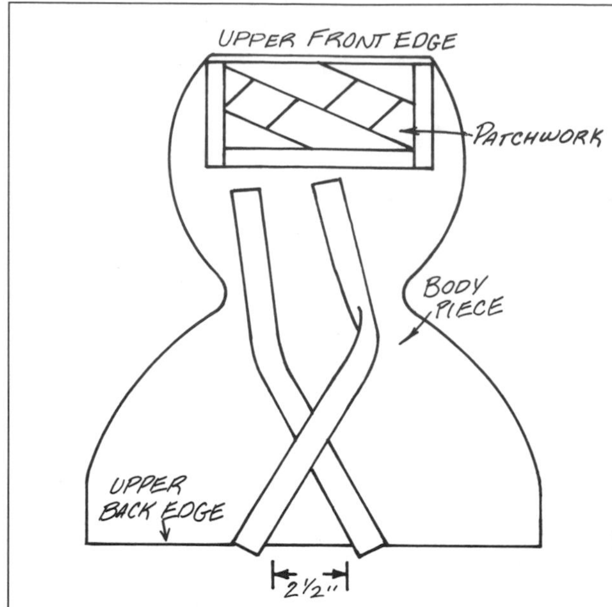

Figure H

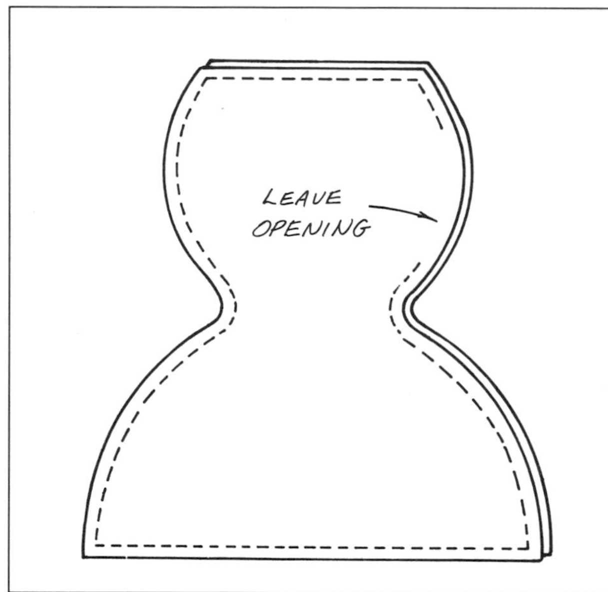

2. Bond the piece of iron-on backing material to the wrong side of the assembled patchwork, following the manufacturer's instructions. Trim the edges of the backing material even with the patchwork.

3. Top and side borders are added to the patchwork, and then you can proceed to assemble the sunsuit. For this assembly, you'll need the white Bib Top and Bib Side Border pieces that you cut earlier. Use the Top Border piece to encase the upper edge of the patchwork. (Refer to the Tips & Techniques section of this book, if necessary, for instructions on encasing raw edges with binding strips.) Trim the ends of the Top Border even with the sides of the patchwork. Use one of the Side Border pieces to encase each side edge of the patchwork; trim the lower ends of these pieces even with the lower edge of the patchwork, but finish the upper ends as described in Tips & Techniques. The lower edge of the bib should remain unbound.

Figure I

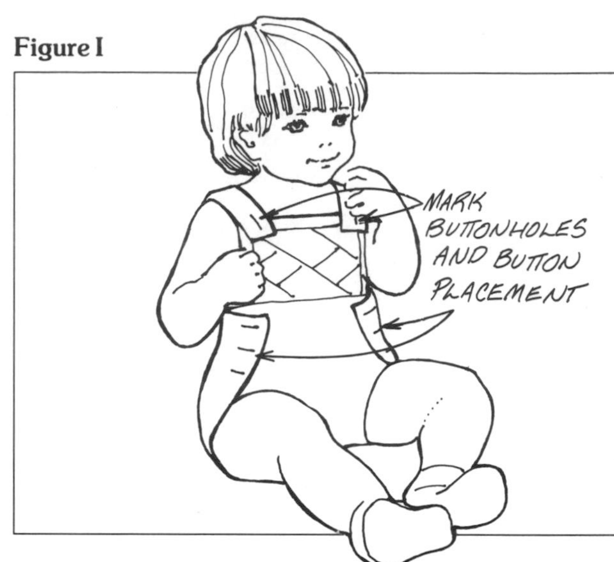

Assembling the Sunsuit

1. To assemble one strap, fold one of the white Sunsuit Strap pieces in half lengthwise, placing right sides together. Stitch the seam along the aligned long edges only, leaving both ends open. Turn the strap right side out and press it flat so that the seam runs along the center of one side. Press the seam allowances to the inside at one end only, and whipstitch the end closed.

2. Repeat the procedures in step 1 to assemble the second strap, using the remaining Sunsuit Strap piece.

3. Place one of the Sunsuit Body pieces right side up on a flat surface. Place the assembled bib and the two straps on top as shown in **Figure G**. The bib should be right side up, and the lower edge of the bib should be aligned with the upper front edge of the Body piece, as

Take Me Home Ensemble – page 83

Winter Ensemble – page 41

Beach Cover-Up & Tote – page 16

Gown & Robe – page 25

Summer Caftan – page 89

Appliqued Jacket & Vest – page 57

Tiny Tot's Sunsuit & Hat – page 50

Puzzle Jacket – page 96

Pinafore & Bonnet – page 66

Acute Caftan – page 10

Christmas Vest – page 75

Figure J

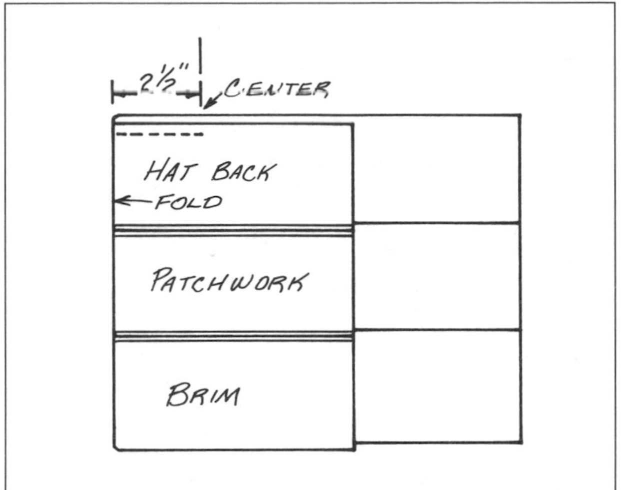

Figure K

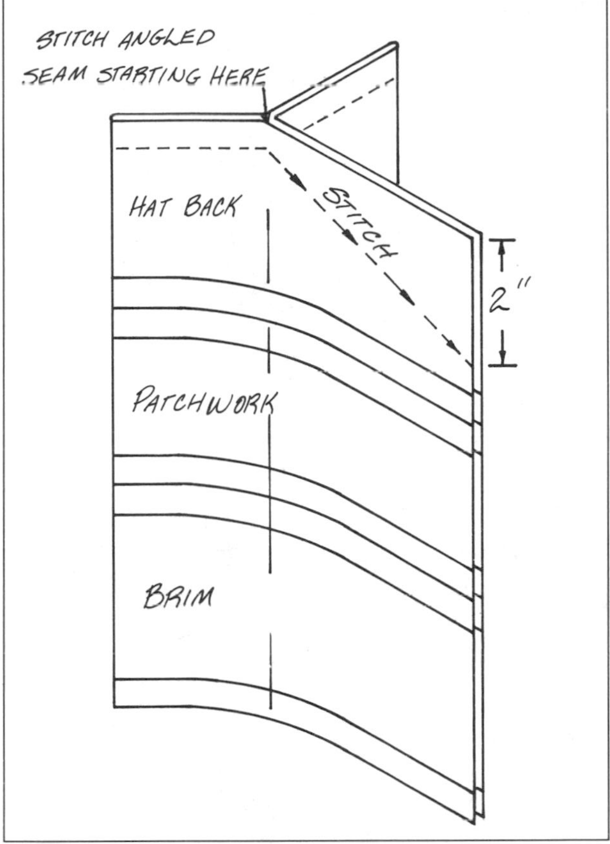

shown. Each strap should be seam-side down and placed at an angle, with the raw open end aligned at the upper back edge of the Body piece. Allow 2½ inches between the straps. Baste the bib and straps in place, close to the respective edges. Temporarily pin the free ends of the straps to the Body piece, out of the way of the side seamlines.

4. Place the remaining Sunsuit Body piece right side down on top of the assembly from step 3. The straps and bib will be sandwiched between the two Body pieces. Pin and then stitch the seams along all outer edges, leaving a 3- or 4-inch opening along one side, as shown in **Figure H**. Clip the curves and corners, and turn the sunsuit right side out through the opening. Press all seams, and press the seam allowances to the inside along the opening edges. Whipstitch the opening edges together.

5. Have your toddler try on the sunsuit to determine placement of the buttons. The bib goes at the front, and the upper back edge of the sunsuit is pulled between the child's legs, and upward. Cross the straps at the back, just above the upper back edge, and pin them together where they cross. Bring each strap to the front, and pin the end underneath the bib. Bring the two ends of the upper back edge around the child's sides, and pin the flaps to the front of the sunsuit (**Figure I**). We used three decorative buttons for each flap, with the buttons sewn to the front of the sunsuit and the buttonholes worked in the flaps. Mark the placement of the buttonholes on each flap, and of the corresponding buttons on the sunsuit front. Mark the placement of the buttonholes on the upper border of the bib, and of the buttons on the straps.

6. Take the sunsuit off your child, and stitch the straps together where they cross at the back. Work the buttonholes at the marked locations on the flaps and bib, and sew the buttons in place.

Assembling the Sun Hat

1. The sun hat consists of outer and lining layers, which are assembled in much the same manner. To assemble the outer layer, you'll need the Hat Patchwork, the Hat Brim piece, and one of the Hat Back pieces. Place the Hat Patchwork and the Hat Brim piece right sides together, aligning one long edge of the Patchwork

Figure L

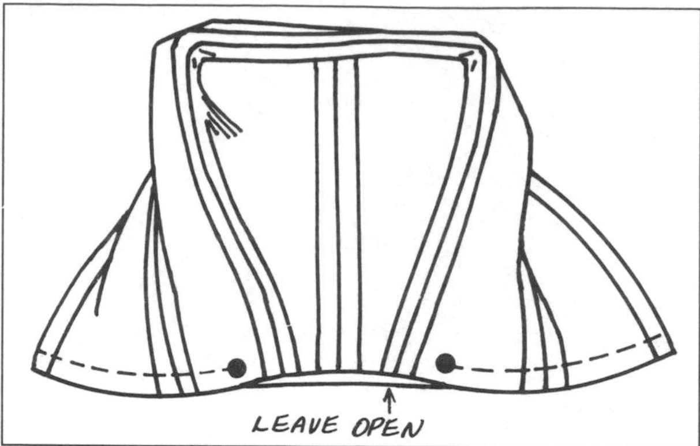

Figure M

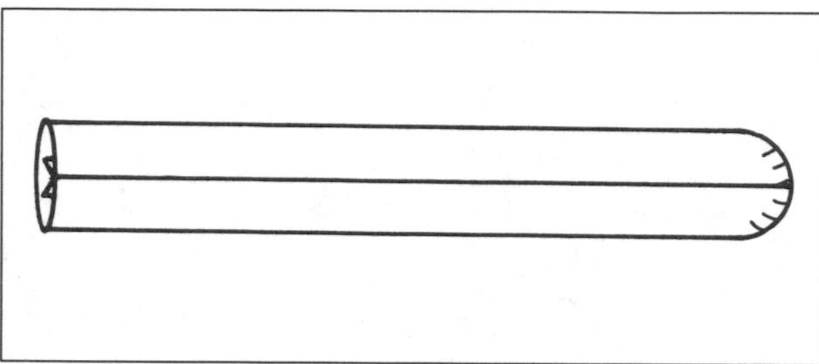

with one long edge of the Brim. Stitch the seam along the aligned long edges, and press open.

2. Place the assembly from step 1 right sides together with one of the Hat Back pieces, aligning the free long edge of the Patchwork with one long edge of the Hat Back. Stitch the seam and press open.

3. Place the assembly from step 2 right side up on a flat surface. Measure from end to end, and mark the center point along the free long edge of the Hat Back piece. Fold one end of the assembly in toward the center, so that the fold line is 2½ inches from the marked center point (**Figure J**). Stitch through both layers of the Hat Back piece, ½ inch from the aligned edges, from the fold line to the center point as shown. Now fold the same end back toward its original position, so it will be out of the way. Follow the same procedures to fold the opposite end of the assembly in toward the center, and stitch in the same manner.

4. Place the two ends of the assembly right sides together as shown in **Figure K**. Stitch an angled seam through both layers of the Hat Back piece as shown, beginning at the point where the stitching lines from step 3 meet, and angling out to the ends of the Hat Back piece. The seam should be about 2 inches wide at the ends of the Back piece. Trim the angled seam allowance evenly to ½ inch, and press open.

5. To assemble the lining layer of the sun hat, you'll need the white Hat Lining and the remaining red Hat Back. Place the two right sides together, aligning one long edge of the Lining with one long edge of the Hat Back. Stitch the seam and press open.

6. Follow the procedures described in steps 3 and 4 to fold this assembly and stitch the Hat Back seams.

7. Turn the outer layer right side out, but leave the lining layer inside out. Place the outer layer inside the lining. (The fabrics should now be right sides together.) Align the long front edges of the two layers, and stitch the seam along the front edges only. Press the seam allowances toward the lining and clip the corners.

8. Realign the layers, still right sides together, so that the long back edges are even. The front seam will now lie on the lining side of the hat, but that's as it should be. Stitch the seam along the aligned back edges as shown in **Figure L**, leaving a 3-inch opening at the center back. Turn the outer and lining layers right sides out through the opening, and press the seam along the back edge. Press the seam allowances to the inside along the opening, and whipstitch the pressed edges together. Tuck the lining inside the outer layer. To press the front edge, fold the Hat Brim piece so that the front seam lies evenly along the lining side of the hat.

9. Fold the Hat Strap piece in half lengthwise, placing right sides together. Stitch the seam along the aligned long edges only, and press the seam open. Turn the strap right side out and press it flat, adjusting the layers so the seam line runs along the center of one side. Turn the seam allowances to the inside at one end, forming a curve (**Figure M**), and whipstitch the end closed. Finish the opposite end in the same manner.

10. Put the sun hat on your child's head, and pin one end of the strap to one front corner of the hat. Bring the strap under the child's chin, and pin the opposite end to the opposite front corner of the hat. Mark the placement of a buttonhole on one end of the strap, and mark the corresponding placement of the button on the hat. Stitch the opposite end of the strap to the hat. Work the buttonhole, and sew on the button.

Appliqued Jacket & Vest

This striking vest and jacket combination is made of black channel-quilted fabric; the vertical quilting lines, done with white thread, create the illusion of pinstripes. The jacket back sports a trio of appliqued geese, and on the vest is a brace of sheep with embroidered flowers.

Materials

For the appliques:

½ yard of 36-inch-wide white cotton fabric for the goose and sheep bodies

Scraps of orange cotton fabric for the goose feet (Three 4 x 4-inch pieces will be enough.)

Scraps of yellow cotton fabric for the goose beaks (Three 1½ x 2-inch pieces will do.)

1 yard of 1-inch-wide striped grosgrain ribbon

½ yard of lightweight fusible interfacing fabric

An embroidery needle and small quantities of embroidery floss in several colors, for the flower design on the sheep applique (We used green, yellow, white, purple, and three shades of pink.)

White thread

For the jacket:

We chose a commercial pattern for the jacket, and purchased the specified amount of black channel-quilted fabric. You may wish to design your own pattern, purchase a commercial one, or even combine elements of several different commercial patterns. If you wish to use channel-quilted fabric, but can not find it in your area, you can make your own. Purchase the required amount of fabric for the outer layer, an equal amount of batting, and an equal amount of backing fabric. The backing fabric can be the same as the outer fabric, or it can be a contrasting color. It's a simple matter to create channel-quilted fabric from the materials you purchased: Place the outer and backing fabrics wrong sides together with the batting between, smooth out the layers, and baste them together securely. Then run straight parallel lines of quilting stitches (by hand or machine), spaced at about 1-inch intervals, across the fabrics.

Lining: There are two ways to approach the inside of your jacket. If you want it fully lined, choose a pattern for a lined jacket, and purchase the specified amount of lining fabric. If you'd rather not deal with a full lining, purchase a couple of packages of seam binding tape in a color that matches the backing side of the channel-quilted fabric. The binding tape can be used to cover the seam allowances on the inside of the jacket.

For the vest:

Pattern: We made our own, but you may wish to purchase a commercial pattern. We have provided instructions for making and sizing your own vest pattern in the Tips & Techniques section of this book.

1¾ yards of 44- or 45-inch-wide channel quilted fabric; or purchase an equal amount each of outer fabric, batting, and backing fabric to create your own channel-quilted fabric (If you will be using a commercial pattern, the amount of fabric required may vary.)

Lining: We used 6 yards of seam binding tape and 3 yards of 1-inch-wide rickrack to cover the seam allowances on the inside of the vest. The binding tape is the same color as the backing side of the channel-quilted fabric, and the rickrack is the same color as the outer side. If you prefer a fully lined vest, purchase an amount of lining fabric equal to the amount of channel-quilted fabric for the vest, instead of binding tape and rickrack.

THE JACKET

Preliminary Assembly

Follow the pattern manufacturer's instructions to cut the pieces and assemble the jacket. When cutting the pieces, keep in mind that the channel quilting lines are like stripes; you want them to run in the same direction on all pieces, except perhaps on the pockets. Most folks prefer the lines to run vertically, because vertical lines make one look taller and slimmer. If you will be lining the jacket, go ahead and assemble the lining separately, but do not install it in the jacket until the appliques have been done. If you will be using binding tape to cover the seam allowances inside the jacket, they should be installed before the appliques are done.

Adding the Appliques

1. Scale drawings for the geese are provided in **Figure A**. Enlarge the drawings to make full-size patterns.

2. The body, feet, and beak for each goose are cut from different fabrics. Cut apart each goose pattern to separate the body portion from the feet and beak, along the dividing lines indicated on the scale drawings.

1 square = 1 inch **Figure A**

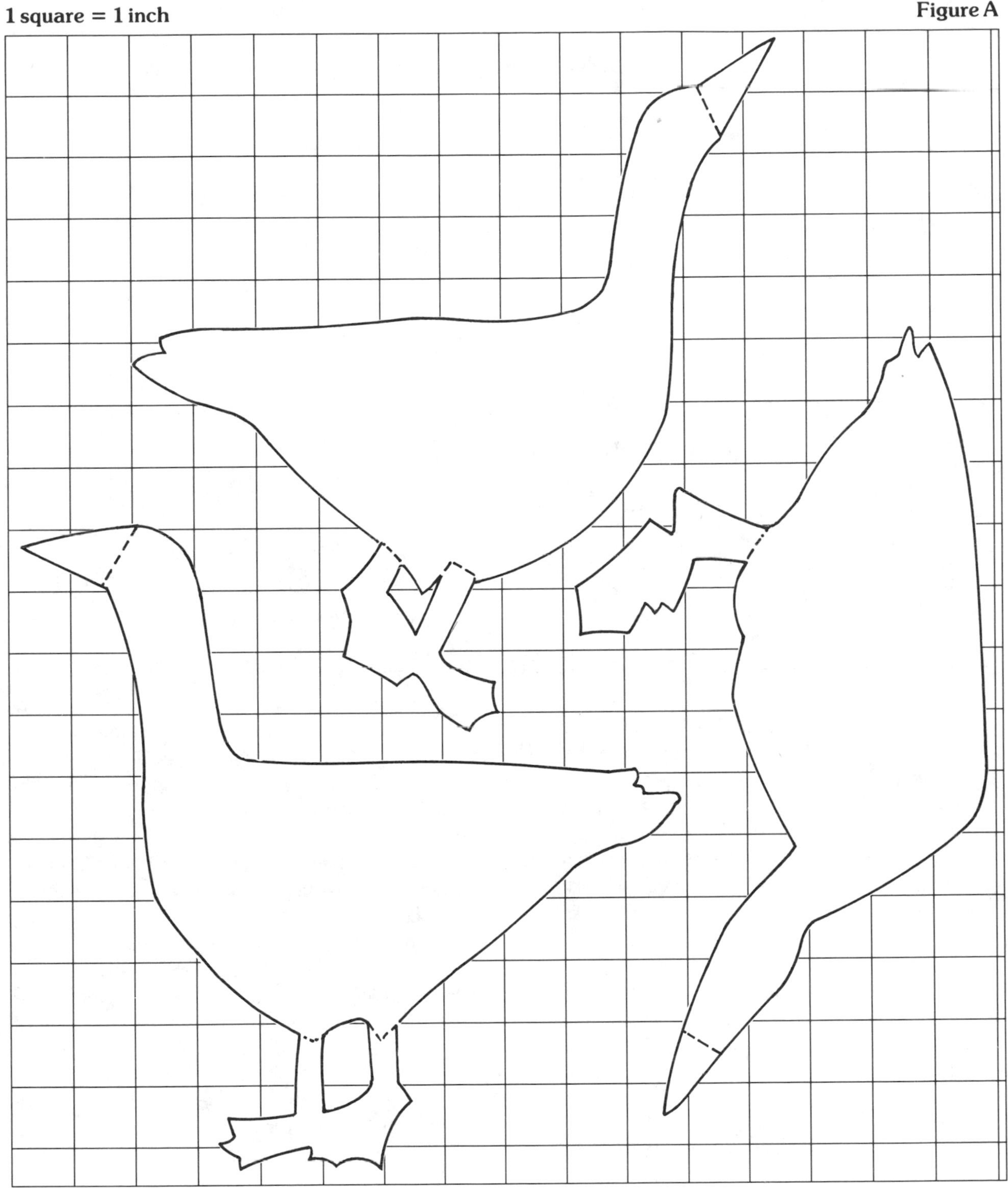

Figure B

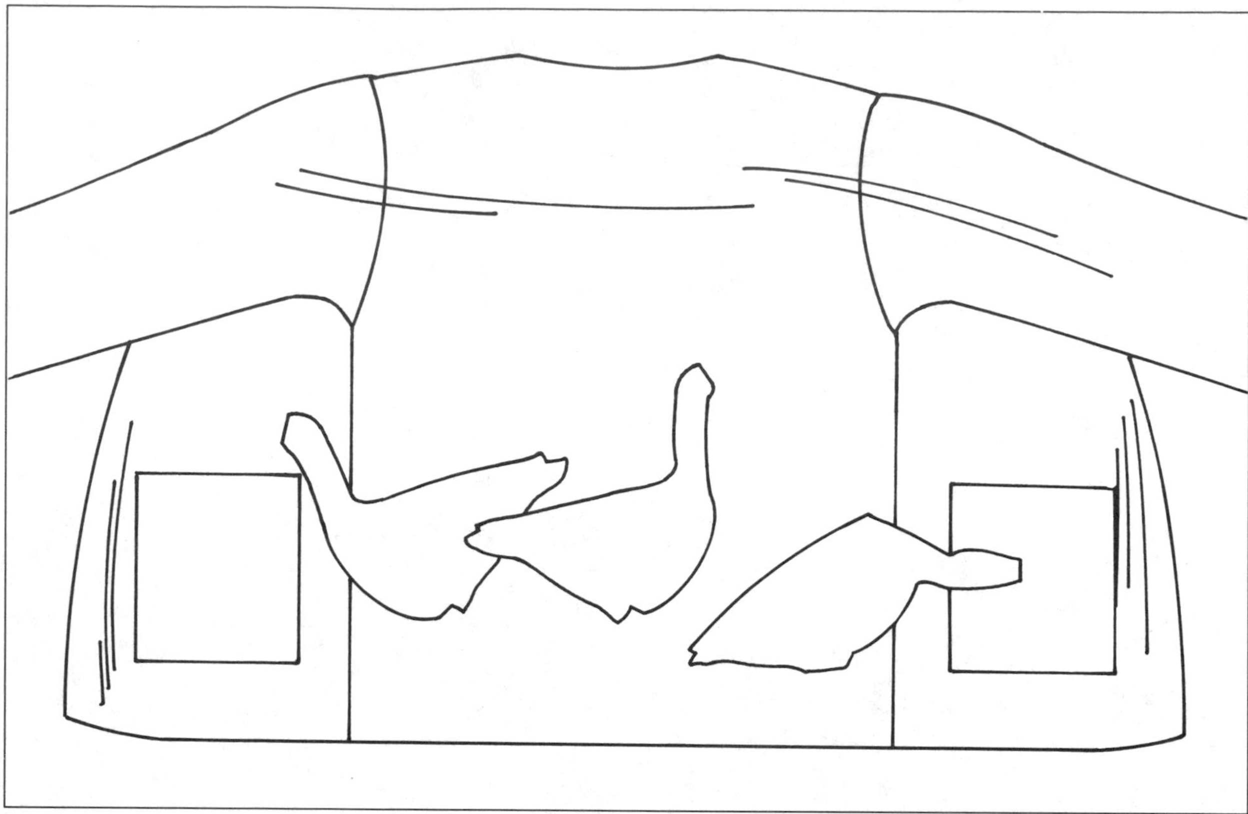

Cut one of each goose body from white fabric. Cut the feet for each goose from orange fabric, and the beak from yellow fabric.

3. Cut a matching piece of fusible material for each fabric piece that you cut in step 2.

4. Open the assembled jacket so that the front sections are spread straight outward from the back, and place the jacket right side up on a flat surface. Arrange the fabric goose body pieces on the jacket as you would like them to appear. The arrangement we used is shown in **Figure B**; as you can see, we allowed the design to wrap around the side seams to the jacket front on each side. When you have the arrangement you like, place a matching piece of fusible material underneath each goose body, and follow the instructions that came with the fusible material to bond the pieces to the jacket. Follow the same procedures to bond the fabric beaks and feet in place.

5. Use a closely-spaced zigzag setting on your machine, and stitch over the edges of the applique pieces. We used white thread for the bodies, yellow for the beaks, and orange for the feet.

6. We added additional lines of zigzag stitching to create wing and feather details on the bodies, and outlines on the feet, as shown in **Figure C**. This technique is not difficult, but it does take some practice; you don't want to have to rip out even an inch-long segment of closely spaced zigzag stitches, because it leaves the fabric looking slightly chewed. Practice on fabric scraps, and if you still do not feel confident you can leave off the detail stitching or add details using fabric markers or acrylic paint.

7. We added ribbon appliques to create a three-dimensional effect (**Figure D**). Cut a 12-inch length of ribbon, tie a loose half-knot at the approximate center, and cut each end at an angle. Place the ribbon across

Figure C

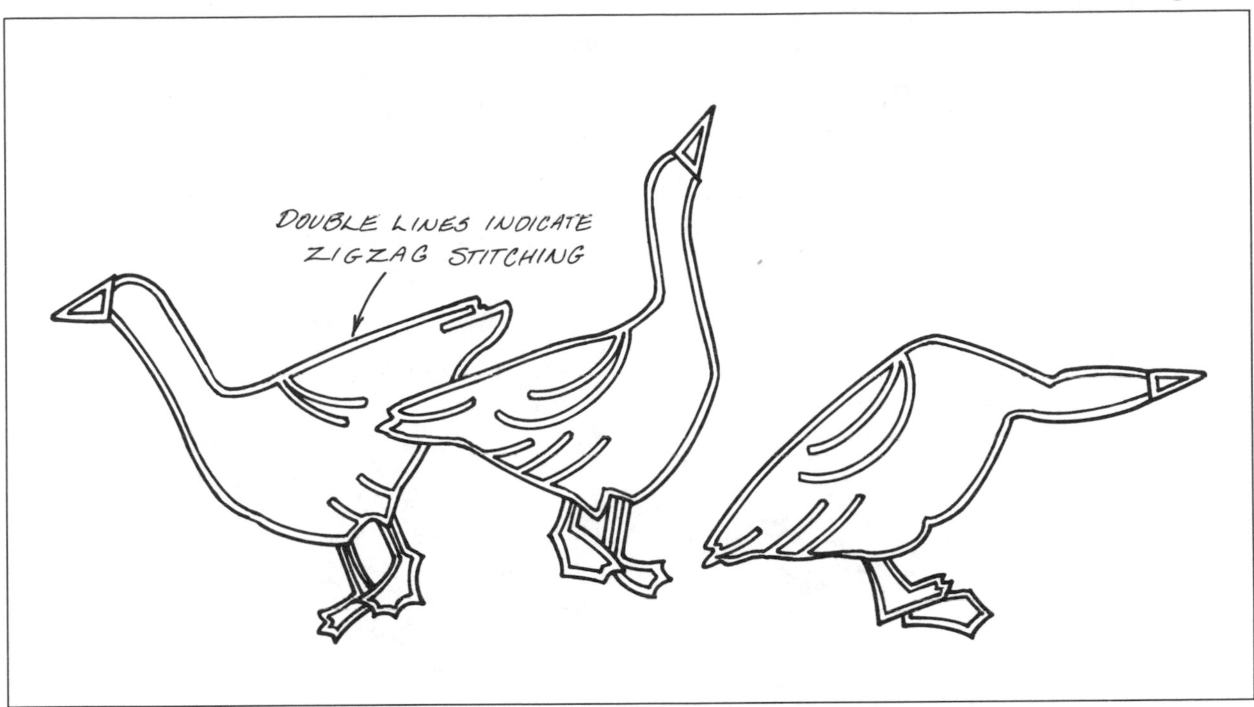

Figure D

Figure E

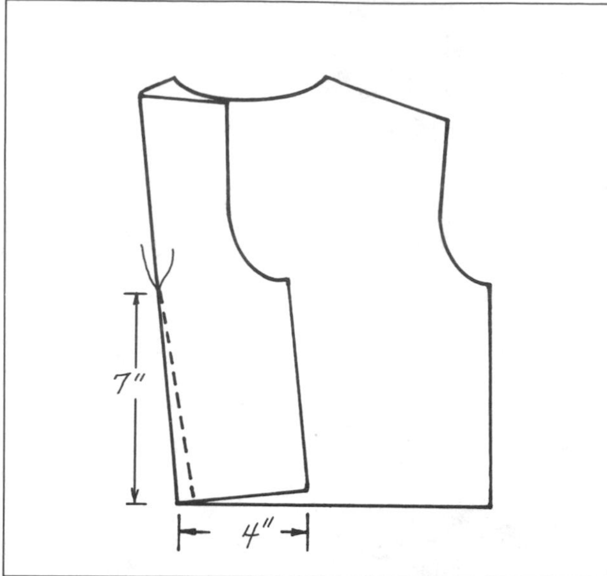

the neck of one goose applique, as shown on the left-hand goose in **Figure D**. Pin the ends of the ribbon to the jacket and zigzag stitch over the edges and ends. Do not stitch over the knotted portion at the goose's neck.

8. Use the remaining length of ribbon for the longer applique, shown on the right in **Figure D**. Cut each end at an angle and tie a half-knot about 4 inches from one end. Pin the ribbon to the jacket as shown and zigzag in place, leaving selected portions unstitched for the three-dimensional effect.

THE VEST

We have provided instructions for making the vest exactly as we did. If you purchased a commercial pattern, disregard our instructions for cutting and assembling the vest pieces. Follow the pattern manufacturer's assembly instructions, and then refer to our instructions for adding the appliques. If you are going to line the vest, do so after the appliques have been added.

Cutting the Pieces

1. Refer to the Tips & Techniques section of this book, and make full-size patterns for the Vest Front and Vest Back. If your vest will be unlined, add 1-inch hem allowances to the armhole and outer edges of each piece, but add only the normal ½-inch seam allowances to the shoulder and side edges. If the vest will be lined, add only the normal ½-inch allowances to all edges of each pattern.

2. Cut two Vest Front pieces and one Vest Back piece from channel-quilted fabric. If you are going to line the vest, cut the same pieces from lining fabric as well.

3. Cut two Pocket pieces, each 4¾ x 4¾ inches, from channel-quilted fabric.

Assembling the Vest

1. We stitched two darts at the lower edge of the Vest Back to make the bottom of the vest more fitted. Place the Vest Back piece right side up on a flat surface and fold one side in toward the center as shown in **Figure E**. The fold line should be about 4 inches from the side edge. Adjust the two layers of fabric so they are even at the lower edge. Run an angled stitching line, beginning at the lower edge approximately ¾ inch from the fold, and ending about 7 inches above the lower edge at the fold, as shown. Tie off the threads at the top of the dart. Slit a 4-inch segment of the dart along the fold line, from the lower edge upward. Press the slit portion of the dart open, and press the upper portion flat. Fold the opposite side edge of the Vest Back in toward the center, and stitch a dart near that side in the same manner. If you are going to line your vest, perform the same procedures on the lining-fabric Vest Back piece.

2. To prepare one Pocket piece, cut a 4¾-inch length of seam binding tape and press one edge open. Pin the tape and Pocket piece right sides together, aligning the pressed-open edge of the tape with one edge of the Pocket piece. (This will be the upper edge of the pocket, so you must decide at this point whether you want the channel quilting lines to run vertically or horizontally on the pocket.) Stitch the seam along the fold line of the tape, and stitch across the tape ½ inch from each end (**Figure F**). Clip the two upper corners, turn the binding tape to the wrong side of the Pocket piece along the seam line, and press the seam. Clip the two lower corners and press the side and lower edges of the Pocket piece to the wrong side of the fabric along the seam lines.

3. Pin the pocket to one of the Vest Front pieces, about 2½ inches from the lower edge and 4 inches

Figure F

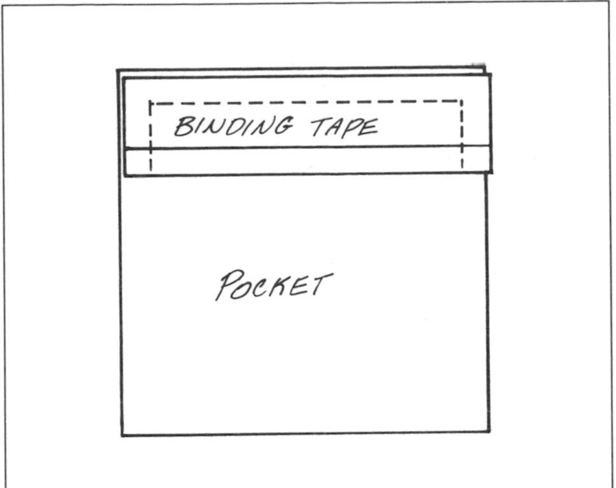

Figure G

Figure H

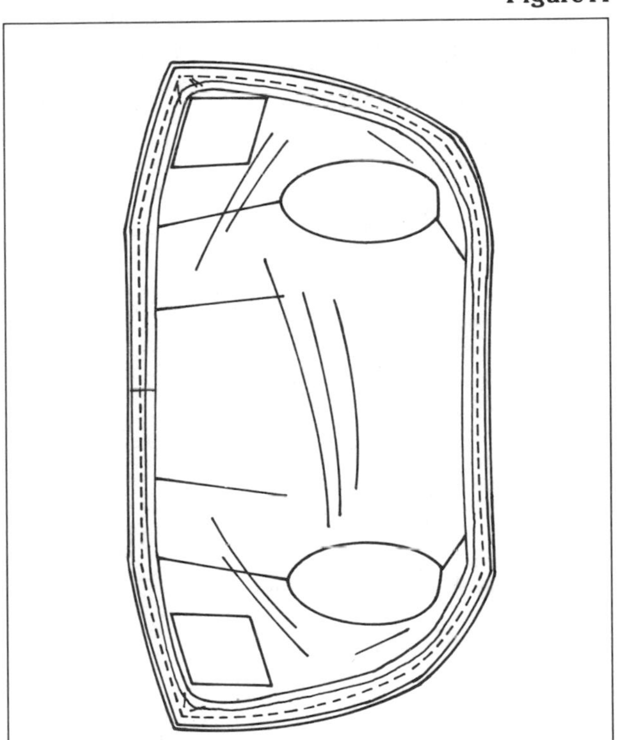

from the center front edge. Topstitch close to the side and lower edges of the pocket.

4. Repeat the procedures in steps 2 and 3 to make a second pocket, using the remaining channel-quilted Pocket piece and another length of seam binding tape. Topstitch the pocket to the other Vest Front piece.

5. Place the Vest Back piece right side up on a flat surface, and place the two Vest Front pieces right sides down on top. Stitch the shoulder and side seams on each side, as shown in **Figure G**. Press the seams open. If you are lining your vest, perform the same procedures on the lining pieces, and skip the remaining steps in this section.

6. Cut four lengths of seam binding tape, each the same length as the shoulder seams. Use one length to cover each shoulder seam allowance. (Refer to Tips & Techniques if you're not certain how to go about this.) Cut additional lengths of binding tape and follow the same procedures to cover the side seam allowances and the darts.

7. Measure the length of the entire outer edge of the vest, and cut a length of seam binding tape 1 inch longer than the measurement. Press open one edge of the tape, and press a ½-inch-wide hem to the wrong side of the tape at one end. Start with the hemmed end and pin the tape to the vest, beginning and ending at the center of the lower back. The tape and vest should be right sides together, and the pressed-open edge of the tape should be aligned with the outer edge of the vest. Lap the unhemmed end of the tape over the hemmed end at the starting point. Stitch along the fold line of the tape, all the way around the vest, as shown in **Figure H**.

Figure I

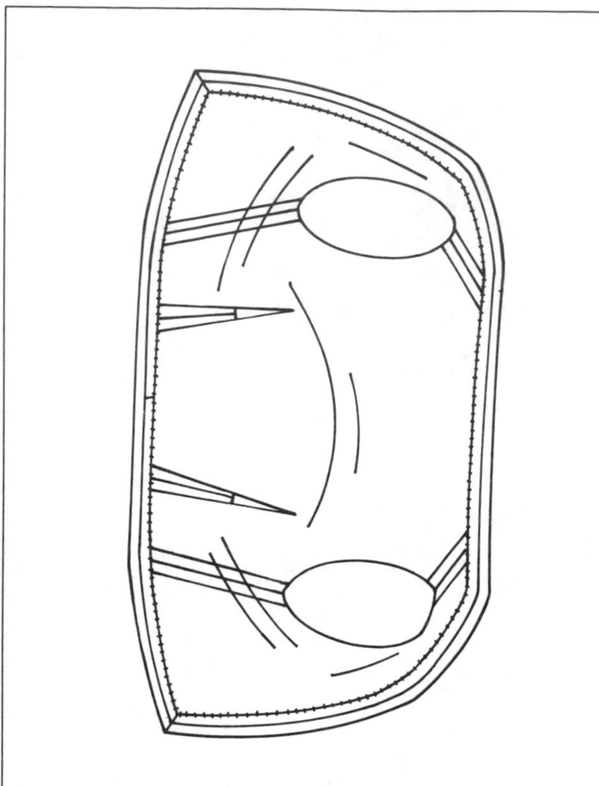

8. Turn the tape and another ½ inch of the vest fabric to the wrong side of the vest all the way around the outer edge, forming a hem (**Figure I**). It may be necessary to clip the tape in some spots to make it lie flat. The tape should be folded neatly at the corners. Press the hem and hand stitch the free edge of the tape to the wrong side of the vest.

9. Follow the procedures described in steps 7 and 8 to hem each armhole edge of the vest.

10. We hand stitched wide rickrack over the binding tape around the outer hem and around each armhole. This is not absolutely necessary, but it will cover the spots where you clipped the tape and will add interest to the inside of the vest.

Adding the Appliques

1. A scale drawing for the double sheep applique is provided in **Figure J**. Enlarge the drawing to make a full-size pattern, and cut one sheep piece from white fabric. The circular cutout shown on the scale drawing will serve as one sheep's face. Cut the circular spot from the fabric sheep piece where indicated.

2. Use the fabric sheep piece as a guide to cut a matching piece from fusible material.

3. Bond the white sheep applique to the vest back

Figure J

1 square = 1 inch

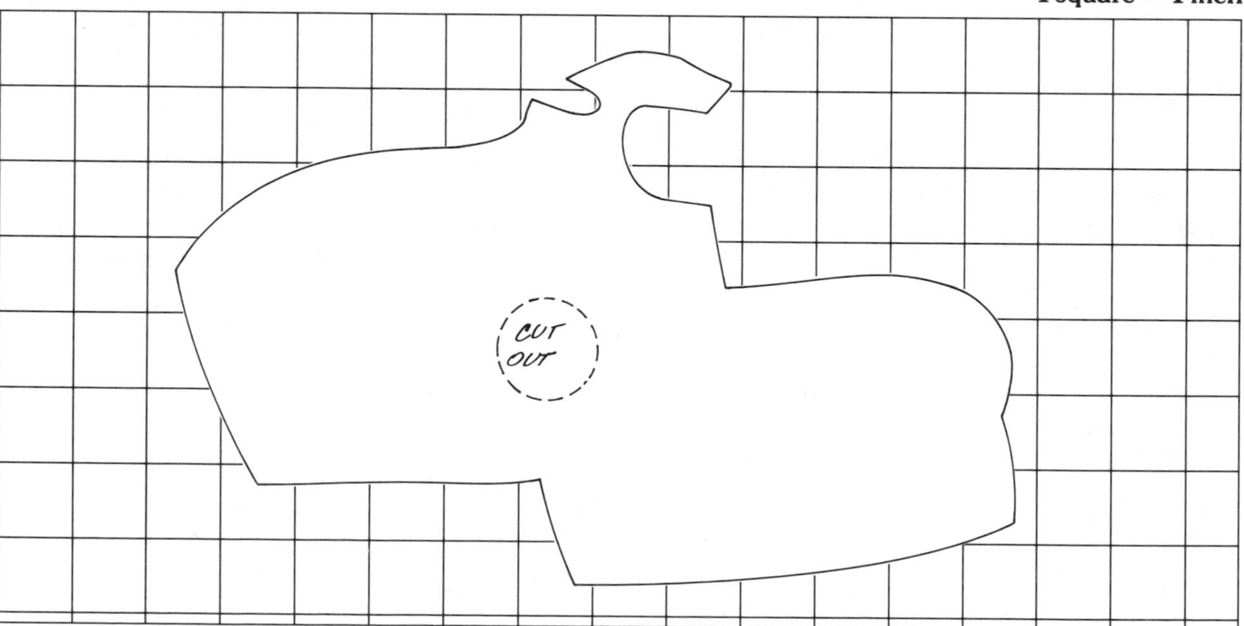

as you did the geese on the jacket back. Use a closely-spaced zigzag setting, and machine stitch over all outer edges of the applique.

4. Add detail zigzag stitching as shown in **Figure K**.

5. We added embroidered flowers to the applique as shown in **Figure L**. Instructions are provided in Tips & Techniques for working the satin stitch and French knots, if you need help in that area. We have indicated the color scheme we used.

6. If you are going to line your vest, place the assembled outer and lining layers right sides together and stitch the seam around the aligned outer edges, leaving a 4-inch opening along the lower back edge. Turn the layers right sides out through the opening, press the seams, and press the seam allowances to the inside along the opening. Whipstitch the opening edges together. Press the seam allowances to the inside around each armhole clipping where necessary. Whipstitch the pressed lining and outer-layer edges together around each armhole.

Figure K

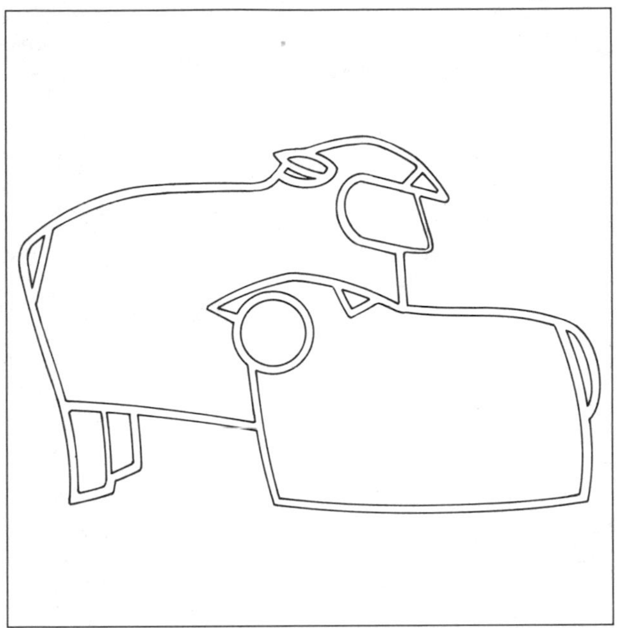

Figure L

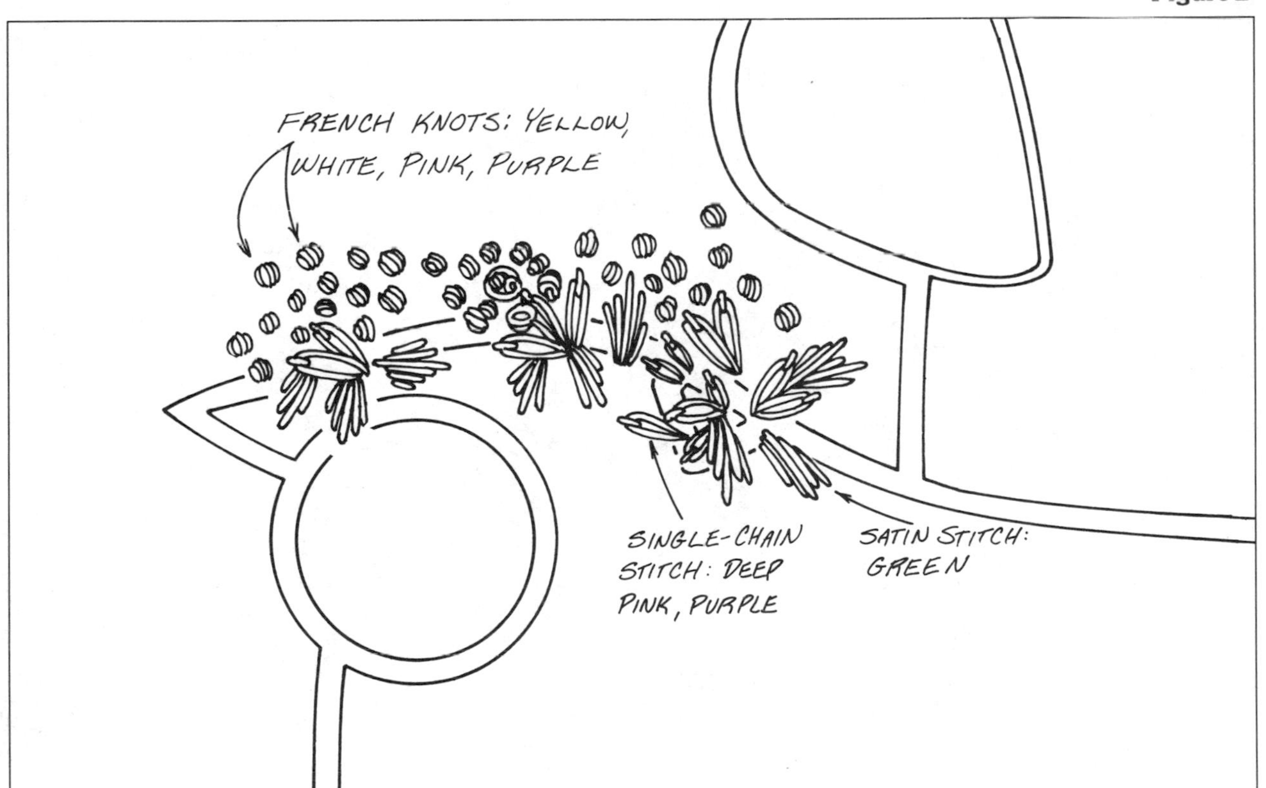

Pinafore & Bonnet

If your lively young lady has a large fabric doll, this cute little combo might fit them both! The pinafore features bias patchwork along the bib and lower border, with tie-straps at the shoulders and sides for ease in getting it on and off. The simple bonnet is made of eyelet fabric embellished with layers of colorful ribbon and white lace.

Figure A

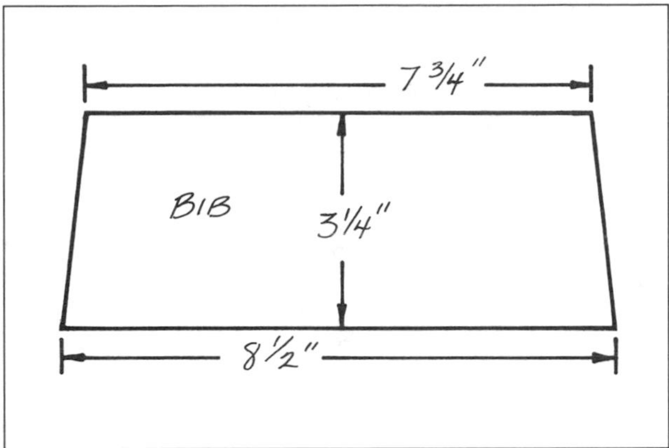

Materials

For the pinafore:

2 yards of 45-inch-wide lightweight white cotton fabric
Lightweight cotton fabrics, all 36 inches wide, for the patchwork: 1/4 yard of pink, 1/8 yard of blue, and 1/8 yard of yellow
White thread

For the bonnet:

9 x 17-inch piece of white eyelet fabric
3 1/2 yards of 1 3/4-inch-wide white lace trim
2 yards of 1-inch-wide striped grosgrain ribbon, in colors that coordinate with the patchwork fabrics
1 yard of 3/4-inch-wide white satin ribbon
White thread

Cutting the Pinafore Pieces

1. Cut the pieces listed below from white fabric. Label each piece for easy identification.

Skirt – 12 x 45 inches, cut two
Border A – 1 3/4 x 45 inches, cut two
Border B – 2 x 45 inches, cut two
Border Lining – 3 3/4 x 45 inches, cut two
Strap – 6 1/2 x 8 1/2 inches, cut eight
Border C – 1 1/2 x 8 1/2 inches, cut one
Border D – 1 3/4 x 8 1/2 inches, cut one
Bib – 3 1/4 x 8 1/2 inches, cut three
Bib Binding – 2 x 8 inches, cut two
Side Binding – 2 x 15 1/2 inches, cut four
Hem Binding – 2 x 45 inches, cut two

2. A diagram of the Bib pattern is provided in **Figure A**. Trim each of the three Bib pieces as shown. (You may wish to make a full-size paper pattern first, but it is not absolutely necessary.)

3. Cut two straight strips from pink fabric (not on the bias), each 3 1/2 x 36 inches.

4. Cut two straight strips from blue fabric and two from yellow fabric, each 1 3/4 x 36 inches.

Assembling the Patchwork

Note: All seam allowances are 1/2 inch unless otherwise specified in the instructions.

The pink, blue, and yellow strips are sewn together side by side to form the basic patchwork fabric. Bias strips are cut from the assembled patchwork fabric, and these strips are then sewn together end to end to achieve the desired lengths. This type of assembly is described in detail in Tips & Techniques, so refer to that section of the book for instructions if you need help at any point. General instructions are provided below.

1. Sew together one pink and one blue strip, side by side, offsetting the ends by 3 inches. Trim the seam allowances to 1/4 inch, and press open. The assembly should now look like the one shown in **Figure B**.

2. Stitch a yellow piece to the free long edge of the blue piece in the same manner, offsetting the ends by only 3/4 inch in the same direction. The assembly should now look like the one shown in **Figure C**.

3. Add a second pink piece, offsetting the ends by 3/4 inch in the same direction; then a second blue piece, offsetting the ends by 2 1/2 inches in the same direction; then a second yellow piece, offsetting the ends by 3/4 inch in the same direction. Trim all allowances and press all seams open. The completed assembly should now look like the one shown in **Figure D**.

4. Cut bias strips from the assembled patchwork fabric as shown in **Figure E**. Each strip should be 2 inches wide, measured perpendicularly to the diagonal cutting lines. The distance between the diagonal cutting lines will be 2 3/4 inches, if you measure straight across the upper free edge of the topmost pink piece, as shown. You should be able to get twelve complete patchwork strips from the assembled fabric.

5. Piece together five of the patchwork bias strips,

Figure B

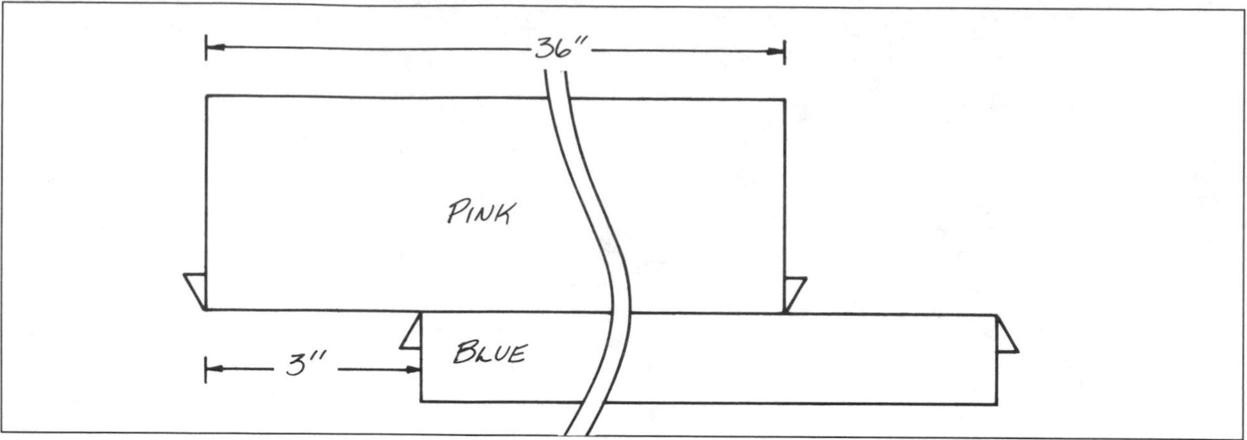

Figure C

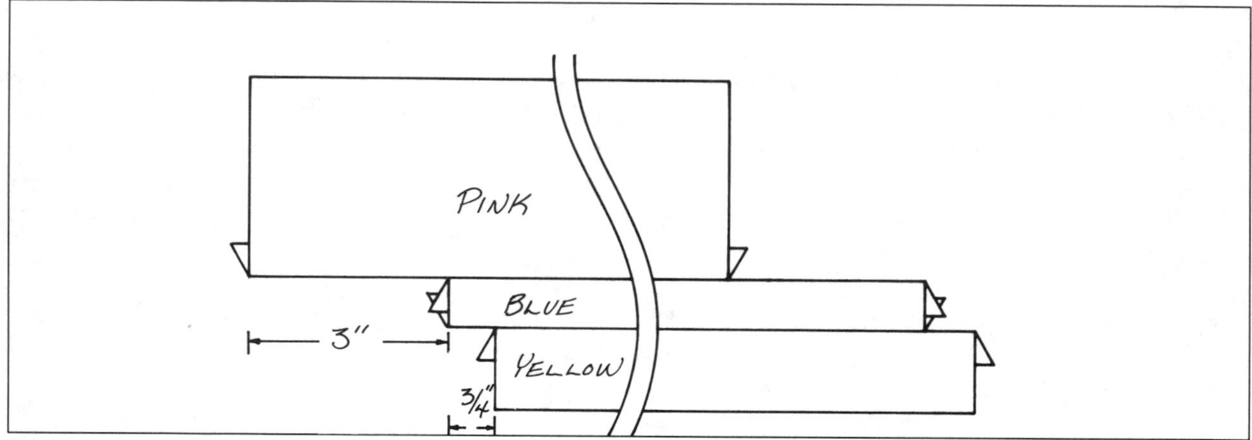

Figure D

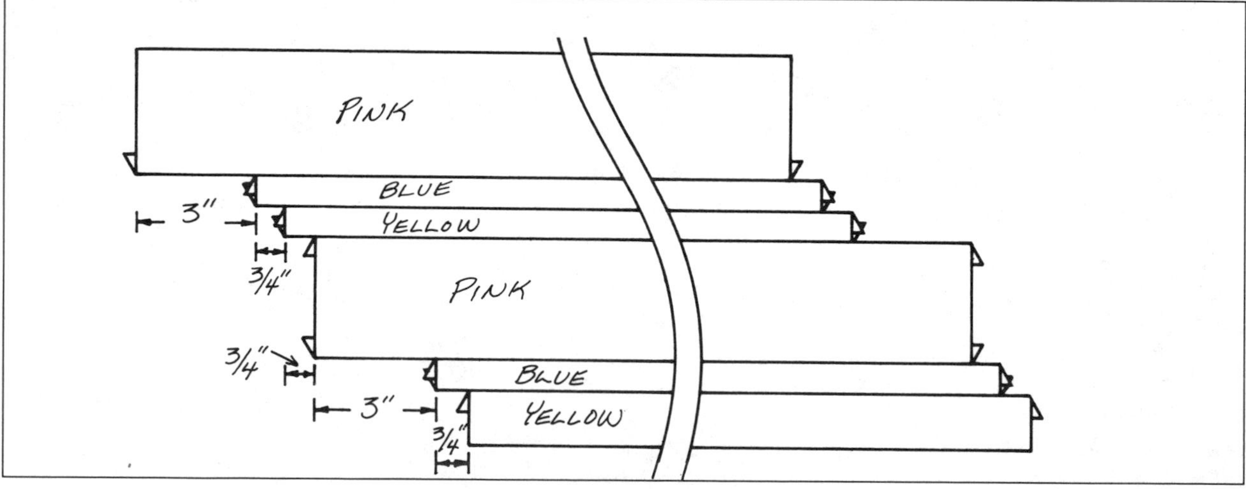

Figure E

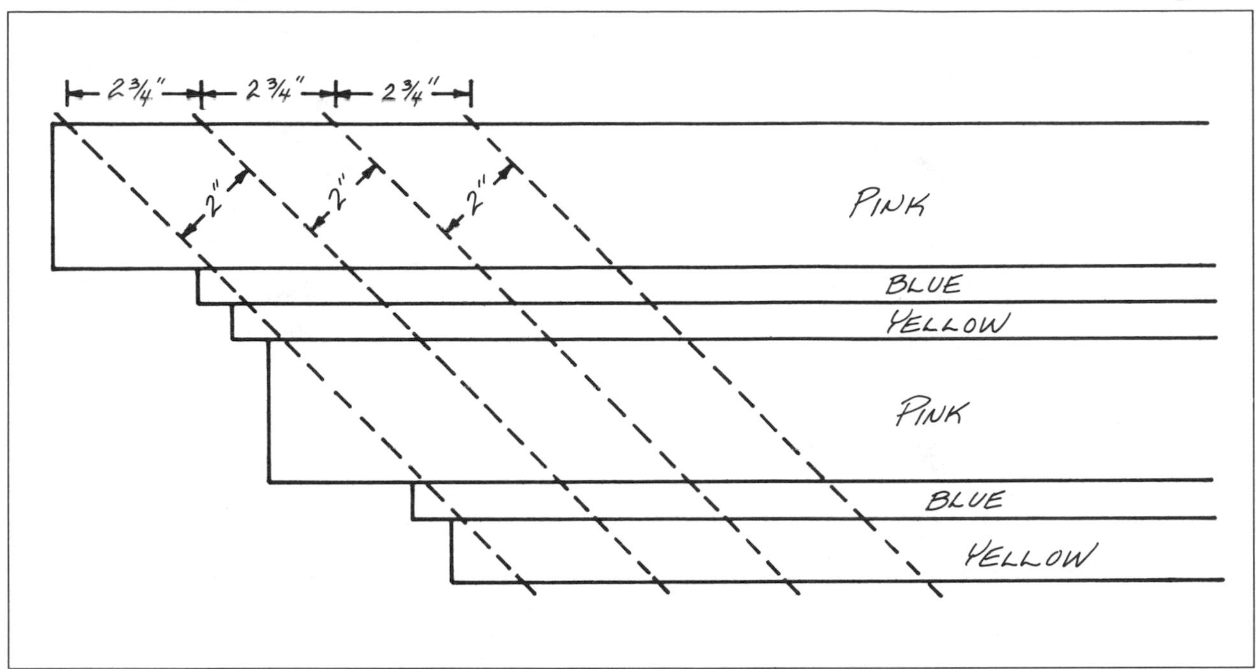

Figure F

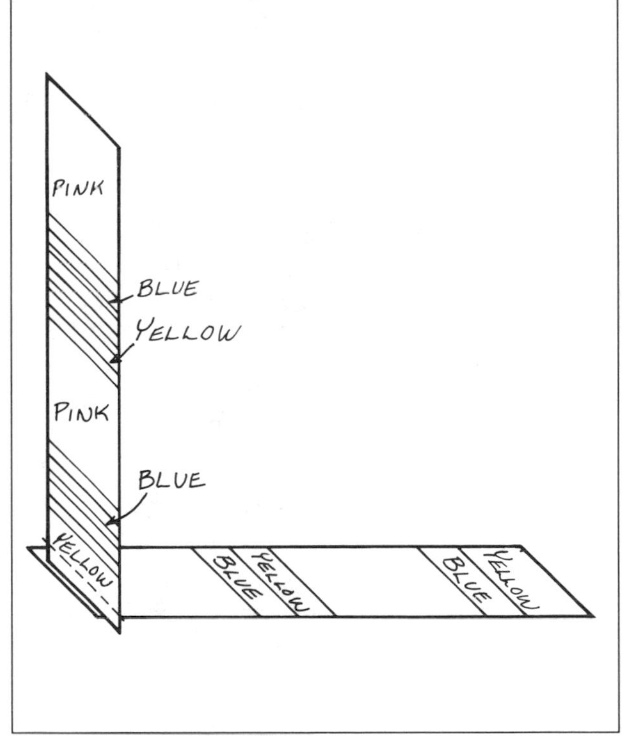

end to end, to form one long strip for the pinafore front border. Detailed instructions for piecing strips with angled ends are provided in Tips & Techniques. **Figure F** shows two strips being sewn together in the proper manner, so the color progression will remain consistent along the assembled strip. Trim all seam allowances to 1/4 inch, and press all seams open.

6. Piece together another five patchwork bias strips, end to end, for the pinafore back border.

7. Piece together the remaining two patchwork bias strips, end to end, to form a strip for the front bib.

Assembling the Pinafore

The front and back pinafore sections are exactly alike, except that the back bib has no patchwork trim. We'll begin with the front section.

1. To make the bib, you'll need the Border C piece, the Border D piece, one Bib piece, and the shortest patchwork strip. Trim and square off the ends of the patchwork strip, so that it measures 8½ inches long.

2. Place the patchwork strip and the Border C piece right sides together, and stitch the seam along one long

Figure G

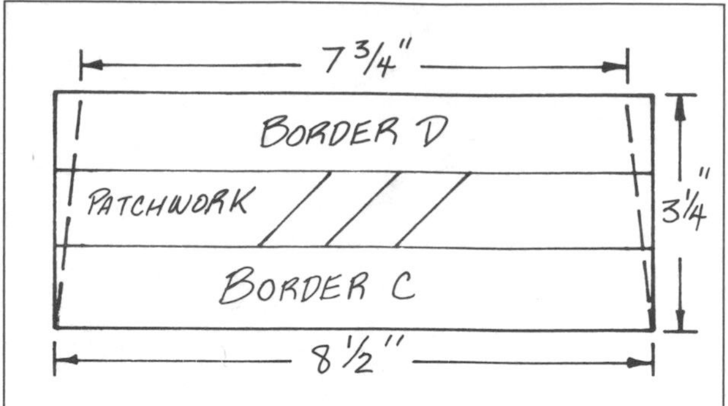

Figure H

Figure I

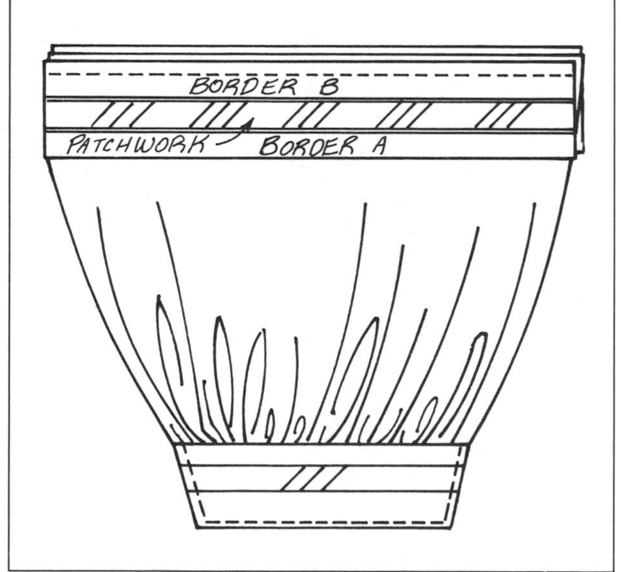

edge. Trim the seam allowances to 1/4 inch, and press the allowances toward the patchwork. Stitch the Border D piece to the free long edge of the patchwork strip in the same manner, trim, and press. This assembly will serve as the bib front. Trim the ends of the assembled bib front to match the size and shape of the white Bib piece, as shown in **Figure G**.

3. Gather one long edge of one white Skirt piece, so that it measures 8½ inches long. (See Tips & Techniques for gathering instructions, if necessary.) The edge will be very tightly gathered, as it is quite a bit longer than 8½ inches to start with. Adjust the gathers evenly, and baste them in place.

4. Place the white Bib piece right side up on a flat surface, with the longest edge at the top. Place the Skirt piece right side up on top, aligning the gathered edge of the Skirt with the longest edge of the Bib. Place the assembled bib front right side down on top of the Skirt, aligning the longest edge of the bib front with the aligned edges of the Bib and Skirt pieces. Stitch the seam as shown in **Figure H**. Turn both the front and back bibs upward, so that they are wrong sides together, and press the seam. Baste the front and back bibs together close to the side and upper edges.

5. The lower border is made in much the same way as the bib. You'll need one of the longer patchwork strips, one Border A piece, one Border B piece, and one Border Lining piece. First, trim and square off the ends of the patchwork strip, so that it is 45 inches long. Stitch the strip to the Border A and Border B pieces, as you did the patchwork and border pieces for the front bib assembly.

6. Place the Border Lining piece right side up on a flat surface. Place the bib-and-skirt assembly right side up on top, aligning the long lower edge of the skirt with one long edge of the Border Lining piece. Place the patchwork border assembly on top of the skirt, right side down, aligning the free long edge of the Border B piece with the aligned edges of the skirt and Border Lining. Stitch the seam as shown in **Figure I**. Turn the patchwork border assembly and the Border Lining downward, so that they are wrong sides together, and press the seam. Baste the front and lining borders together close to each raw edge.

7. To finish the edges of the front pinafore section, you'll need one Bib Binding piece, two Side Binding pieces, and one Hem Binding piece. Instructions for encasing raw edges with binding tape are provided in the Tips & Techniques section of this book. Use the Bib Binding piece to encase the top raw edges of the bib, and trim the ends of the Binding piece even with the sides of the bib. Use the Hem Binding piece to encase the lower raw edges of the border in the same manner. Use one of the Side Binding pieces to encase each side edge of the pinafore, and finish the ends of these bindings as specified in Tips & Techniques.

8. We contoured the straps to give them a softer look. A scale drawing for the Strap pattern is provided in **Figure J**. Enlarge the drawing to make a full-size pattern.

9. To make one strap, fold one of the Strap pieces in half lengthwise, placing right sides together. Place the Strap pattern on top, and cut the contours. Stitch the seam all the way around the long contoured edge, leaving the straight short edge open and unstitched (**Figure K**). Clip the curves and turn the strap right side out. Press the strap flat, and press the seam allowances to the inside along the straight edge. Whipstitch the pressed edges together. Make three more straps in the same manner, using three of the remaining white Strap pieces.

10. Placement of the straps on the pinafore is shown in **Figure L**. Stitch the square end of one strap to the wrong side of the pinafore bib, so that the outer edge of the strap is even with the outer edge of the side binding. Stitch a second strap to the bib, even with the opposite side. Stitch a third strap to the wrong side of the pinafore, so that it extends outward from one side edge at the bib-to-skirt seam, as shown in **Figure L**. Stitch the fourth strap to the opposite side edge of the pinafore in the same manner.

11. The pinafore back section is made exactly like the front section, with one exception: The bib has no patchwork, so it consists of two white Bib pieces. Follow the procedures described in steps 3 through 10 to make the pinafore back section, substituting a white Bib piece for the patchwork front bib assembly in step 4.

12. Tie together the back and front shoulder straps on each side of the pinafore. You can tie them in square

1 square = 1 inch **Figure J**

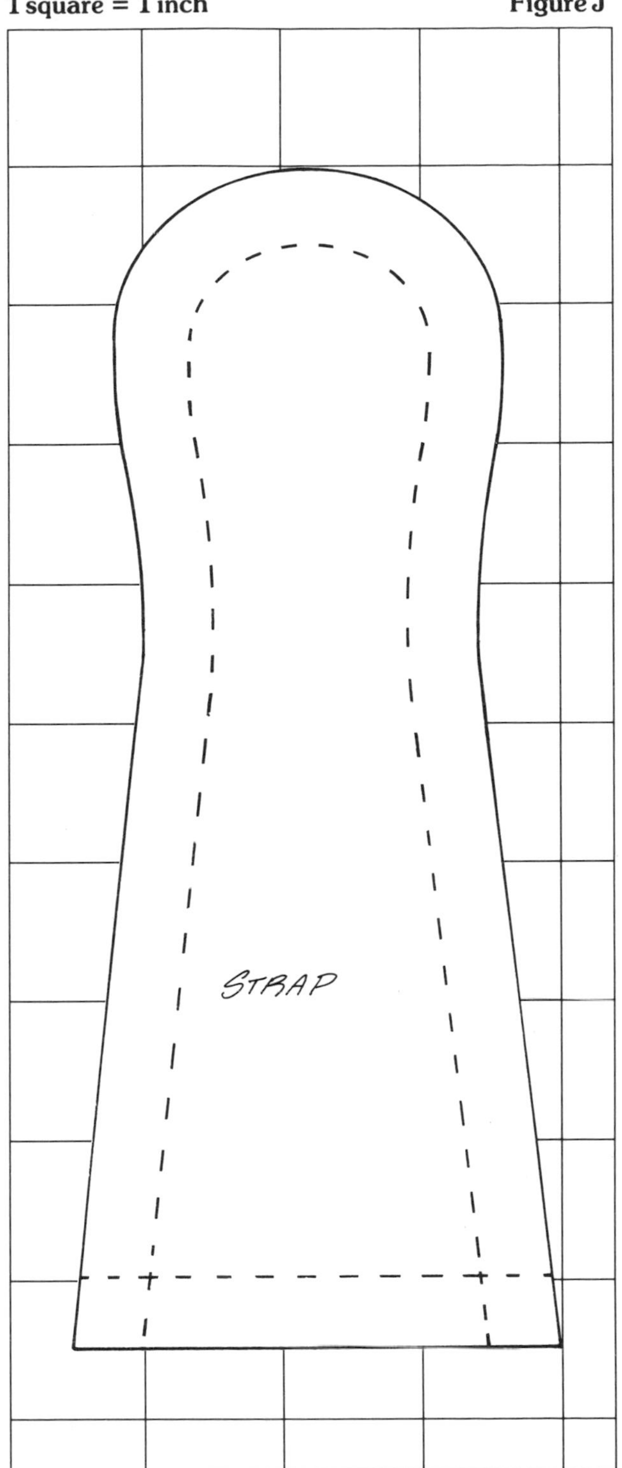

Figure K

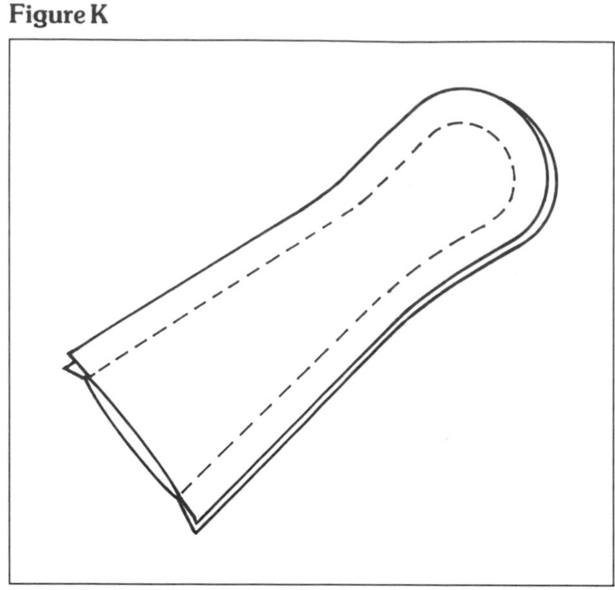

Figure L

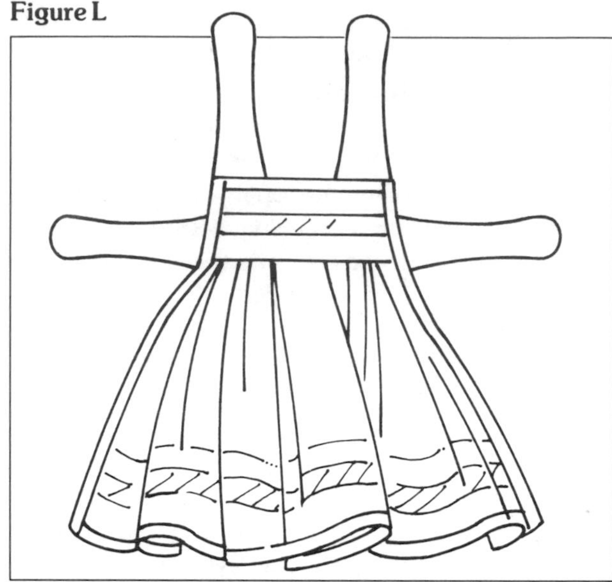

Figure M

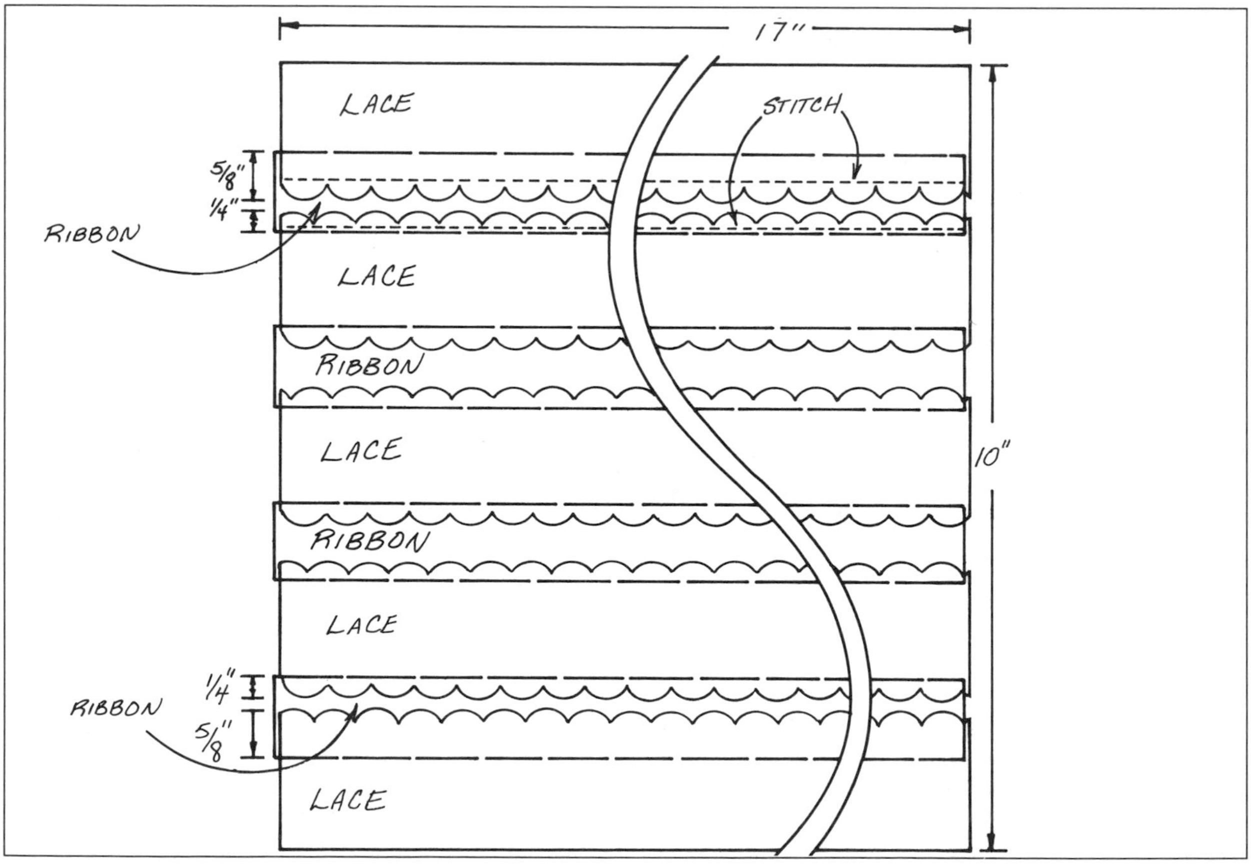

17"
10"
LACE
STITCH
5/8"
1/4"
RIBBON
LACE
RIBBON
LACE
RIBBON
LACE
1/4"
RIBBON
5/8"
LACE

knots, because the shaped ends of the straps will make the knots look like bows. Slip the pinafore over your child's head, and tie together the front and back underarm straps on each side.

Assembling the Bonnet

The fabric for the outer layer of the bonnet consists of lengths of ribbon and lace sewn together. The eyelet fabric is used for the lining layer.

1. Cut five 17-inch lengths of lace trim, and four 17-inch lengths of grosgrain ribbon. Place all of the ribbons right side up on a flat surface, side by side with 1 inch of space between each two ribbons. Place the lengths of lace on top as shown in **Figure M**, lapping the edges of the lace over the ribbons by about 1/4 inch on each side. For the two outer lengths of lace, make the overlap about 5/8 inch, as shown. The overall width of the assembly should be 10 inches. Pin or baste the layers together along each overlapped edge, and then run a single line of machine stitches along each edge to secure the ribbons and lace together.

2. To form the squared-off back of the bonnet, fold the assembled outer bonnet fabric in half widthwise and mark the center point on one long edge. Place the assembly right side up on a flat surface, and fold one end in toward the center, so that the fold line is 2 inches from the marked center point (**Figure N**). Stitch through both layers of the lace strip, 1/2 inch from the aligned edges, beginning at the fold and ending at the marked center point as shown. Fold the same end back toward its original position, so it will be out of the way. Follow the same procedures to fold the opposite end in toward the center, and stitch in the same manner.

3. Place the two ends of the outer bonnet assembly right sides together as shown in **Figure O**. Stitch the seam through both layers of the lace strip as shown, beginning at the point where the stitching lines from step 2 meet, and running straight along the aligned edges to the ends of the strip. This is the center back seam.

4. Turn the outer bonnet right side out. The free long edge will be the front edge of the bonnet. Fold the front lace strip back over the assembly along the line of stitches that joins it to the adjacent ribbon, placing right sides together, and baste across both ends to hold the lace in place, as shown in **Figure P**.

Figure N

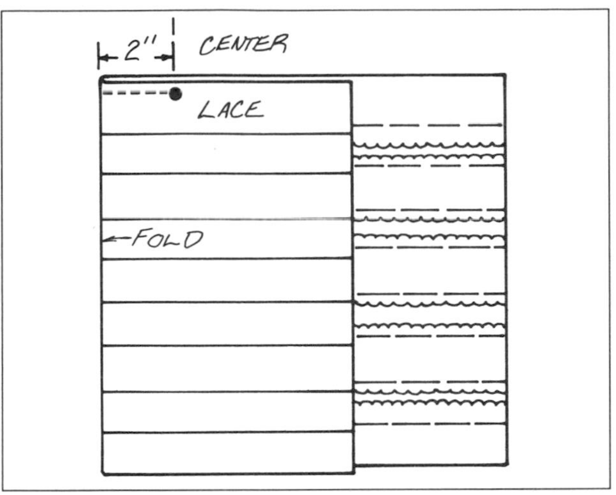

Figure O

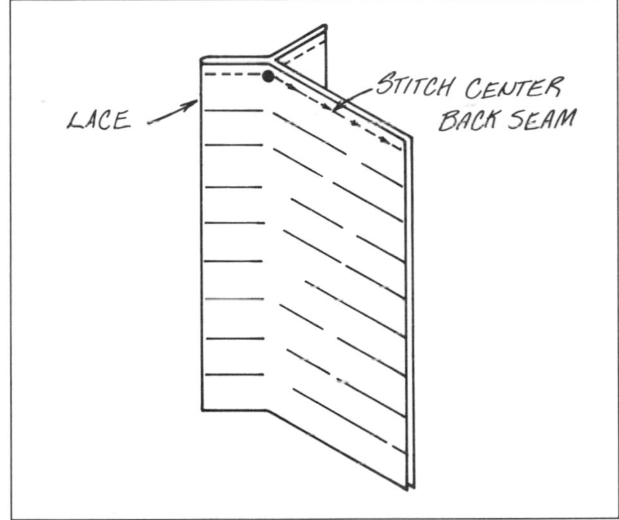

5. To create the bonnet lining, mark the center point along one long edge of the eyelet fabric, and then fold and stitch the fabric to form the back seams as you did the outer bonnet fabric in steps 2 and 3. Leave the lining turned wrong side out.

6. Place the outer bonnet inside the lining. If each was turned as specified in steps 4 and 5, the layers should now be right sides together. (The front lace strip that was turned back in step 4 will be sandwiched between the two layers.) Stitch the seams along the aligned outer edges, leaving a 3-inch opening at the

Figure P

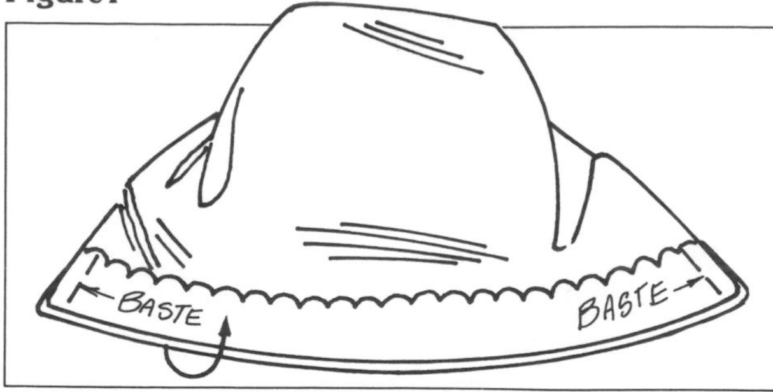

Figure Q

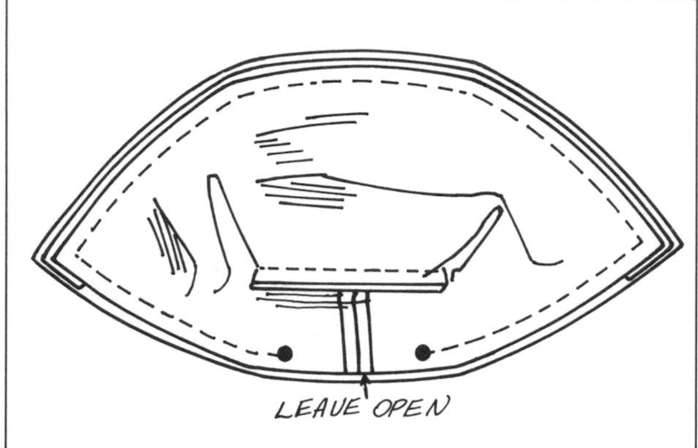

Figure R

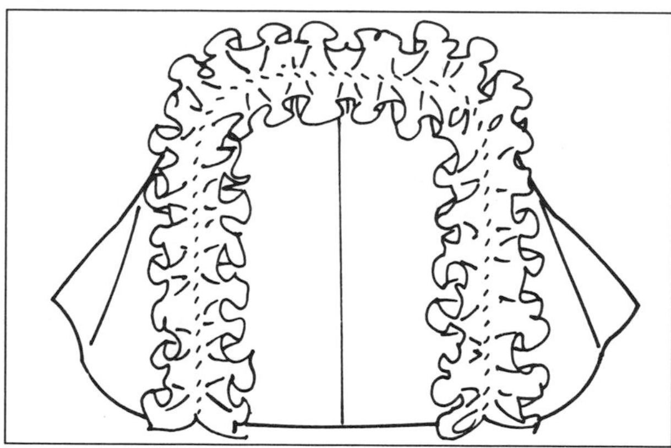

center back (**Figure Q**). Clip the corners and turn the layers right sides out through the opening. The front lace strip should be turned backward over the right side of the outer layer, and the lining should be tucked inside the outer layer. Press the seams, and press the seam allowances to the inside along the opening. Whipstitch the opening edges together.

Figure S

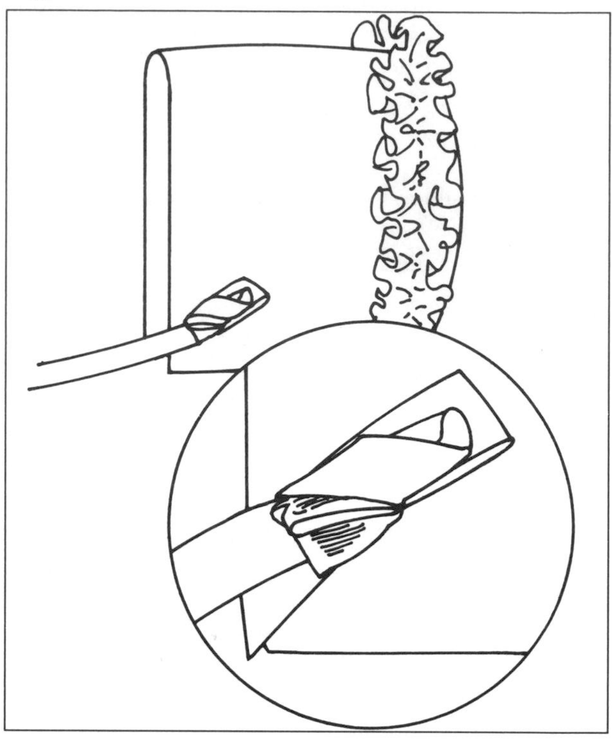

7. Cut a 1-yard length of lace trim, and turn each end under about ½ inch, forming a hem at each end. Gather the trim along the lengthwise center line so that it is 15 inches long, adjust the gathers evenly, and baste over the center line to hold the gathers in place. Pin the gathered trim to the back of the bonnet as shown in **Figure R**. The center line of the trim should be placed along the horizontal back seam of the bonnet, and should run parallel to the vertical center back seam, straight downward from each end of the horizontal seam. Hand stitch the trim to both layers of the bonnet, along the gathered center line.

8. Cut an 18-inch length of white satin ribbon for one of the ties. Fold one end of the ribbon into several loops, forming a rosette as shown in **Figure S**. Tack the rosette to the outside of the bonnet at one front corner, with the free end of the tie extending downward as shown. Cut the free end of the ribbon at an angle. Follow the same procedures to create the second tie, using the remaining 18-inch length of ribbon, and tack it to the opposite front corner of the bonnet.

Christmas Vest

We made this cheerful string-quilted vest in bright Christmas colors for the holiday season. Eyelet trim lends a soft, frilly accent to the straight, geometrical lines of the vest design and quilting strips. The same pattern can be made up in spring or fall colors for almost any occasion.

Materials

2⅜ yards of 36-inch-wide fabric for the patchwork (We used ½ yard of red calico, and ⅜ yard each of five different fabrics: green calico; white calico; red with white pin dots; a small geometric print in red, green, and white; and white eyelet fabric.)

5 yards of gathered white eyelet trim, 1 inch wide

2 yards of 36-inch-wide lining fabric (We used the same white calico as we did for the patchwork.)

28 x 50-inch piece of lightweight batting

White thread

Cutting the Pieces

1. Scale drawings for the vest Front, Back, and Gusset patterns are provided in **Figure A**. Enlarge the drawings to make full-size patterns, and make any necessary size alterations (see Tips & Techniques). Note that this design is slightly different than most standard vests, which consist of only front and back pieces. For this vest, a wide underarm gusset joins the front and back pieces on each side, so take this into consideration when you are altering the patterns to fit. Note also that the Back and Gusset patterns are half patterns, so the full-size pieces cut from them will be twice as wide as the patterns. Transfer the yoke lines indicated on the scale drawings to the Front and Back patterns.

2. Cut two Front pieces, one Back piece, and two Gusset pieces from lining fabric. Put aside the rest of the lining fabric, which will be used later for bias hem binding strips.

3. Cut a total of fifty-one straight strips, not on the bias, from the patchwork fabrics. Each strip should be 2 inches wide and 18 inches long. We cut twelve from red calico; nine each from eyelet fabric, the geometric print, and white calico; and six each from green calico and pin-dot fabric.

ASSEMBLING THE PATCHWORK

Several strips are sewn together side by side to create the fabric for each outer vest piece. The patchwork assemblies are then trimmed to match the pattern pieces. All seams are ⅜ inch unless otherwise specified.

The Vest Fronts

1. The first patchwork assembly will serve as the fabric for the lower portion of one Vest Front piece. The strips will run vertically. Sew together six different strips, side by side and even at both ends, for this assembly. Our arrangement is shown in **Figure B**. (Refer to Tips & Techniques if you're not certain how to go about stitching the strips together properly.) When you have all six strips sewn together, place the Vest Front pattern on top to make certain the patchwork assembly is at least as wide as the pattern. The patchwork will not be as long as the pattern, because a yoke section will be added to the top to achieve the length, so you need not be concerned with length at this point. If the assembled patchwork is not as wide as the pattern, add one or more additional strips to achieve the width. (**Note:** If it is necessary to add more strips than specified for any of these assemblies, select the colors you wish to add, and cut the extra strips from leftover fabric.)

2. The second patchwork assembly will serve as the fabric for the yoke portion of the same Vest Front piece. The strips will run horizontally. Measure the width of the assembly from step 1. Choose four strips for the yoke assembly (our arrangement is shown in **Figure C**), and trim all four strips to the measured length. Stitch together these four strips, side by side and even at both ends, as shown in **Figure C**. Now measure the distance across the assembled yoke strips, and measure the vertical distance between the very top of your Vest Front pattern and the yoke line. The measurement across the assembled strips should be at least ½ inch longer than the pattern measurement. If it is not, add one or more strips to achieve the length.

3. Place the step 1 assembly right side up, with the strips running vertically. Place the step 2 assembly right side down on top, with the strips running horizontally. One long edge of the horizontal assembly should be aligned with one short edge of the vertical assembly. Stitch a ½-inch-wide seam along the aligned edges (**Figure D**), and press the seam open.

4. Place the Vest Front pattern on top of the assembly from step 3, and adjust it so that the seam that joins the vertical and horizontal fabric sections is aligned with the yoke line on the pattern. Trim the patchwork assembly to match the shape of the pattern.

5. Repeat the procedures in steps 1 through 4 to create the second outer Vest Front piece. We arranged

1 square = 1 inch **Figure A**

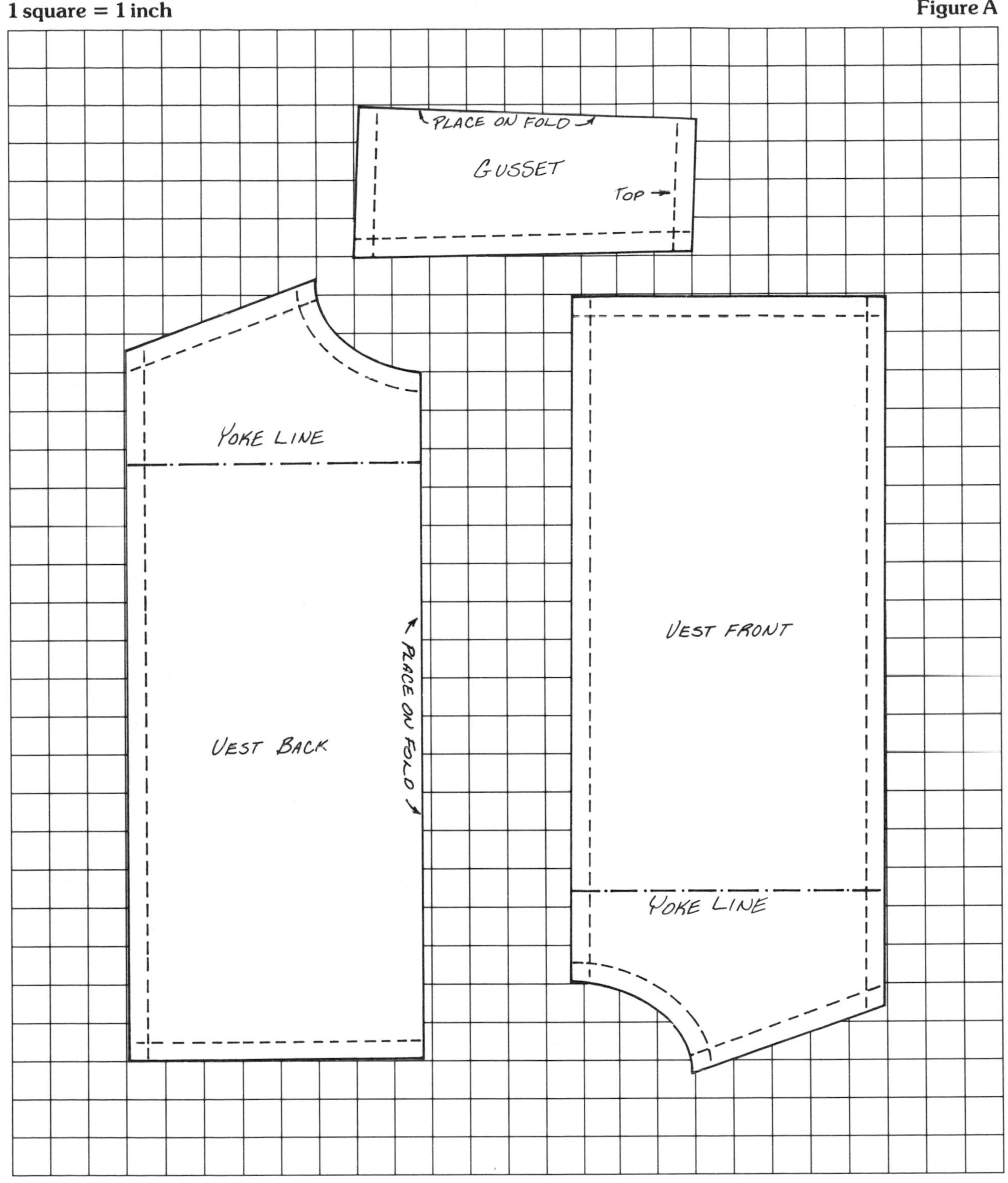

Figure B

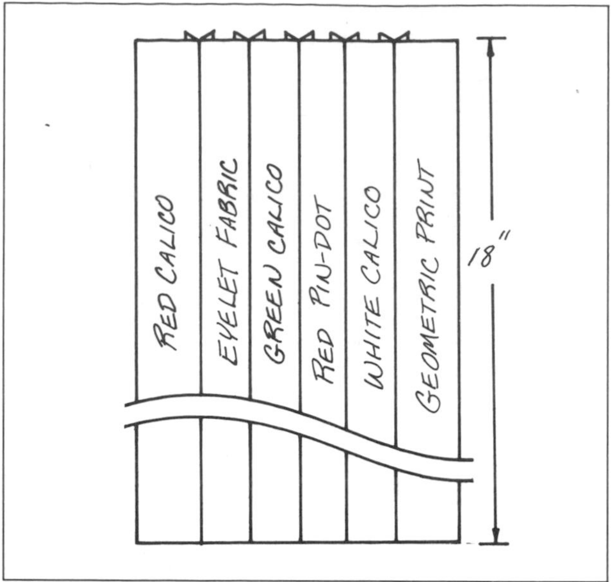

Figure C

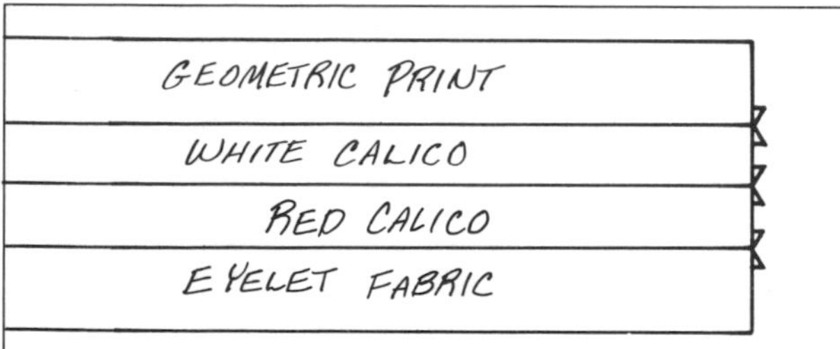

Figure D

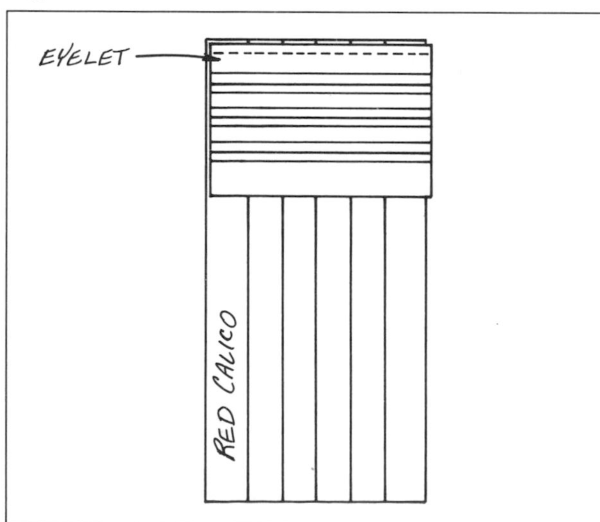

the colors so that the two Front pieces are mirror images of each other, as shown in **Figure E**. Keep this in mind when you stitch the horizontal and vertical assemblies together (step 3). Keep in mind also that you must use the Vest Front pattern upside down when you trim the assembled patchwork to match, so the overall shape will be a mirror image of the first Vest Front piece.

The Vest Back

1. The next patchwork assembly will serve as the fabric for the lower portion of the Vest Back piece. The strips will run vertically. We made two assemblies exactly like the ones for the lower portions of the Vest Fronts, and joined them with a red calico strip to separate the matching center strips of each half. The finished assembly is shown in **Figure F**. Compare your finished assembly with your Vest Back pattern to make certain it is wide enough, and add one or more strips if necessary. Remember that the Vest Back pattern is a half pattern, so the fabric assembly should be at least twice as wide as the pattern.

2. Assemble four strips to serve as the yoke portion of the Vest Back piece. The strips will run horizontally. We repeated the color arrangement that we used for the yoke front assemblies. Measure across the assembled strips to be certain they will cover the yoke area of the Vest Back pattern (the vertical distance between the topmost edge of the pattern and the yoke line, plus ½ inch), and add more strips if necessary.

3. Sew together the vertical and horizontal assemblies for the Vest Back as you did those for each Vest Front, and press the seam open.

4. Fold the patchwork Vest Back assembly in half lengthwise. Place the Vest Back pattern on top, aligning the center back "place on fold" pattern edge with the fold of fabric. Adjust the pattern to align the seam that joins the vertical and horizontal fabric sections with the yoke line on the pattern. Pin the pattern in place and trim the patchwork assembly to match, but do not cut along the fold line.

The Gussets

1. The final patchwork assemblies will serve as the fabric for the two Gusset pieces. The strips will run horizontally. Measure the width of your Gusset pattern

Figure E

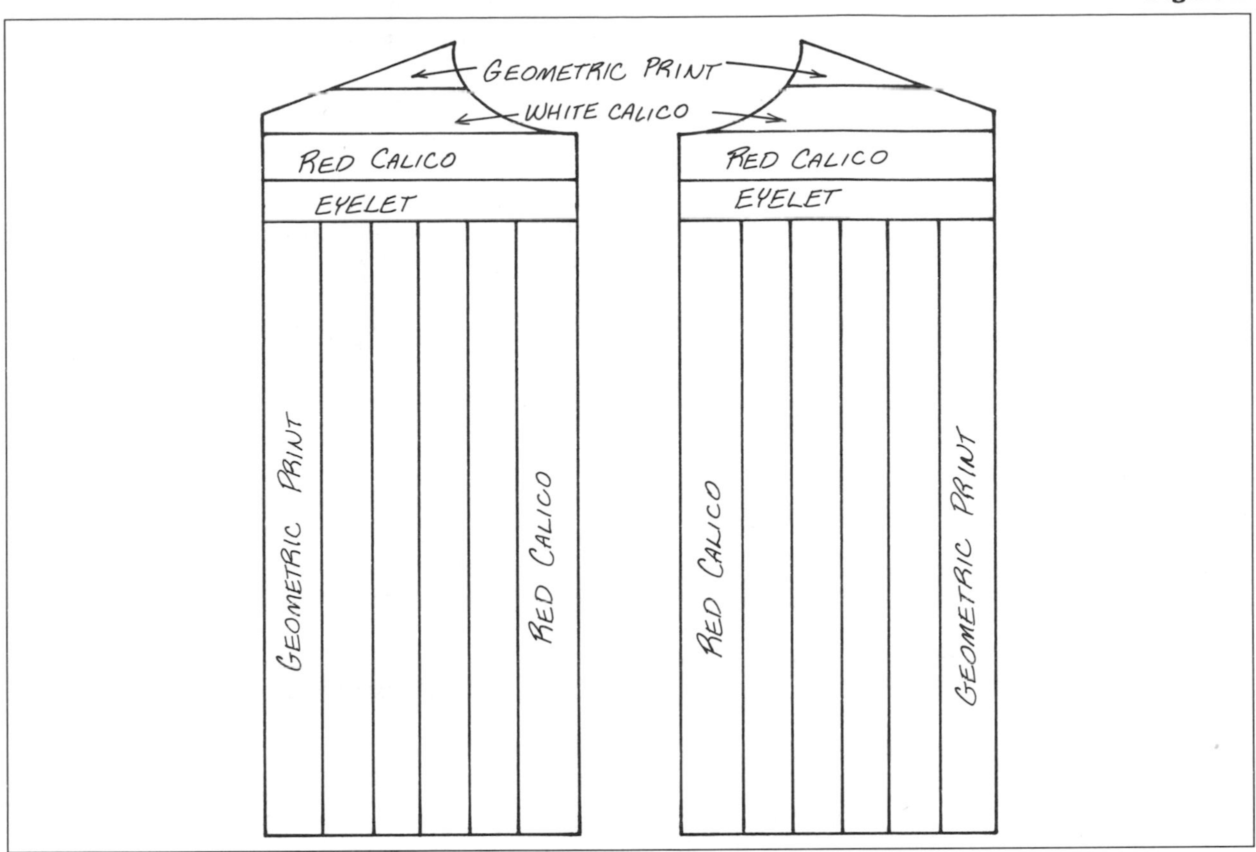

Figure F

GEOMETRIC PRINT
WHITE CALICO
RED PIN-DOT
GREEN CALICO
EYELET FABRIC
RED CALICO
WHITE CALICO
RED CALICO
EYELET FABRIC
GREEN CALICO
RED PIN-DOT
WHITE CALICO
GEOMETRIC PRINT
18"

Figure G

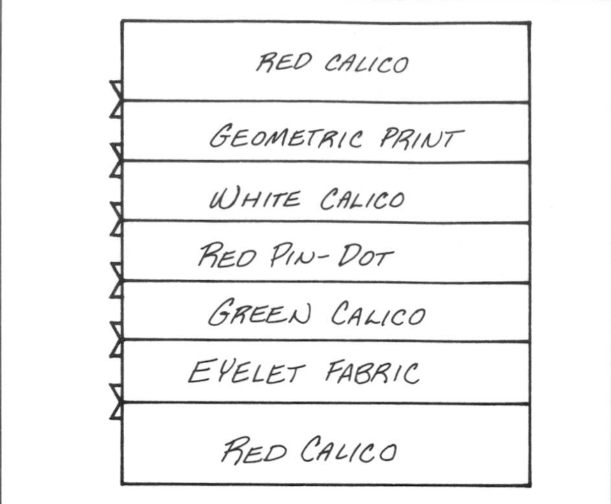

Figure H

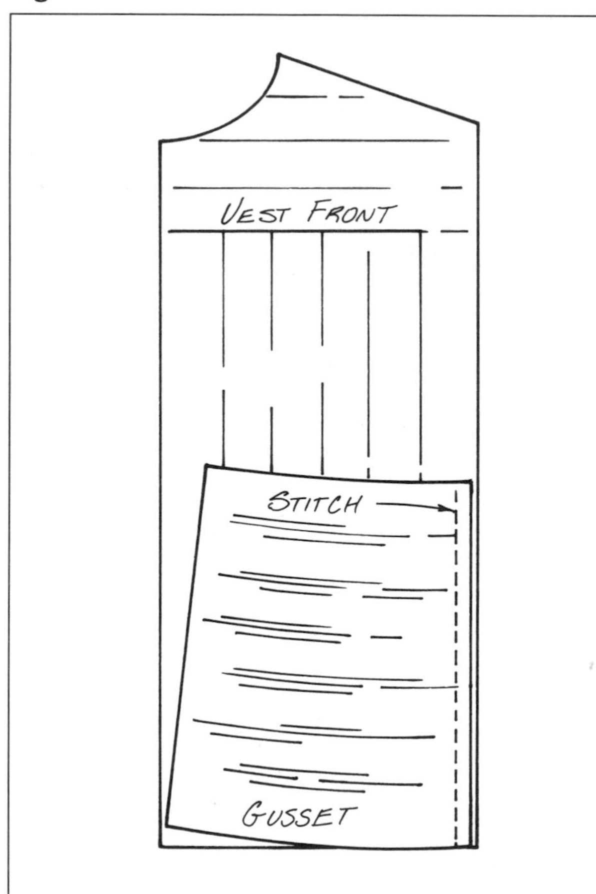

along the lower edge, and multiply this measurement by 2. Trim seven strips to this length for each Gusset assembly. Our color arrangement is shown in **Figure G**. Assemble the seven strips for each Gusset piece. Measure across the strips to be certain they will cover the length of the Gusset pattern, and add more strips if necessary.

2. Fold one of the patchwork Gusset assemblies in half lengthwise and pin the Gusset pattern on top, aligning the "place on fold" pattern edge with the fold of fabric. Trim the patchwork to match the shape of the pattern. Repeat these procedures to trim the second patchwork assembly to match the Gusset pattern.

ASSEMBLING THE VEST

The patchwork pieces are sewn together to create the outer layer of the vest, and the lining pieces are sewn together in the same way. The two layers are then quilted, with batting between, and the eyelet trim and hem binding are added.

Outer and Lining Layers

1. For the outer vest assembly, you'll need the patchwork Front, Back, and Gusset pieces. Pin one Front and one Gusset piece right sides together, matching notches, and stitch the side seam as shown in **Figure H**. Press the seam open.

2. Pin the assembly from step 1 to the patchwork Back piece, placing right sides together and aligning the opposite free edge of the Gusset piece with one side edge of the Back. Stitch the seam as shown in **Figure I** and press open.

3. Follow the procedures described in steps 1 and 2 to attach the remaining patchwork Front and Gusset pieces to the opposite side edge of the Back piece. Press all seams open. Leave the shoulder seams unstitched for the time being, but turn each raw shoulder edge to the wrong side of the patchwork along the seam line, and press.

4. For the lining assembly, you'll need the lining-fabric Front, Back, and Gusset pieces. Assemble them as you did the outer pieces in steps 1 through 3, and press all seams open. Leave the shoulder seams unstitched, but press the seam allowance to the wrong side of the fabric along each shoulder edge.

Quilting

1. Place the piece of batting on a flat surface. Place the lining vest layer on top of the batting, and use it as a guide to cut a complete vest piece from batting. Trim the batting piece along the seam lines, so the batting layer will not extend into the seams of the finished vest.

2. Stack the outer and lining layers wrong sides together, with the batting layer sandwiched between. Smooth out the layers so they are all flat and even, and pin them together. Baste the layers together, beginning at the center back and placing your stitches along the center of each strip. Work from the center back all the way around one side to the center front, and then from the center back around the other side to the opposite center front.

3. To quilt, stitch in the ditch by hand or machine. (See Tips & Techniques, if necessary, for instructions on the quilting procedure called "stitch in the ditch.") For best results, begin at the center back and work toward the front on one side and then on the other, as you did for the basting stitches. Quilt along all existing patchwork seam lines in this manner.

4. The shoulder seams are stitched by hand. Align the back and front pressed shoulder edges on one side of the vest, as shown in **Figure J**. Stitch the outer-layer shoulder edges together, using small hidden stitches. Turn the vest and stitch the lining-layer edges together. Perform the same procedures to join the shoulder edges at the other side of the vest.

Finishing

1. Measure the entire outer edge of your vest, and cut a length of eyelet trim 5 inches longer than the measurement. Press a ½-inch-wide hem to the wrong side of the eyelet at one end. Baste the eyelet to the vest, placing right sides together, as shown in **Figure K**. Begin with the hemmed end of the eyelet, placing it at the center of the lower back edge. The bound edge of the trim should be aligned ¼ inch from the outer edge of the vest, and the scalloped edge should extend in toward the center of the vest, as shown. Allow a generous amount of eyelet at each corner, so it will lie flat when it is turned outward. Lap the unhemmed end of the eyelet over the hemmed end, and trim it so that the overlap is only about ½ inch.

Figure I

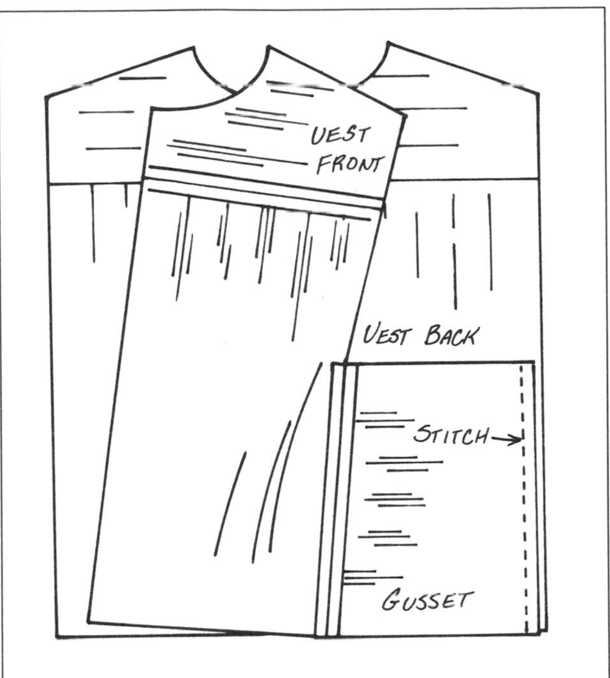

Figure J

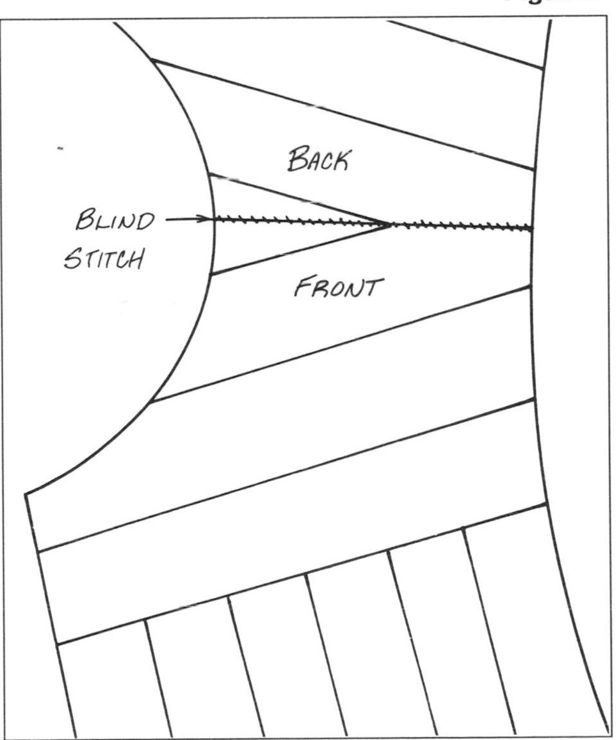

Figure K

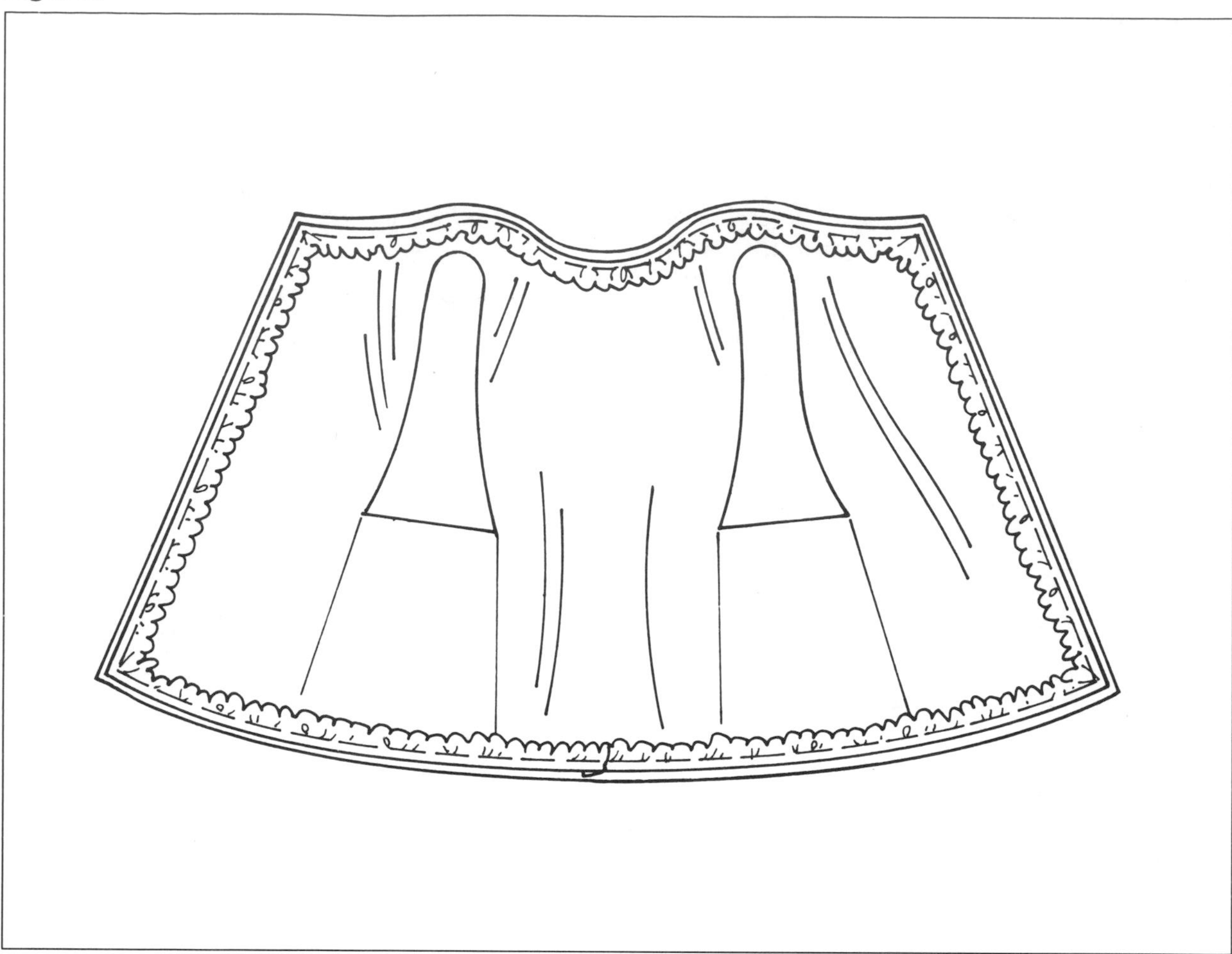

2. Cut 1-inch-wide bias strips from leftover lining fabric, and piece them together end to end to form one long strip. (See Tips & Techniques, if necessary, for instructions on cutting and piecing together bias strips.) The assembled strip should be at least 1 inch longer than the measurement around the outer vest edge.

3. Press a ½-inch-wide hem to the wrong side of the strip at one end only. Baste the bias strip right side down over the eyelet trim, around the outer edge of the vest. One long edge of the strip should be even with the bound edge of the eyelet, and the opposite long edge of the strip should extend in toward the center of the vest. Begin with the hemmed end, at the center of the lower back edge of the vest, and finish by lapping the unhemmed end over the hemmed one.

4. Stitch through all layers (bias strip, eyelet trim, and vest), all the way around the vest, ½ inch from the outer edge. Turn the bias strip and the eyelet outward, and press all seam allowances toward the vest, clipping where necessary. Trim the seam allowances of the vest layers to ¼ inch. Press a ¼-inch-wide allowance to the wrong side of the bias strip along the free long edge, and then turn the strip to the wrong side of the vest so that the eyelet forms a border around the edge. Whipstitch the pressed edge of the strip to the lining side of the vest.

5. Follow the procedures in steps 1 through 4 to bind and trim each armhole edge of the vest.

Take-Me-Home
Ensemble

Here's something for a brand-new person to wear home from the hospital or out on a visit. The tiny jacket actually is just a lined rectangle of fabric; the illusion of sleeves is created by simple tacked folds on each side, so you don't have to wrestle your infant into it. The bonnet is also a very simple assembly. Because most mothers-to-be don't have much time for complex sewing jobs, we made the ensemble from prequilted fabric.

Figure A

1 square = 1 inch

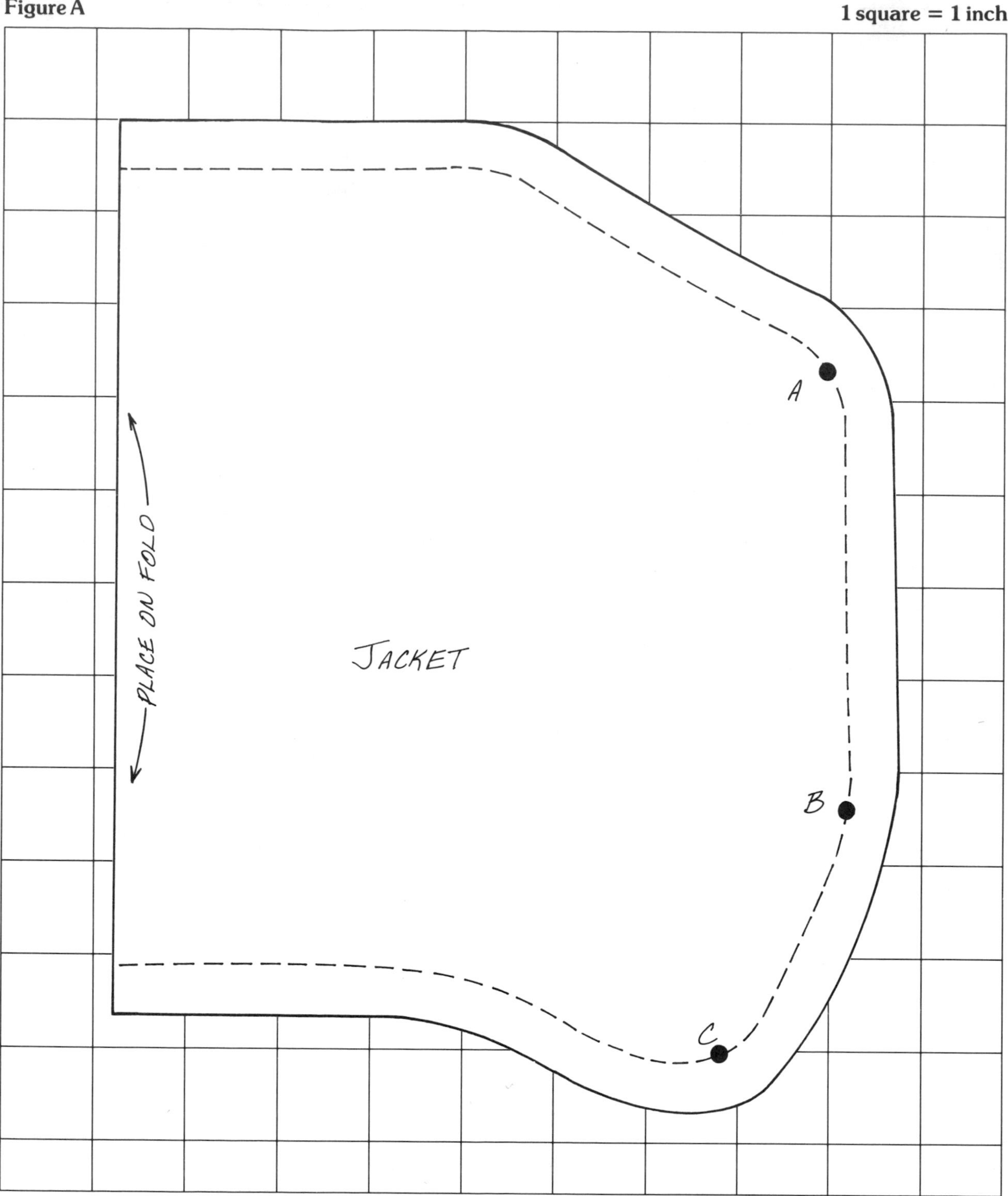

Materials

3/8 yard of 36-inch-wide prequilted fabric for the outer pieces (We used pink gingham.)
3/8 yard of 36-inch-wide baby flannel for the linings (We used white.)
2 yards of 3/4-inch-wide gathered white eyelet trim
1½ yards of 3/8-inch-wide decorative satin ribbon (We used pink ribbon with tiny decorative loops along the edges.)
Thread to match the outer fabric

Cutting the Pieces

1. A scale drawing for the Jacket pattern is provided in **Figure A**. (We fibbed a little – it's not exactly a rectangle, but close enough.) Enlarge the drawing to make a full-size pattern.

2. A full-size pattern for the Bonnet Back is provided in **Figure B**. Trace the drawing onto pattern or tracing paper, so you won't have to cut up your book.

3. You now have all the patterns you need. Cut the pieces as listed below, from the specified fabrics.

Outer fabric:

Jacket – cut one
Bonnet Back – cut one
Bonnet Brim – cut one, 4½ x 12 inches

Lining fabric:

Cut the same pieces and quantities as you did from the outer fabric.

Making the Jacket

1. Place the outer-fabric Jacket piece right side up on a flat surface. Pin and then baste eyelet trim along the outer edges as shown in **Figure C**. The bound edge of the eyelet should be placed about 1/4 inch from the Jacket edge, and the scalloped edge of the eyelet should extend in toward the center. Begin and end at the center of the lower edge, overlap the ends by about 1/2 inch, and turn each raw end back over itself.

2. Place the lining-fabric Jacket piece right side down on top of the assembly from step 1. The outer and lining Jacket pieces should be right sides together, with the eyelet trim sandwiched between. Stitch the seam all the way around the outer edges, but leave a 3-inch opening along the lower edge. Clip the curves, turn the jacket right side out, and press. The eyelet trim should now extend out from the jacket, forming a border. Press the seam allowances to the inside along the opening edges, and whipstitch the edges together.

3. Refer back to the scale drawing for the Jacket pattern (**Figure A**), and note the corners marked A and B. To form the "sleeve" on one side, fold the jacket lengthwise, placing lining sides together and aligning corners A and B. Take a couple of tacking stitches through all thicknesses of fabric, just inside the aligned corners, as shown in **Figure D**.

4. Cut a 9-inch length of ribbon, and fold it into a double loop as shown in **Figure E**. Tack through all layers where indicated, and trim the long end at an angle, as shown.

5. Tack the ribbon bow to the jacket as shown in **Figure F**, over the spot where you tacked the jacket layers together to form the sleeve. You should stitch through

Figure B

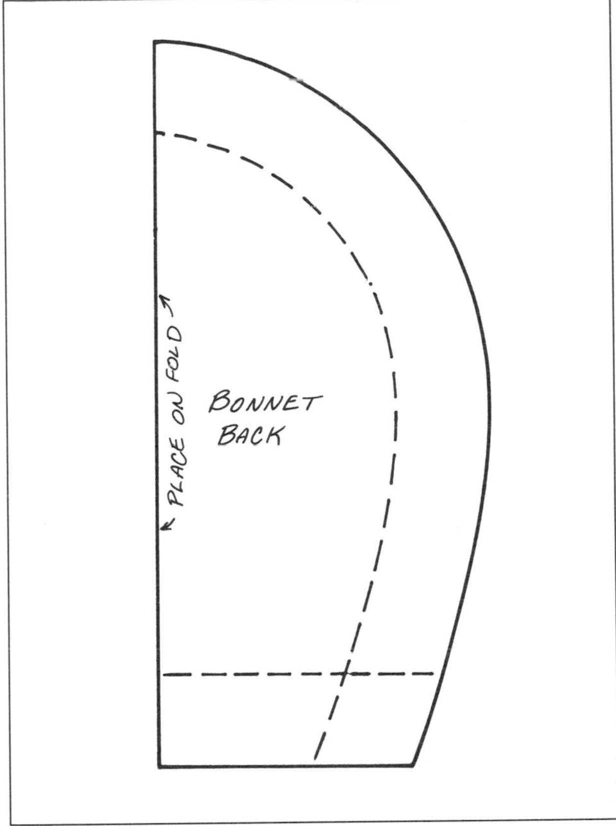

Figure C

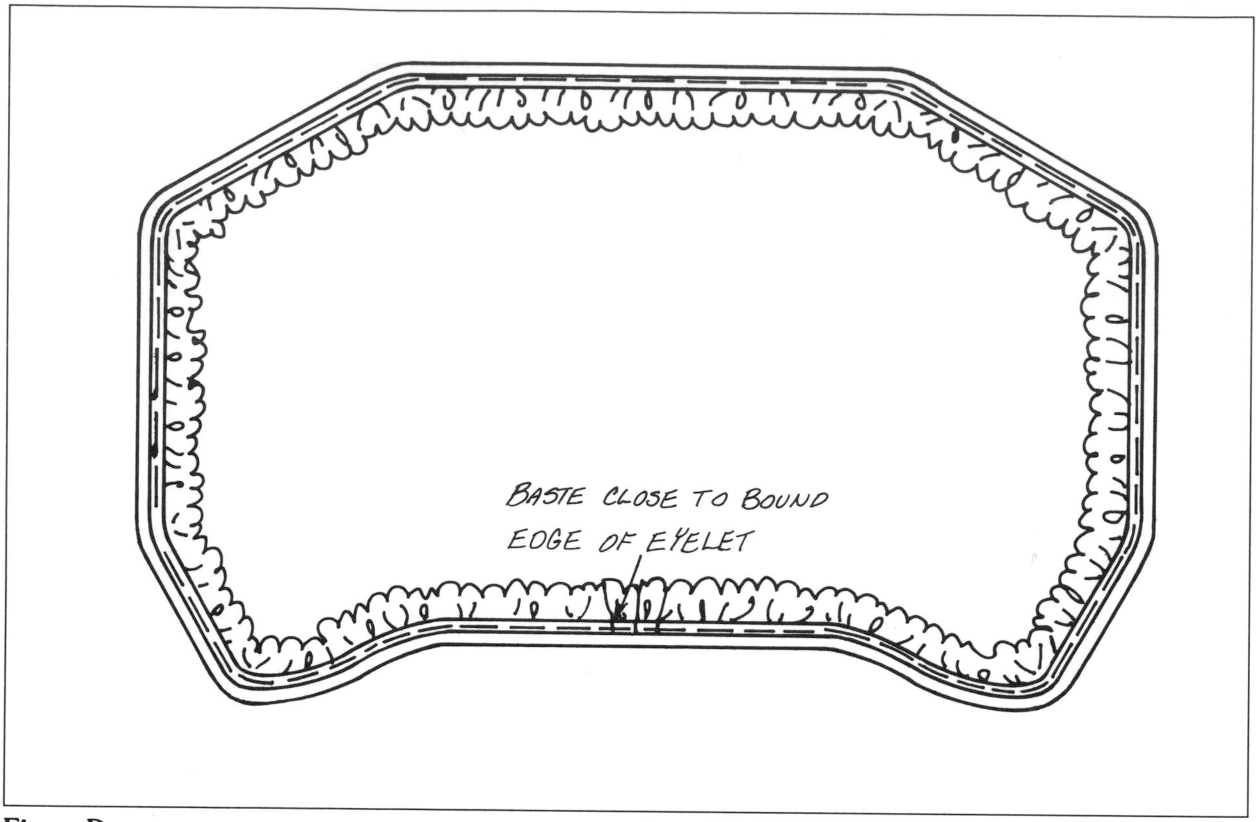

BASTE CLOSE TO BOUND
EDGE OF EYELET

Figure D

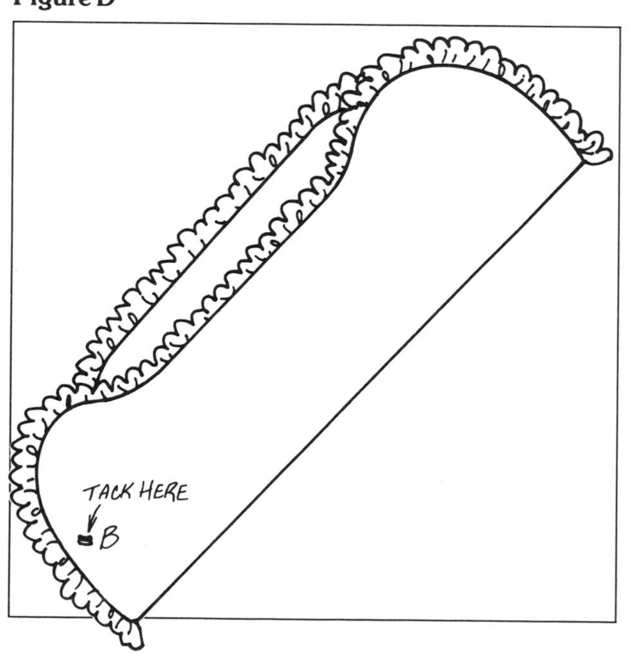

Figure E

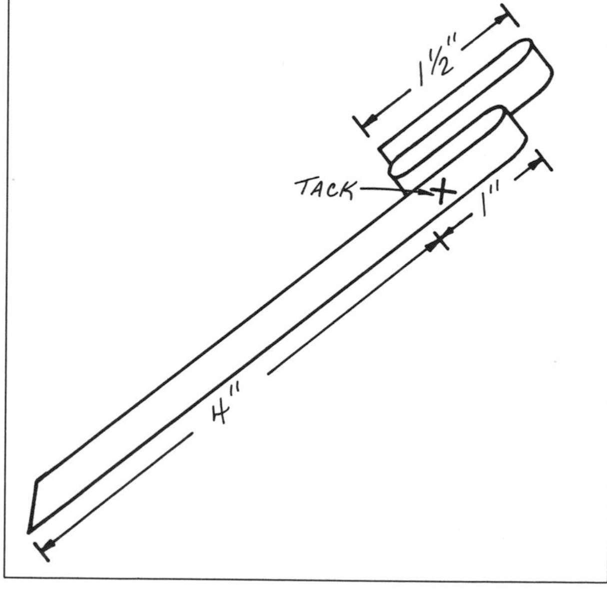

Figure F

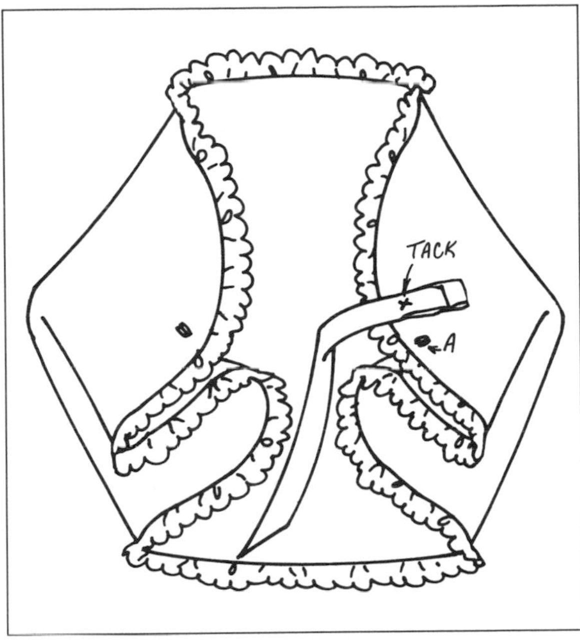

Figure G

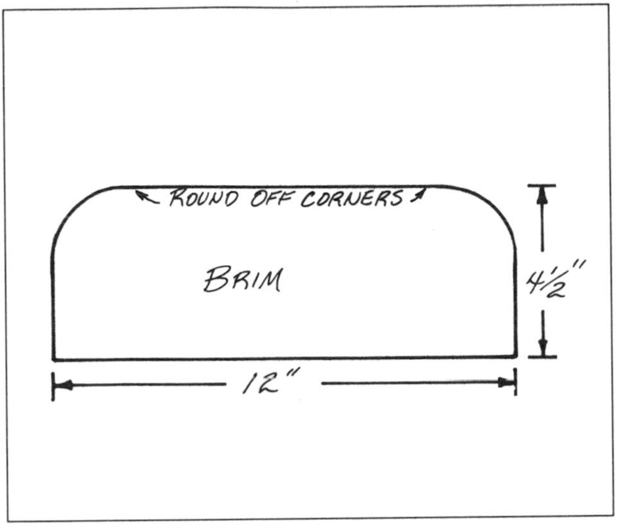

Figure H

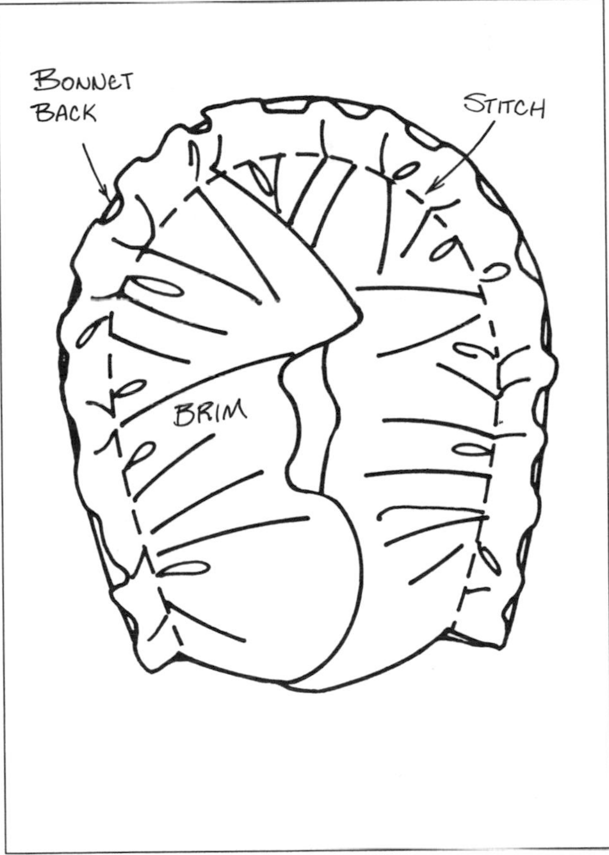

the same layers as you did for the sleeve.

6. Repeat the procedures in steps 3 through 5 to create the sleeve on the other side of the jacket. Fold each side of the jacket as shown for the right side in **Figure F**, and tie together the long ends of the ribbons.

Making the Bonnet

1. Round off two corners of the outer-fabric Brim piece as shown in **Figure G**. They should be the corners of one long edge, not the two corners of one end. Use the contoured piece as a guide to round off two corresponding corners of the lining-fabric Brim piece.

2. Gather the opposite long edge of the outer-fabric Brim piece, so that it is the same length as the long curved edge of the Bonnet Back piece. (See Tips & Techniques for instructions on making gathers.) Adjust the gathers evenly, and baste over the gathers to hold them in place.

3. Pin the outer-fabric Brim and Back pieces right sides together, aligning the gathered edge of the Brim with the long curved edge of the Back. Stitch the seam as shown in **Figure H**. Clip the curves, and press the seam allowances toward the Back piece.

Figure I

Figure J

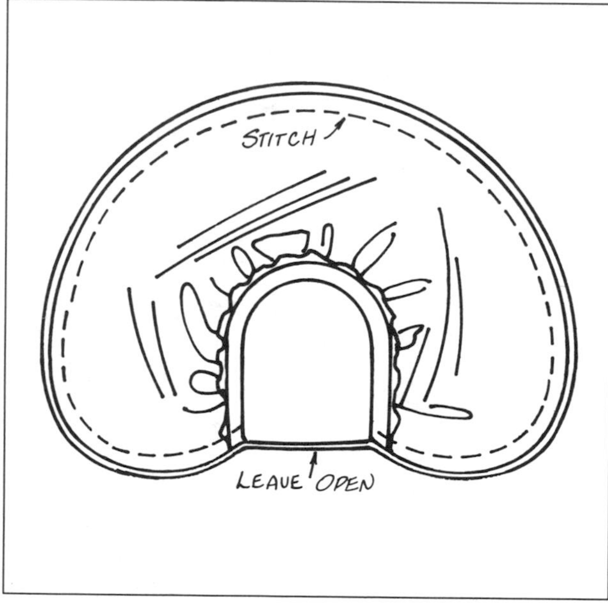

Figure K

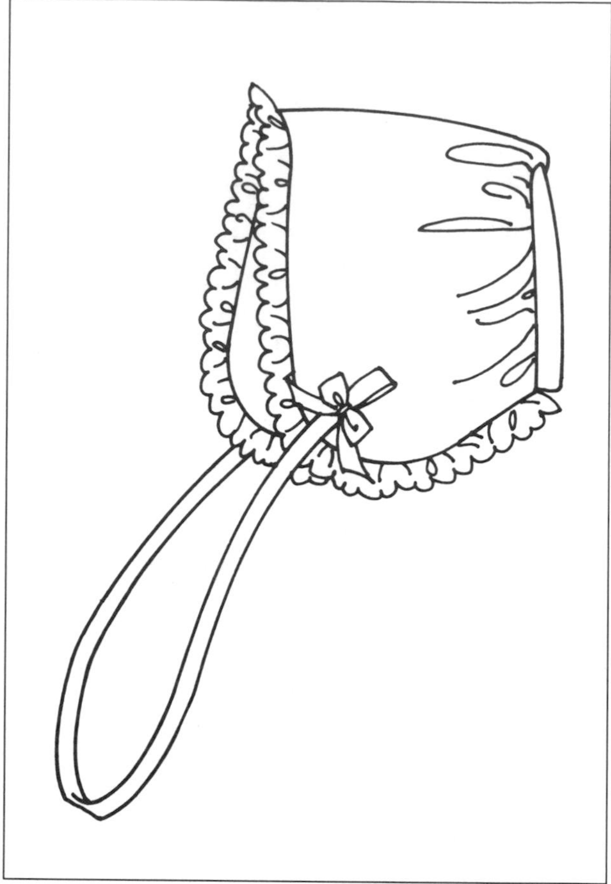

4. Repeat the procedures in steps 2 and 3 to gather and join the lining-fabric Brim and Back pieces.

5. Pin and baste eyelet trim to the right side of the outer Brim piece, beginning at one side of the Back piece and working all the way around the front edge of the Brim to the other side of the Back piece. Place the eyelet as you did for the jacket assembly, and turn each raw end of the eyelet back over itself (**Figure I**).

6. Pin the lining and outer assemblies right sides together (the eyelet will be sandwiched between). Stitch the seam all the way around the outer edges, leaving it open and unstitched along the straight lower edges of the Back pieces, as shown in **Figure J**. Clip the curves, turn the bonnet right side out, and press. Press the seam allowances to the inside along the opening edges, and whipstitch them together.

7. Use the remaining 1-yard length of ribbon as the tie. We simply tied a bow at each end of the ribbon, and tacked the bows to the outside of the bonnet as shown in **Figure K**. The ribbon can be left uncut, and the center portion tied in a half-knot under your infant's chin.

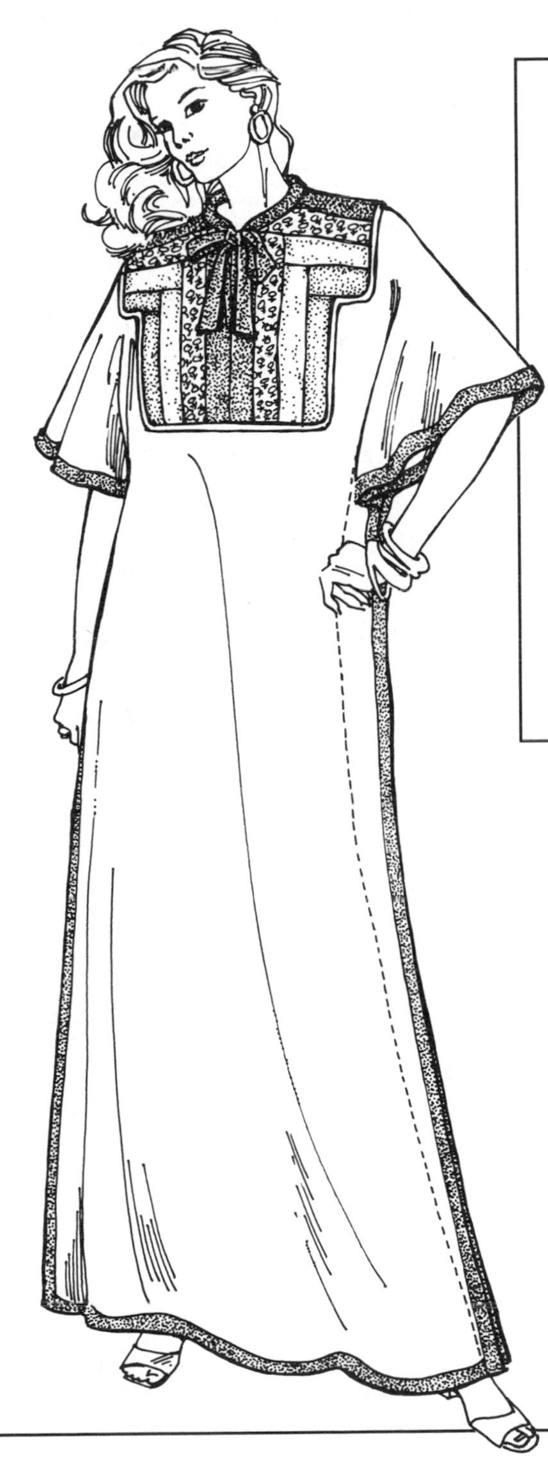

Summer Caftan

This lightweight caftan is the perfect cover-up for warm summer weather. The quilted patchwork yoke adds a lovely personal touch, and provides a way for you to use some of those small fabric remnants that have been stashed away in a closet!

Figure A

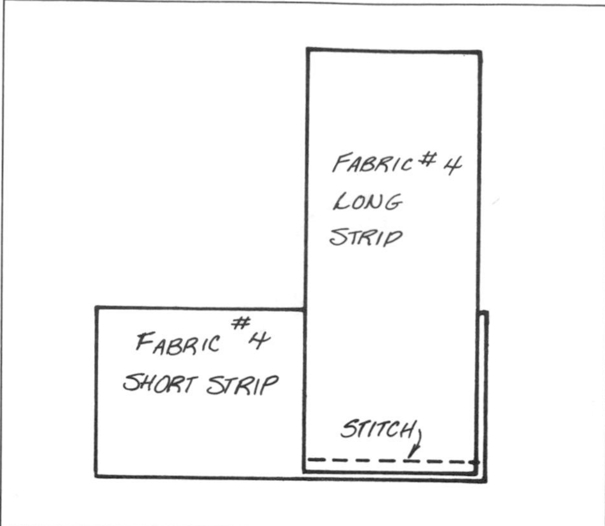

Materials

3 yards of 44- or 45-inch-wide lightweight fabric for the caftan (We used an ivory-colored cotton-poly blend.)

For the patchwork yoke, you'll need about ½ yard each of two different fabrics and ¼ yard each of two others. We used a solid green, a calico print on a peach-colored background, a lighter solid peach, and a light beige, all the same weight and fiber content as the caftan fabric.

11 yards of seam binding tape in a color to match one of the patchwork fabrics (We used green.)

4 yards of narrow corded piping in a color to match one of the patchwork fabrics (We used beige.) If you prefer, you can make your own corded piping, using one of the same fabrics that you are using for the patchwork. (See Tips & Techniques for instructions on making corded piping.)

24 x 40-inch piece of lightweight batting

Thread to match the fabrics

Cutting the Fabric

In order to make the instructions easier to follow, we have numbered the fabrics that are cut and sewn together to form the patchwork yoke. The two fabrics of which you need ½ yard each are numbered 1 and 2. The two fabrics of which you need ¼ yard each are numbered 3 and 4. (For our caftan, solid green was #1, calico was #2, light peach was #3, and beige was #4.) Cut the patchwork pieces listed below, from the specified fabrics.

Fabric #1:

Cut four pieces, each 3¼ x 15¼ inches
Cut four pieces, each 3¼ x 11½ inches

Fabric #2:

Cut four pieces, each 3¼ x 13 inches
Cut four pieces, each 3¼ x 9¼ inches

Fabric #3:

Cut four pieces, each 3¼ x 10¾ inches
Cut four pieces, each 3¼ x 7 inches

Fabric #4:

Cut four pieces, each 3¼ x 8½ inches
Cut four pieces, each 3¼ x 4¾ inches

Assembling the Patchwork

The patchwork pieces are sewn together in L-shaped pairs to form four identical sections. The sections are then sewn together to complete the patchwork. **Figure D** shows one of the sections, and **Figure G** shows the complete patchwork assembly. All seams are ½-inch wide unless otherwise specified in the instructions.

1. Begin by sewing together two of the pieces you cut from fabric #4: one of the shorter and one of the longer pieces. Place the two pieces right sides together at right angles (**Figure A**), aligning one end of the longer strip with one edge of the shorter strip as shown. Stitch the seam, trim the seam allowances to ¼ inch, and press the seam open.

2. Place the L-shaped assembly from step 1 right side up on a flat surface. Place one of the longer strips of fabric #3 right side down on top (**Figure B**), aligning one long edge of the #3 strip with the longest edge of the first assembly. Stitch the seam, trim the seam allowances to ¼ inch, and press the seam open.

3. Place the assembly from step 2 right side up on a flat surface. Place one of the shorter strips of fabric #3 right side down on top (**Figure C**), aligning one long edge of the #3 strip with the upper edge of the assem-

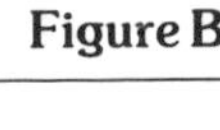

Figure B

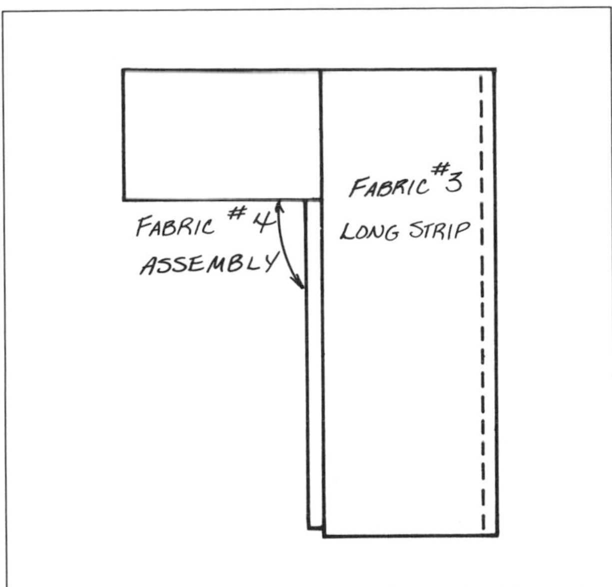

bly as shown. Stitch the seam, trim the seam allowances to ¼ inch, and press the seam open.

4. Stitch one of the longer fabric #2 strips to the longest edge of this assembly, placing right sides together as you did in step 2. Trim and press open.

5. Stitch one of the shorter fabric #2 strips to the upper edge of this assembly, placing right sides together as you did in step 3. Trim and press open.

6. Stitch one of the longer fabric #1 strips to the longest edge of this assembly, trim and press.

7. Stitch one of the shorter fabric #1 strips to the upper edge of this assembly, trim and press as you did before. This completes the first patchwork section, which should look like the one shown in **Figure D**.

8. Repeat the procedures in steps 1 through 7 to make one identical yoke section.

9. The third yoke section must be a mirror image of the first two. Begin as you did for the first section, by stitching together one long and one short strip of fabric #4, but arrange the pieces and stitch the seam as shown in **Figure E**. Trim and press open as before.

10. Stitch one of the longer fabric #3 strips to the longest edge of this assembly, trim and press open.

11. Stitch one of the shorter fabric #3 strips to the upper edge of this assembly, trim and press open.

Figure C

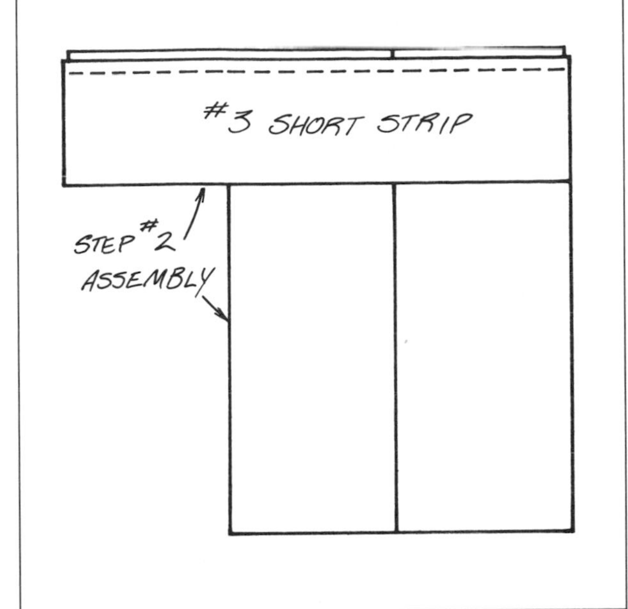

Figure D

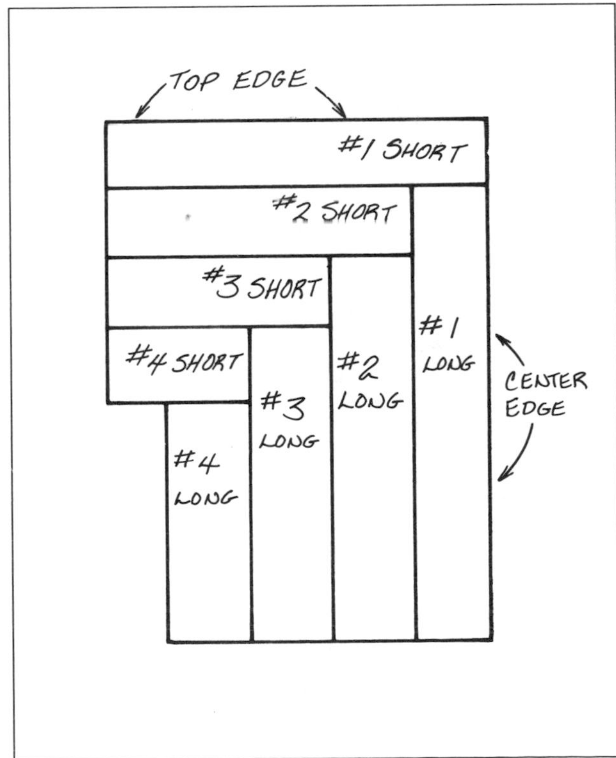

Figure E

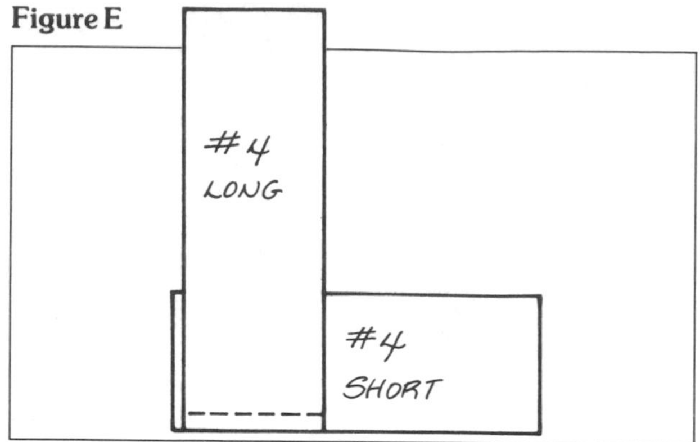

Figure F

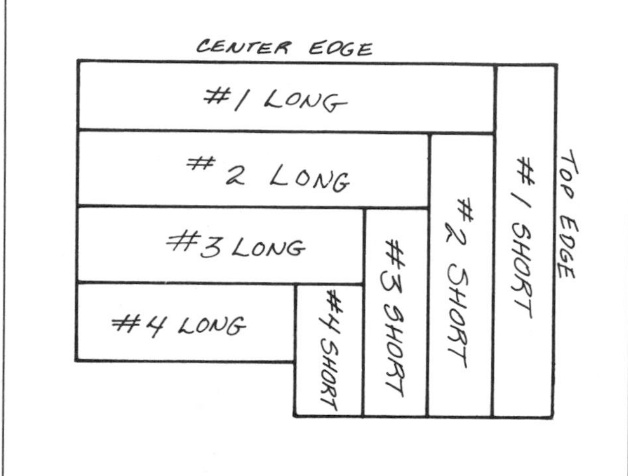

Figure G

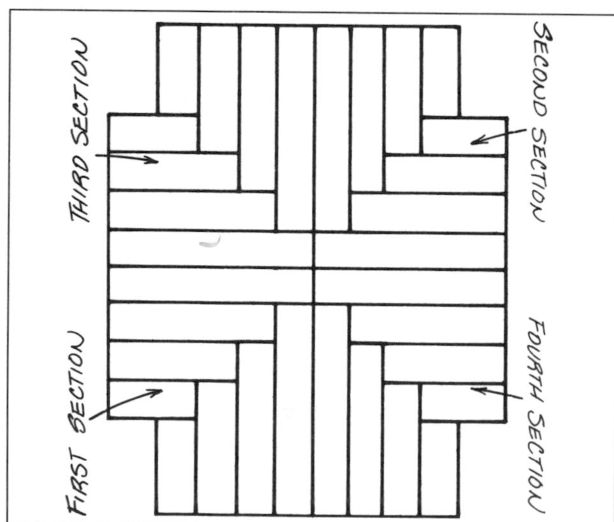

Figure H

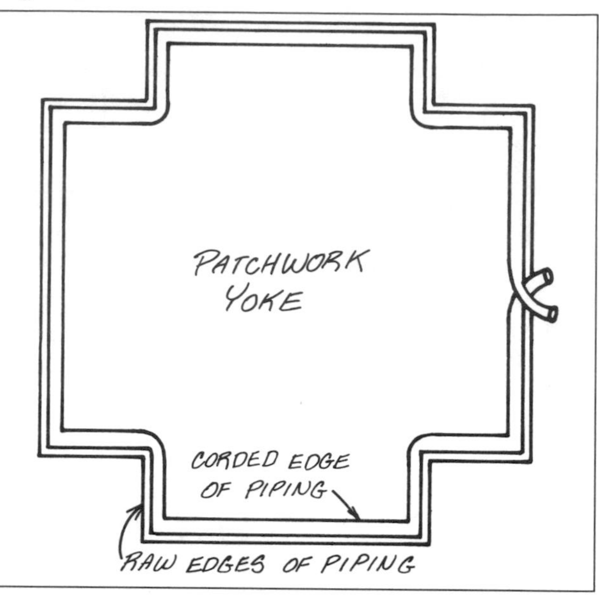

12. Continue adding strips just as you did for the first two sections, so that the complete patchwork section looks like the one shown in **Figure F**.

13. Repeat the procedures in steps 9 through 12 to make the fourth and final patchwork section.

14. Place the first and third sections right sides together. Be sure they are turned so that the top edges are aligned and the center edges are aligned. Stitch the seam along the upper edges, trim the seam allowances, and press open.

15. Repeat the procedures in step 14 to stitch the second and fourth sections together.

16. Place the two patchwork assemblies right sides together and stitch the seam along the long center edges. Trim the seam allowances and press open. The completed patchwork should now look like the diagram in **Figure G**.

Finishing the Patchwork

We added piping around the edges of the patchwork yoke for a more finished look.

1. Place the assembled patchwork right side up on a flat surface. Begin at the center of one side edge, and pin the piping to the patchwork as shown in **Figure H**. The straight edges of the piping should be even with the

Figure I

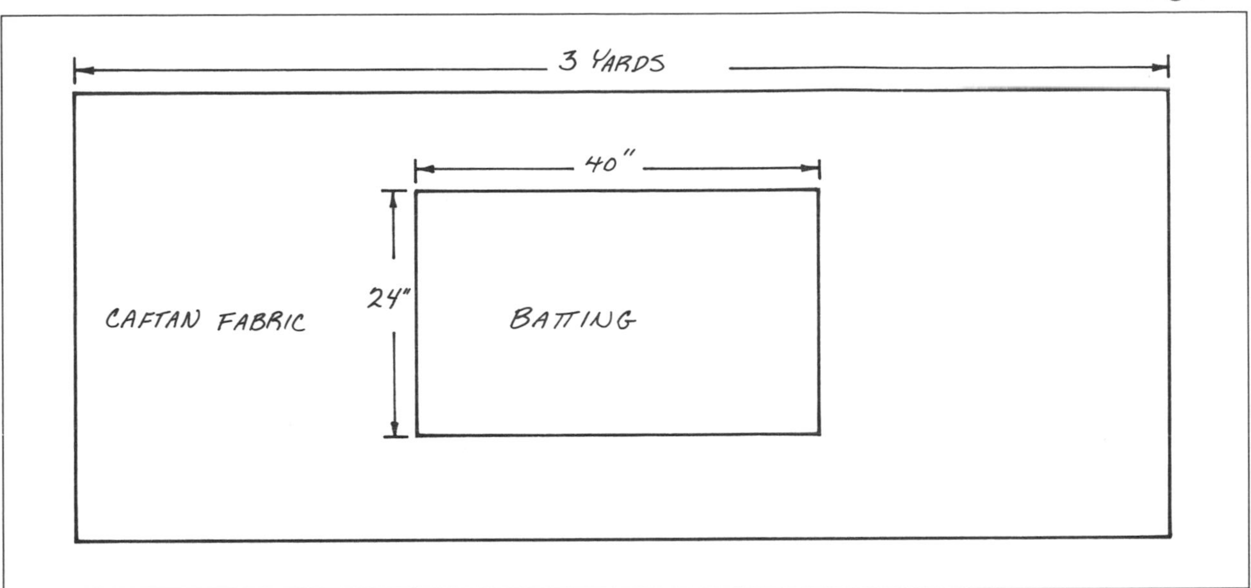

Figure J

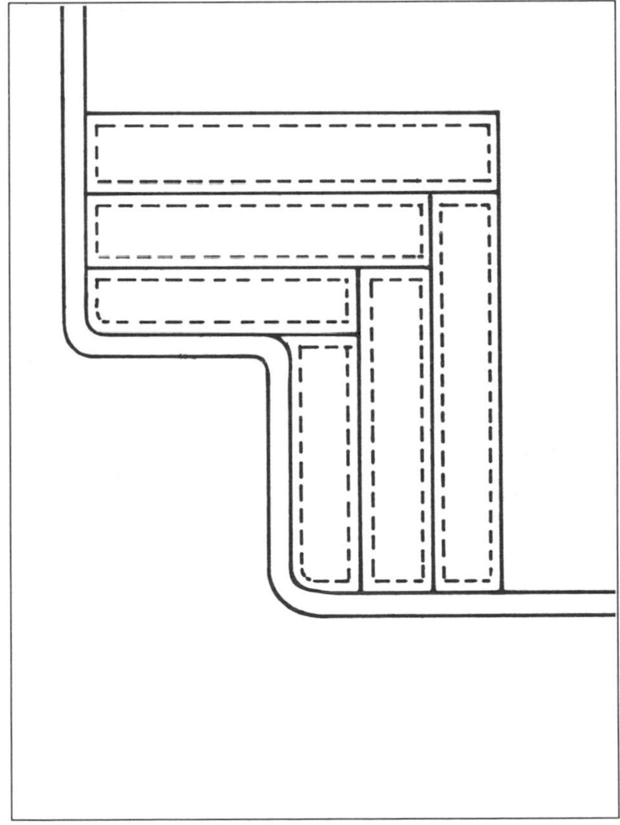

outer edges of the patchwork, and the corded edge of the piping should extend in toward the center as shown. Overlap the ends of the piping as shown.

2. Use a zipper foot attachment on your machine to stitch the piping to the yoke, so that you can stitch as close as possible to the corded portion of the piping.

3. Turn and press the raw edges of the yoke and the straight edges of the piping to the wrong side of the yoke, so that the corded edge of the piping forms a border around the patchwork.

Assembling the Caftan

1. Place the 3-yard length of caftan fabric right side up on a flat surface. Center the piece of batting on top as shown in **Figure I**. Center the patchwork yoke on top of the batting, right side up, and pin all layers together. Trim the batting just inside the piped edges of the yoke. Baste all layers together, working from the center of the yoke out to each corner. Run a few additional lines of basting stitches vertically and horizontally across the yoke, so that the layers will remain smooth and even as you quilt.

2. You can quilt by hand or machine, whichever is your preference. We quilted by hand, close to each existing patchwork seam as shown in **Figure J**. The

Figure K

Figure L

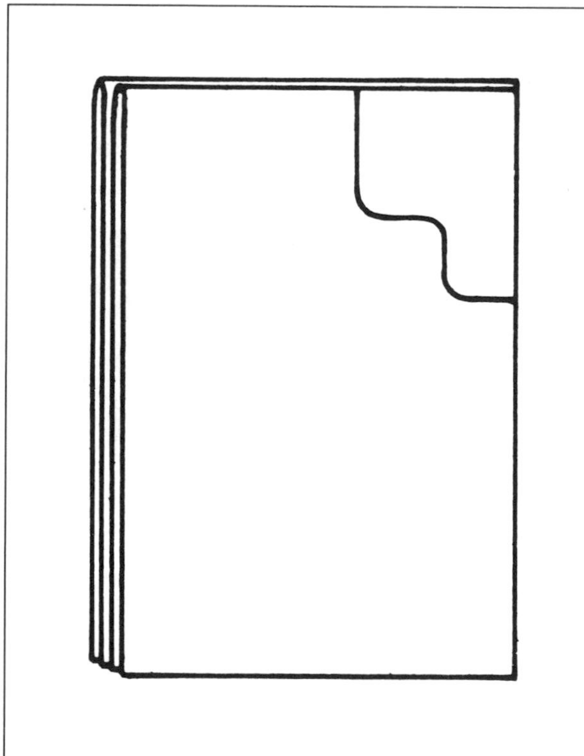

quilting stitches should pass through all layers: patchwork, batting, and caftan. We used a zipper-foot attachment to topstitch through all thicknesses, just inside the corded piping. When you have completed the quilting, remove all basting stitches.

3. The neck opening is made by cutting out the center of the caftan and yoke, and binding the edges. First, fold the caftan in half widthwise, placing wrong sides together. The fold should run along the crosswise center seam of the patchwork yoke (**Figure K**). Now fold the caftan in half again, this time lengthwise, so that it is folded in even quarters. The lengthwise fold should run along the lengthwise center seam of the patchwork (**Figure L**).

4. To make a pattern for the Neck Cutout, draw one-quarter of a 6-inch-diameter circle. Use the square corner of a piece of paper as the center of the circle, as shown in **Figure M**. (See Tips & Techniques for instructions on making circular patterns.) Cut out the pattern and place it on top of the folded caftan, aligning the square corner of the pattern with the folded center point of the caftan as shown in **Figure L**. Cut through all layers of the caftan along the curved edge.

Figure M

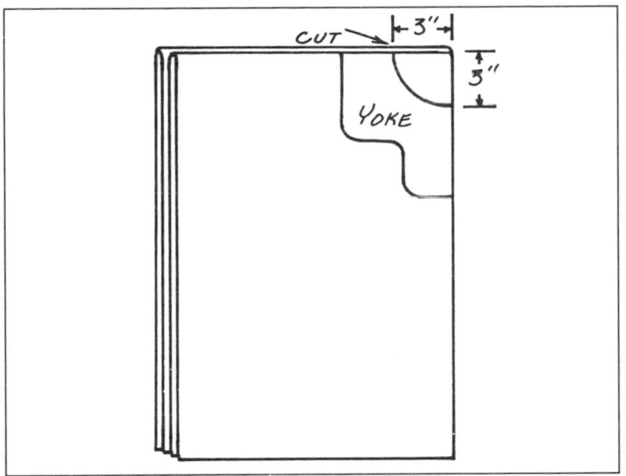

5. Open out the caftan completely and cut a straight slit along the center front yoke seam, from the curved neck opening downward. The slit should be about 5 inches long (**Figure N**).

6. Cut a 5-inch length of seam binding tape, and use it to encase one raw edge of the slit. (See Tips & Techniques for specific instructions on encasing raw edges with seam binding.)

7. Cut a 5½-inch length of binding tape, and use it to encase the remaining raw edge of the slit, folding the strip under at the bottom.

8. Cut a 1½-yard length of binding tape, and use it to encase the circular neck edge of the caftan, leaving equal extensions at each front corner to use as ties. Hem the ends of the strip, and stitch the long edges together from the neck opening to the end of each tie.

9. Use a length of binding tape to encase each outer edge of the caftan.

10. When all edges have been finished, you're ready for the final step, which is sewing the side seams. Fold the caftan in half widthwise, placing wrong sides together. Measure 13 inches down from the shoulder fold and 6½ inches in from one side edge, as shown in **Figure O**, and mark this point. Pin the front and back caftan layers together and run a line of straight machine stitches through both layers of the caftan from the marked point down to the lower corner, as shown.

11. Repeat the procedures in step 10 to create the closure along the opposite side edges of the caftan.

Figure N

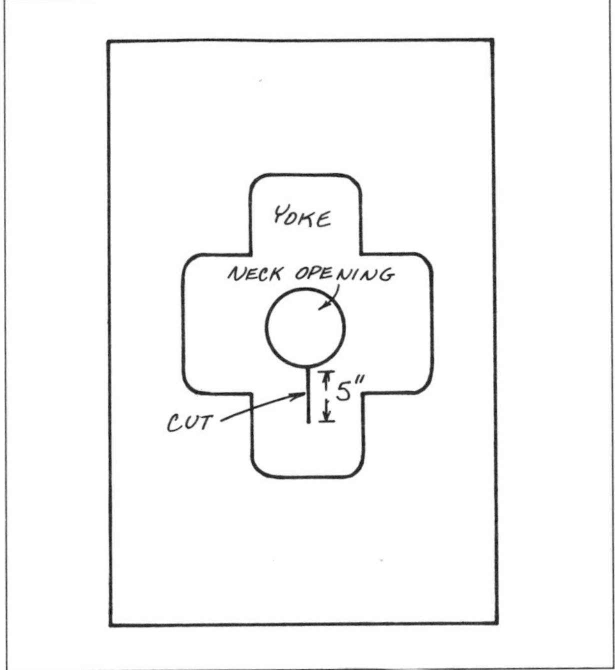

Figure O

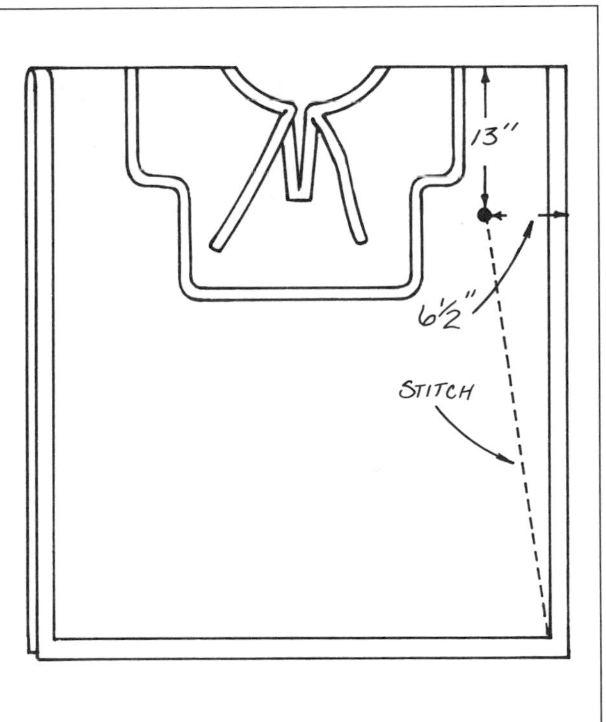

Puzzle Jacket

This wondrous jacket is the state of the art in the world of patchwork. It contains string-quilted sections, fan-quilted sections, checkerboard patchwork, and just about every other type of geometric patchwork you can imagine. If you are a beginner, practice on other projects before attempting this one. Full-color front and back photographs can be found in the color section of this book.

Materials

Note: We have specified the types, colors, and amounts of fabric required to reproduce this jacket exactly as is. Light blue is the primary color, and the patchwork is done in six bright colors: red, orange, pale yellow, Kelly green, deep royal blue, and purple. You may wish to use different fabrics, or to rearrange the patchwork designs, alter them, or design your very own puzzle jacket using different patchwork assemblies altogether. If you opt for an original design, we suggest that you read through these instructions, because many of the basic techniques will be the same.

5 yards of medium-weight light blue cotton fabric, 45 inches wide

3/4 yard of 45-inch-wide medium-weight cotton fabric in each of the following solid colors, for the patchwork: red, orange, yellow, Kelly green, deep royal blue, and purple

3 yards of 45-inch-wide lightweight cotton fabric in a multicolored plaid that picks up the colors of the patchwork fabrics, for the jacket lining

3 yards of 45-inch-wide muslin

A metal jacket zipper that will separate at the bottom, 22 inches long

1/2 yard of 1/2-inch-wide elastic

Thread to match the primary color (light blue); and one or two other colors for the patchwork assemblies

CUTTING THE PIECES

1. Scale drawings for the Jacket Front, Jacket Back, Collar, Sleeve, and Pocket patterns are provided in **Figure A**. Enlarge the drawings to make full-size patterns, and alter the patterns to fit, if necessary.

2. Cut two Jacket Fronts, one Jacket Back, one Collar, and two Sleeves from muslin. These pieces will serve as backing fabric for the patchwork outer jacket pieces. The patchwork strips will be cut during the assembly process.

3. Cut from lining fabric the same pieces as specified in step 2.

4. Cut from light blue fabric two Pocket pieces.

ASSEMBLING THE PATCHWORK

The outer jacket pieces are composed of patchwork assemblies string-quilted with solid filler strips. The various patchwork assemblies are made first. Because there will be lots of patchwork floating around when you have completed the steps in this section, we suggest that you devise a system for keeping them organized as they are sewn. You might find it convenient to use five boxes, labeled Left Front, Right Front, Left Back, Right Back, and Sleeves. As each patchwork assembly is completed, simply label it as specified and place it in the appropriate box. If you need additional information on how to go about performing any of the procedures in this section, please refer to Tips & Techniques. All patchwork seams are 1/4 inch unless otherwise specified, and all seam allowances should be pressed in one direction (not open) during each assembly step.

The Diagonal Checkerboards

1. The first assembly is a green and royal blue diagonal checkerboard, which appears on both jacket fronts and on both sides of the jacket back; it is a standard Seminole patchwork assembly. To create the checkerboard for the left front, cut two straight strips from royal blue fabric, each 1 3/8 x 17 inches; and one strip from green fabric, 1 1/8 x 17 inches. Stitch a blue strip to each long edge of the green strip, even at both ends. Cut straight across this assembly at 1 1/8-inch intervals, as shown in **Figure B**.

2. Now stitch together the resulting short patchwork strips side by side, offsetting each successive strip by one square in the same direction, as shown in **Figure C**. Note that the green squares should be corner-to-corner, as shown. Stitch together all of the short strips in this manner.

3. Mark a straight cutting line across the assembly, 3/8 inch above the aligned upper corners of the green squares, as shown in **Figure D**. Mark a second straight cutting line 3/8 inch below the lower corners of the green squares, and cut across the assembly along each marked line.

4. To finish the first checkerboard, narrow border strips are sewn to the long edges. Cut two straight green

Figure A

1 square = 1 inch

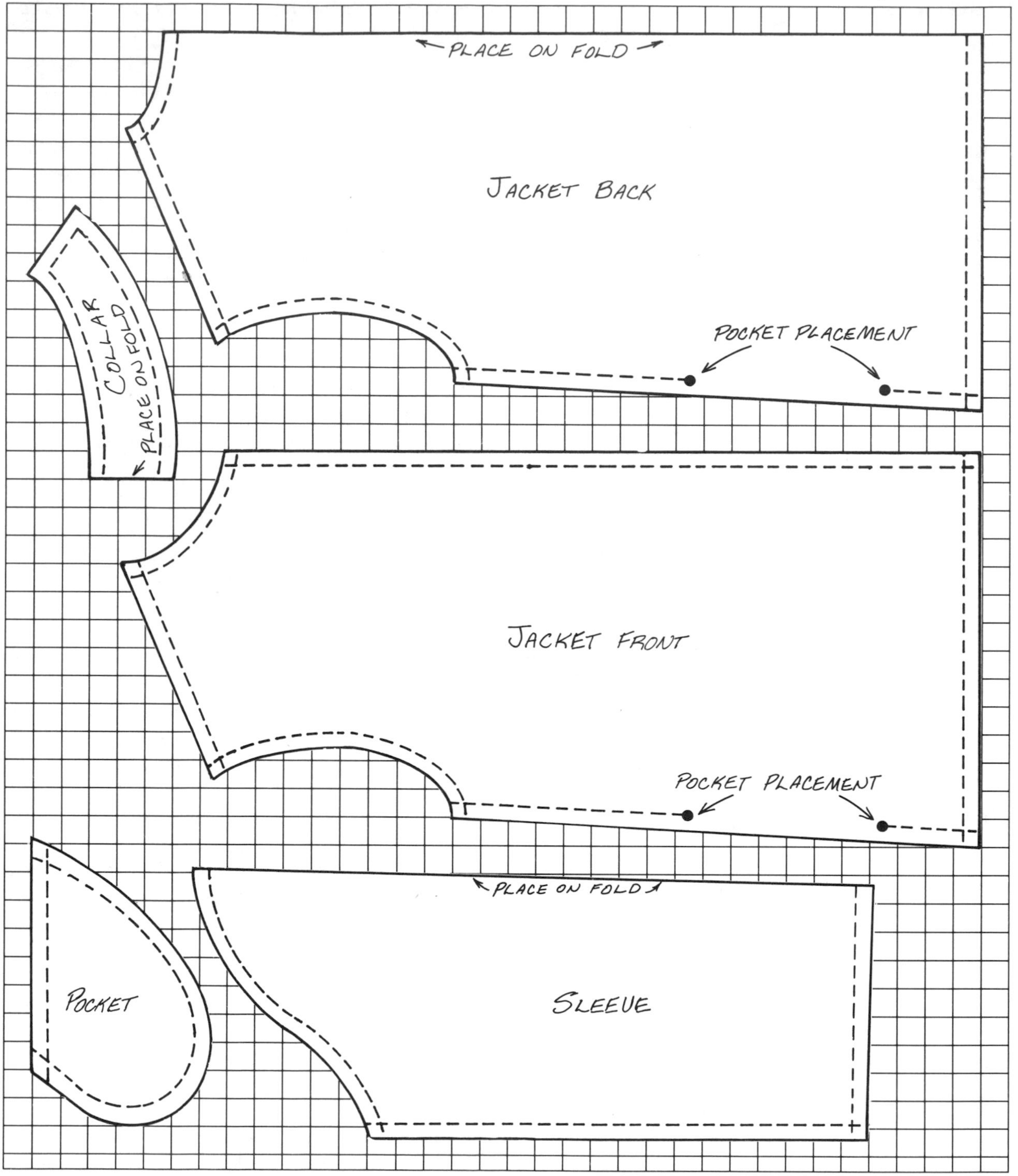

Figure B

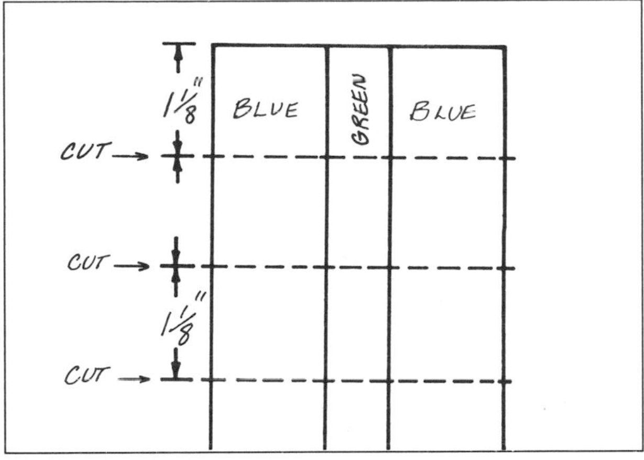

Figure C

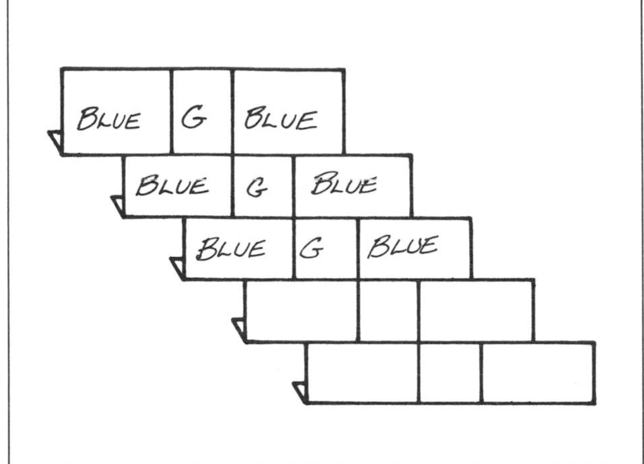

Figure D

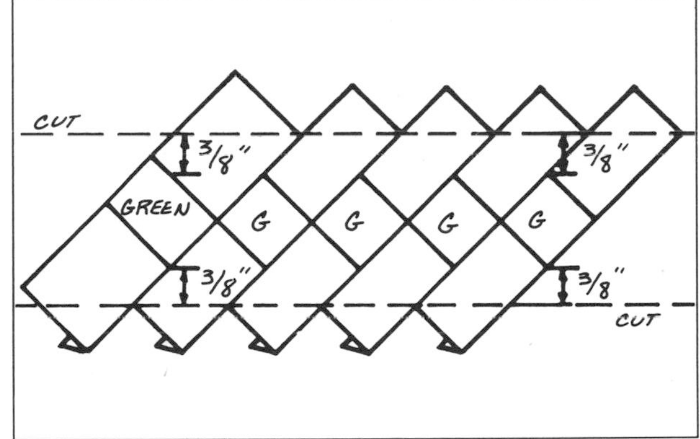

strips, each ⅞ inch wide and the same length as the checkerboard. Place one of the strips and the checkerboard right sides together, aligning one long edge of the strip with one long edge of the checkerboard. Stitch the seam ¼ inch from the aligned edges. Turn the border strip outward and press the allowances toward the strip. Border the opposite long edge of the checkerboard, using the remaining green strip in the same manner. This completes the checkerboard for the left front jacket piece. Label the assembly Left Front A, and file it in the box set aside for the left front assemblies.

5. Now that you have finished one patchwork assembly, we're going to take a short detour and talk for a moment about size; you don't want to end up with patchwork assemblies that are too short to cover the required space, nor do you want to waste a lot of fabric making assemblies that are overly long. You will find diagrams for the individual jacket pieces, showing where the various patchwork assemblies fall, in **Figures** V, X, **BB**, and **GG**. Refer to **Figure V**, which shows the left front jacket piece, and note where Patchwork Assembly A is placed. This space will be filled by the Left Front A assembly that you just made. Measure across your own Jacket Front pattern at about the same place, and compare this measurement with the length of your Left Front A assembly, which probably will be considerably longer than the pattern measurement. (We did that intentionally, so your first assembly would be at least as long as the pattern is wide.) For all of the remaining patchwork assemblies, you may wish to do a few simple calculations before cutting the initial strips, so each assembly will be close to the correct length.

6. Another blue and green diagonal checkerboard appears on the right jacket front, this time as a vertical strip. Placement is shown in **Figure X**, labeled Patchwork Assembly A. Cut two straight royal blue strips, each 1⅜ x 24 inches; and one straight green strip, 1⅛ x 24 inches. Follow the procedures described in steps 1 through 3 to create the checkerboard. Follow the instructions in step 4 to cut and attach ⅞-inch-wide green border strips. Label the assembly Right Front A, and file it in the corresponding box.

7. Blue and green diagonal checkerboards appear on both the left and right jacket backs. Placement is shown in **Figure BB**, labeled Patchwork Assembly A

Figure E

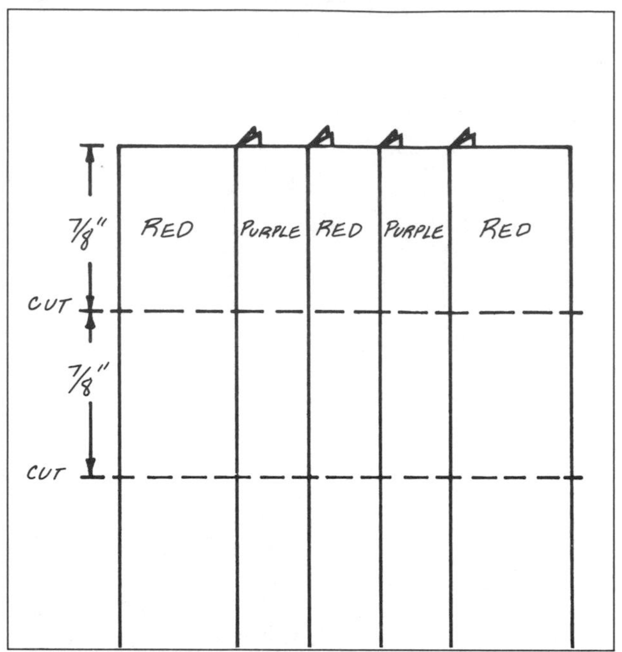

Figure F

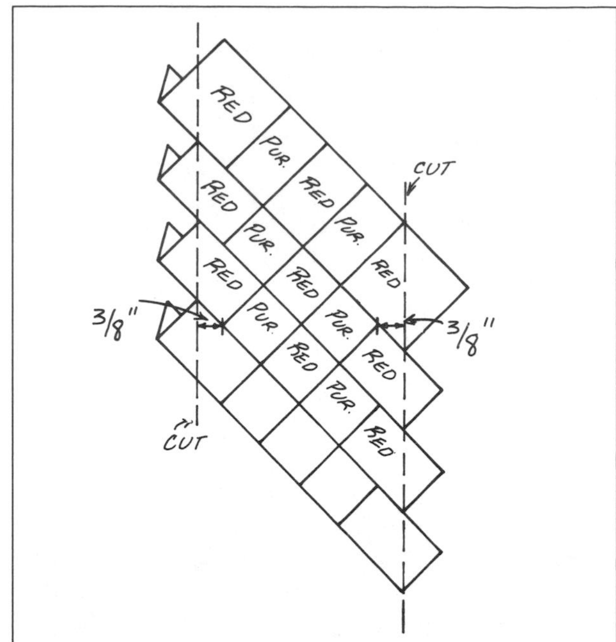

Figure G

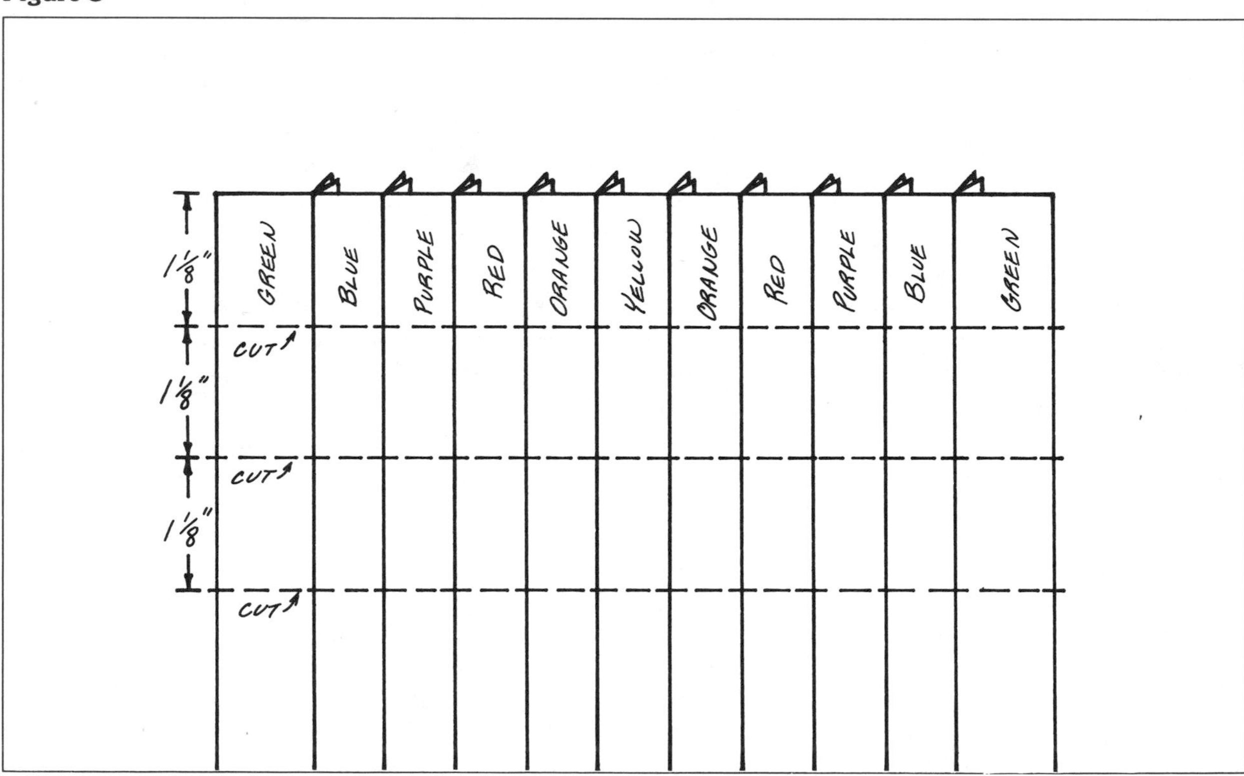

on each side. For the right back assembly, cut two royal blue strips, each 1⅜ x 12 inches; and one green strip, 1⅛ x 12 inches. Assemble the checkerboard as you did the others, and then cut and attach ⅞-inch-wide green border strips. Label the assembly Right Back A, and file it. For the left back assembly, cut two royal blue strips, each 1⅜ x 15 inches; and one green strip, 1⅛ x 15 inches. Assemble the checkerboard, cut and add green border strips, label it Left Back A, and file it.

8. A purple and red diagonal checkerboard appears on the right jacket front. Placement is shown in **Figure X**, labeled Patchwork Assembly B. This diagonal checkerboard is slightly different than the ones you already have made, in that it consists of smaller squares in double rows, but the assembly techniques are the same. Cut three straight red strips and two straight purple strips, each ⅞ x 30 inches. Stitch all five strips together side by side and even at both ends, alternating colors (**Figure E**). Cut across the strips at ⅞-inch intervals, as shown. You should be able to get at least thirty-two patchwork strips from the assembly.

9. Stitch together the resulting patchwork strips side by side, offsetting each successive strip by one square in the same direction, as shown in **Figure F**. Cut across the checkerboard assembly as shown, ⅜ inch above the aligned upper corners of the center squares, and ⅜ inch below the aligned lower corners. Cut two purple border strips, each ⅞ inch wide, and attach them to the checkerboard as you did those for the previous assemblies. Label this checkerboard Right Front B, and file it accordingly.

The Checkerboard Triangles

1. A triangular checkerboard assembly, consisting of all patchwork colors, appears on the left jacket front, the right jacket back, and both sleeves. Size will not matter on any of these. Cut the following straight strips, each 1⅛ x 14 inches: two green, two royal blue, two purple, two red, two orange, and one yellow.

2. Stitch the strips together side by side and even at both ends, in the following order: green, royal blue, purple, red, orange, yellow, orange, red, purple, royal blue, green. When all of the strips have been sewn together, cut across the assembly at 1⅛-inch intervals as shown in **Figure G**. You should be able to get twelve multicolored strips from the assembly.

3. Stitch together the multicolored strips side by side, offsetting each successive strip by one square in the same direction, as shown in **Figure H**. Use all twelve strips for this assembly.

4. The completed assembly should now look like the one shown in **Figure I**. Cut straight across the assembly along the existing seams, where indicated, to create two separate patchwork triangles. Label one Left Front B and the other Right Back B, and file them accordingly.

5. Repeat all of the procedures described in steps 1 through 4 to create two more triangular checkerboards. Label each of these Sleeve B, and file.

The Seminole Squares

1. Seminole squares appear on the right jacket front and the left jacket back. Size will not matter for these.

Figure H

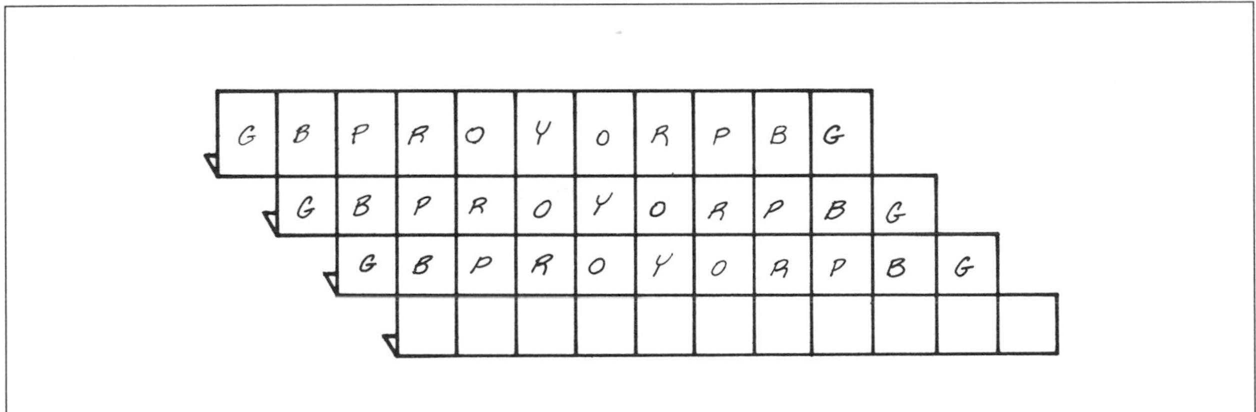

Figure I

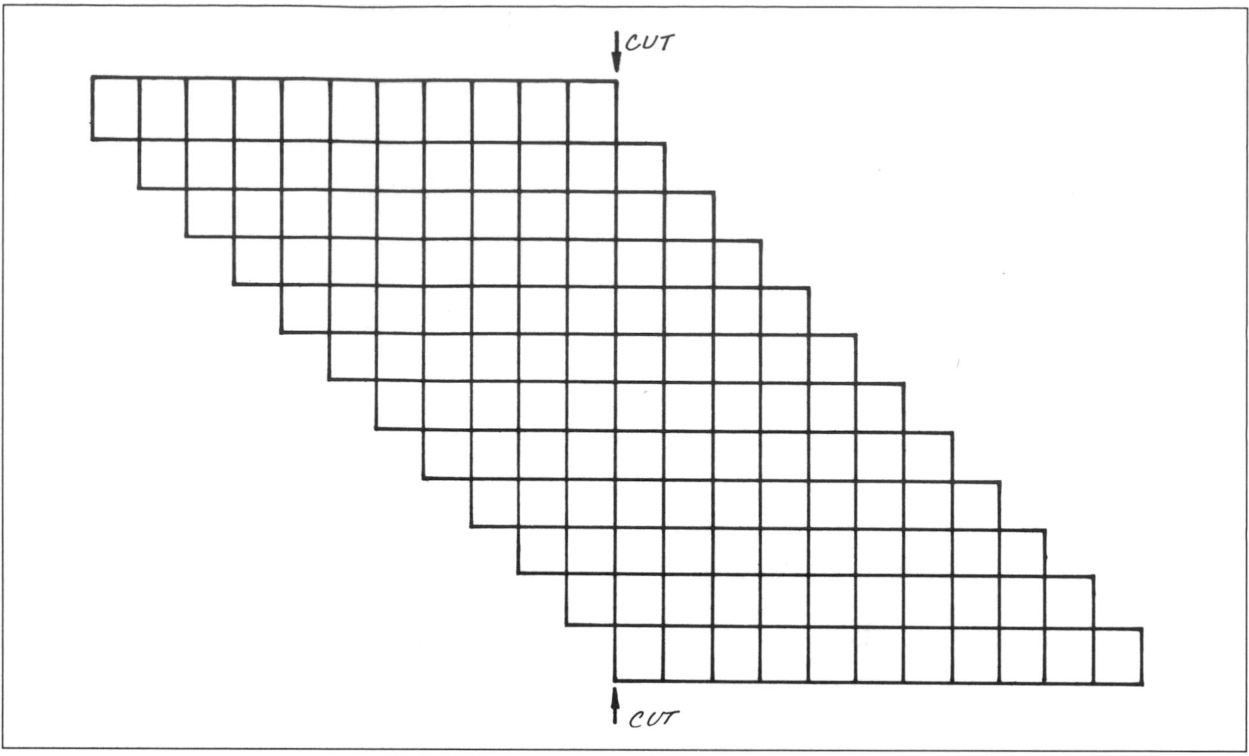

To make the two squares for the right jacket front, cut the straight strips listed here:

Green – cut one, 1⅛ x 6 inches
Red – cut one, ⅞ x 6 inches
Royal blue – cut one, ⅞ x 6 inches
Orange – cut one, 1⅛ x 6 inches
Purple – cut one, 1⅛ x 4 inches
Yellow – cut one, ⅞ x 4 inches
Purple – cut one, ⅞ x 4 inches
Yellow – cut one, 1⅛ x 4 inches

2. Sew together the green, red, royal blue, and orange strips in that order, side by side and even at both ends. Cut across the assembled strips at 1¼-inch intervals. You should be able to get four multicolored strips from the assembly.

3. Sew together the two purple and two yellow strips side by side and even at both ends, alternating colors and placing the wider strips on the outside, as shown in **Figure J**. Cut across the assembly at ⅞-inch intervals, as shown. You should be able to get four strips from the assembly.

4. To create one Seminole square, use two of the multicolored strips that you cut in step 2, and two of the strips that you cut in step 3. Stitch them together side by side and even at both ends, as shown in **Figure K**. The strips from step 2 should be on the outside, turned in opposite directions end for end, so that the color progression is reversed. The strips from step 3 are on the inside, and also should be turned in opposite directions end for end, as shown. This completes one Seminole square. Label it Right Front **C**, and file.

5. Repeat the procedures in step 4, using the multicolored strips that remain, to create a second, identical Seminole square. Label it also Right Front **C**, and file.

6. Six Seminole squares appear on the left jacket back: Three are identical to the ones you already have made, and three are slightly different in color arrangement. Cut the strips listed here:

Figure J

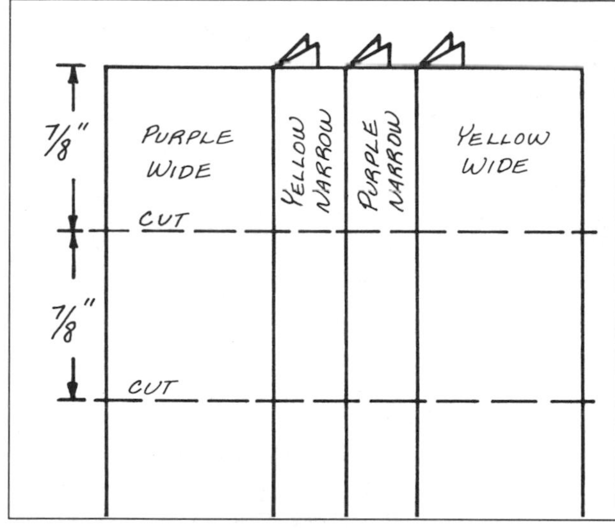

Figure K

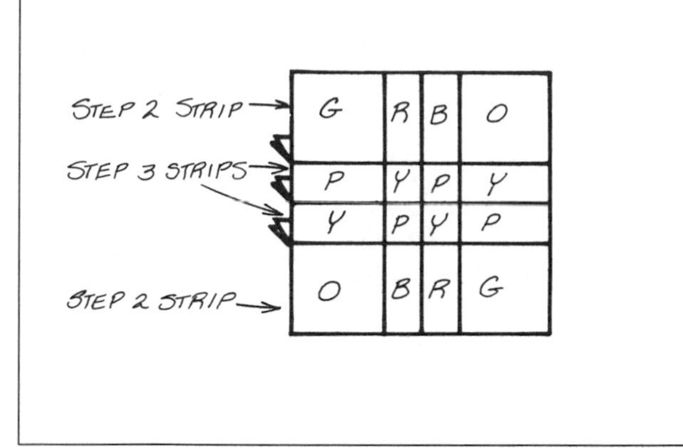

Figure L

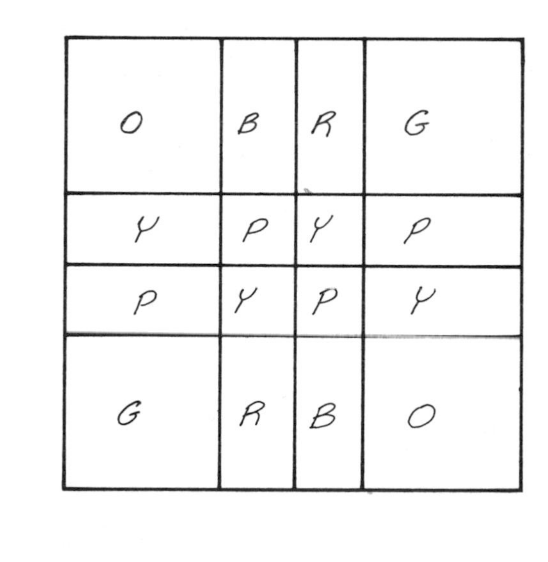

Green – cut one, 1⅛ x 16 inches
Red – cut one, ⅞ x 16 inches
Royal blue – cut one, ⅞ x 16 inches
Orange – cut one, 1⅛ x 16 inches
Purple – cut one, 1⅛ x 12 inches
Yellow – cut one, ⅞ x 12 inches
Purple – cut one, ⅞ x 12 inches
Yellow – cut one, 1⅛ x 12 inches

7. Repeat the procedures described in steps 2 through 4 to create three Seminole squares identical to the first ones you made. Label each of these squares Left Back C, and file.

8. The last three Seminole squares are assembled in the same manner, but the colors are reversed so that the arrangement is a mirror image of the squares you already have made. To make one of these squares, follow the same procedures but arrange the colors so that the finished square looks like the one shown in **Figure L**. Use the remaining strips to create three Seminole squares with this color arrangement, label each of them Left Back C, and file.

The Bicolored Rectangles

These Seminole patchwork assemblies consist of diagonally divided rectangles; each rectangle is half one color and half another color.

1. The first bicolored rectangle assembly appears on both the left jacket front and right jacket back. Placement is shown in **Figures V** and **BB**, labeled Patchwork Assembly C on each. To make the assembly for the left jacket front, cut twelve straight purple strips and twelve straight yellow strips, each 1⅜ x 2 inches.

2. One end of each strip must be cut at an angle, as shown in **Figure M**. Measure along one long edge of a strip, 1⅛ inches from the upper corner, and mark the point. Cut diagonally across the strip from the opposite

Figure M

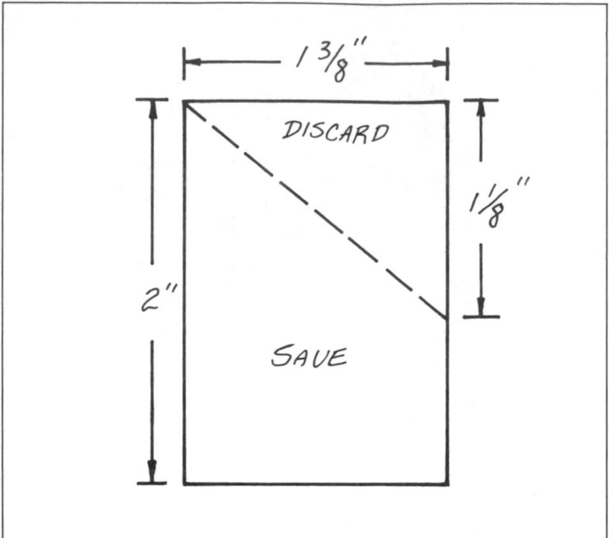

Figure N

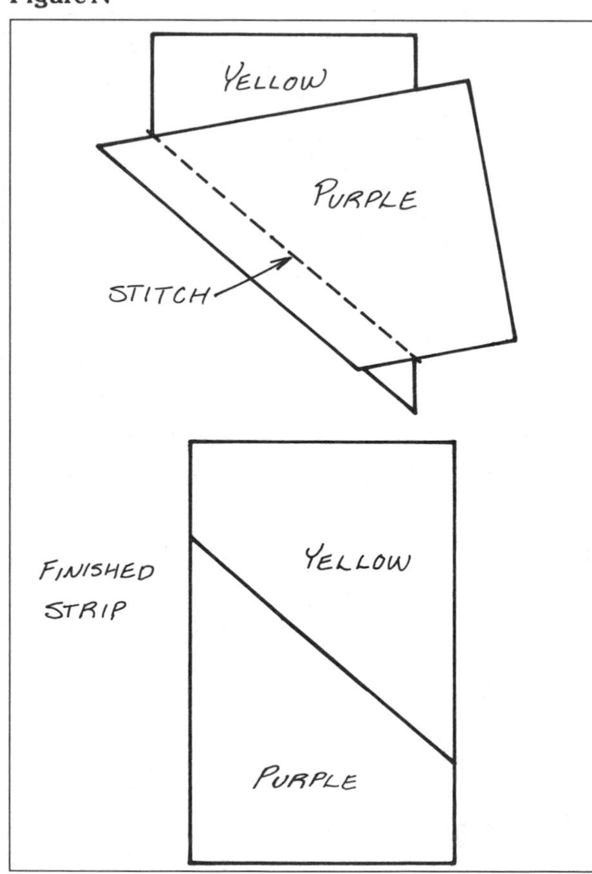

upper corner to the marked point, as shown. Use the angled strip as a guide to trim each of the remaining twenty-three strips. You will be using only the larger portion of each trimmed strip.

3. Sew together one purple and one yellow strip along the angled ends, as shown in **Figure N**. (Detailed instructions for sewing together strips with angled ends are provided in Tips & Techniques, if you need some help with this procedure.) Open out the strips; you should now have a two-colored strip like the one shown in the second diagram, **Figure N**. Trim off the corners of the seam allowances where they extend beyond the long edges of the assembled strip.

4. Repeat the procedures in step 2 to stitch together the remaining purple and yellow strips in pairs.

5. Now stitch together all of the two-colored strips, side by side and even at both ends, as shown in **Figure O**. All strips should be turned the same way end for end, so that the yellow segments are all at the top and the purple segments are all at the bottom, as shown.

6. Mark a straight cutting line across the yellow segments, 3/8 inch above the aligned upper corners of the diagonal seams. Mark a second cutting line across the purple segments, 3/8 inch below the aligned lower corners of the diagonal seams, and cut across the assembly along each marked line.

7. Cut one yellow and one purple border strip, each 7/8 inch wide and the same length as the assembled patchwork. Follow the same procedures as you did previously to stitch the borders to the patchwork; attach the purple border to the yellow edge of the patchwork, and attach the yellow border to the purple edge. Label the assembly Left Front C and file it.

8. Patchwork assembly C for the right jacket back is identical to the one you just made, but it's a little shorter. Cut ten purple and ten yellow strips, each 1 3/8 x 2 inches. Follow the procedures described in steps 2 through 7 to create the finished assembly, label it Right Back C, and file.

9. The third bicolored rectangle assembly appears on the left jacket back. Placement is shown in **Figure BB**, labeled Patchwork Assembly B. Although it is the same type of Seminole strip as the two you just made, it is slightly different. For this assembly, cut one orange and one red strip, each 1 3/8 x 33 inches.

Figure O

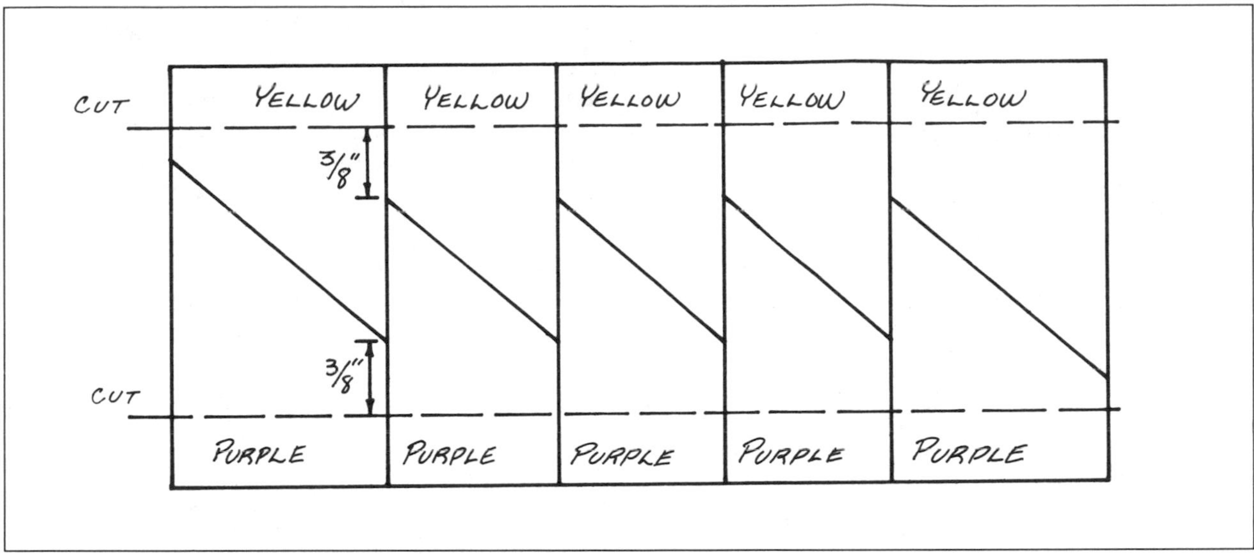

Figure P

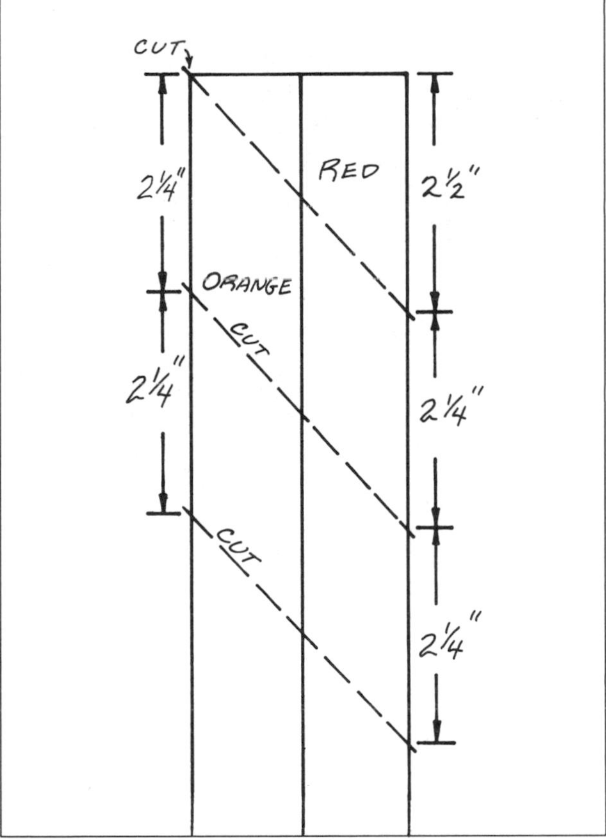

10. Stitch the two strips together side by side and even at both ends. This assembly must now be cut at an angle, as shown in **Figure P**. Place the assembled strips on a flat surface as shown, measure along the right-hand edge 2½ inches from the top, and mark this point. Continue to measure along the same edge from the first marked point, and mark the edge at 2¼-inch intervals all the way to the bottom. Measure along the left-hand edge, beginning at the top, and mark points at 2¼-inch intervals all the way to the bottom. Cut across the strips at an angle between each two successive points on opposite edges, as shown in **Figure P**. You should be able to get thirteen bicolored strips from the assembly.

11. Stitch together the bicolored strips side by side, offsetting each strip by 1¼ inches as shown in **Figure Q**. Note that this placement should align the upper and lower ends of the diagonal seams. Be certain that each strip is turned the same way end for end, so that the color arrangement is the same along the entire assembly, as shown. When all of the bicolored strips have been sewn together, mark a straight cutting line across the orange segments, ⅜ inch above the aligned upper ends of the diagonal seams. Mark a second straight cutting line across the red segments, ⅜ inch below the aligned lower ends of the diagonal seams, as shown. Cut across the assembly along each marked line.

Figure Q

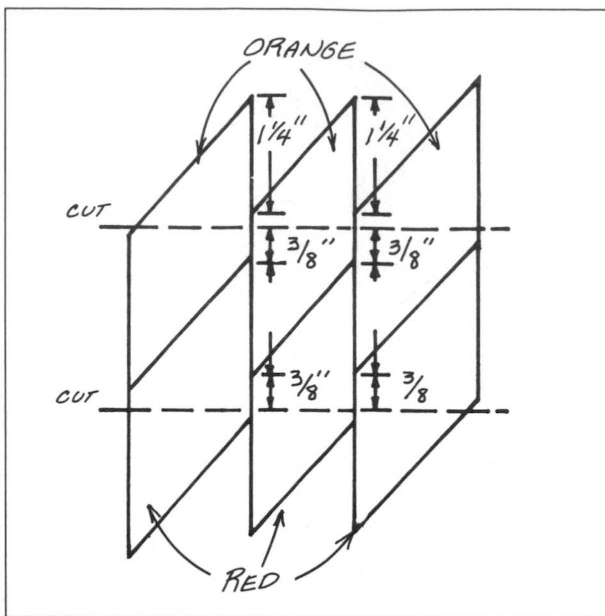

12. Cut one orange and one red border strip, each ⅞ inch wide and the same length as the patchwork assembly. Stitch the orange border to the orange edge of the patchwork, and the red border to the red edge, as you did the other borders. Label the assembly Left Back B, and file it.

13. The final bicolored rectangle assembly appears on each sleeve. Placement is shown in **Figure GG**, labeled Patchwork Assembly A. These assemblies are very similar to the last one you made, but the angle is a bit different. Cut one royal blue and one green strip, each 1¾ x 32 inches. Stitch them together side by side and even at both ends.

14. Measure along one long edge of the assembled strips 3 inches from the top, and mark this point. Continue to measure along the same edge from the first marked point, and mark the edge at 2¼-inch intervals all the way to the bottom. Measure along the opposite long edge, beginning at the top, and mark points at 2¼-inch intervals all the way to the bottom. Cut across the assembled strips at an angle between each two successive points on opposite edges. You should be able to get at least twelve bicolored strips from the assembly.

15. Stitch together the bicolored strips side by side, offsetting each successive strip by 1 inch and turning all strips the same way end for end so the color arrangement remains the same throughout. This assembly should look very much like the one shown in **Figure Q**, except that the ends are offset by 1 inch instead of 1¼ inches, and the colors are blue and green instead of orange and red.

16. Mark a straight cutting line across the green seg-

Figure R

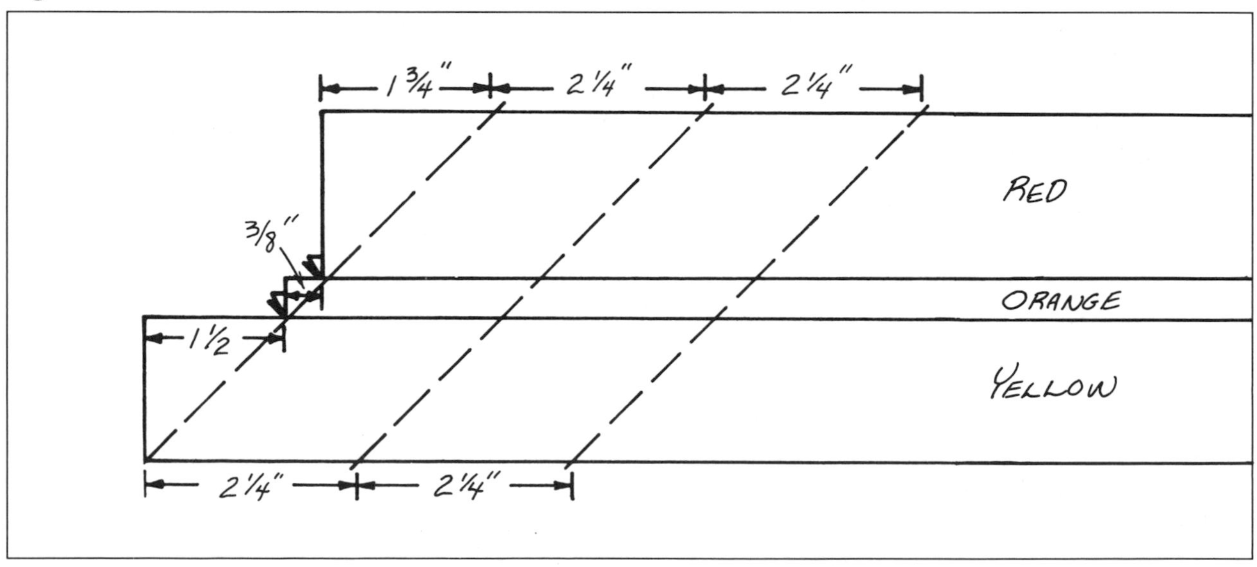

ments, ½ inch from the aligned upper corners of the diagonal seams. Mark a second cutting line across the blue segments, ½ inch from the lower ends of the diagonal seams. Cut along each marked line.

17. Cut one green and one royal blue border strip, each ⅞ inch wide and the same length as the assembled patchwork. Stitch the green border strip to the blue edge of the patchwork, and the blue border strip to the green edge, as you did the previous borders. Label the assembly Sleeve B, and file.

18. Repeat the procedures in steps 13 through 17 to create an identical patchwork assembly. Label it also Sleeve B, and file.

The Tricolored Rectangles

The next two Seminole patchwork assemblies are composed of tricolored rectangles. They are made in the same manner initially but are cut at different angles.

1. The first tricolored rectangle assembly appears on the left jacket front. Placement is shown in **Figure V**, labeled Patchwork Assembly D. For this assembly, cut one straight red strip, 2 x 24 inches; one orange, ⅞ x 24 inches; and one yellow, 1¾ x 24 inches.

2. The three strips are sewn together side by side, with ends offset as shown in **Figure R**. First, stitch together the red and orange strips, offsetting the ends by ⅜ inch. Stitch the yellow strip to the free long edge of the orange strip, offsetting the ends by 1½ inches.

3. Figure R also shows how the assembled strips are marked and cut. Measure along the upper edge of the red strip 1¾ inches from the left-hand end, and mark this point. Measure along the same edge from the first marked point, and mark points at 2¼-inch intervals as shown, all the way to the opposite end. Measure along the lower edge of the yellow strip, beginning at the left-hand end, and mark points at 2¼-inch intervals all the way to the opposite end. Cut diagonally across the assembly between successive marked points on opposite edges, as shown. You should be able to get nine tricolored strips from the assembly.

4. Stitch together the tricolored strips side by side, offsetting the ends by 1¾ inches as shown in **Figure S**. This placement should align the upper and lower ends of the diagonal seams. Make certain that each strip is turned the same way end for end, to keep the color arrangement the same throughout.

Figure S

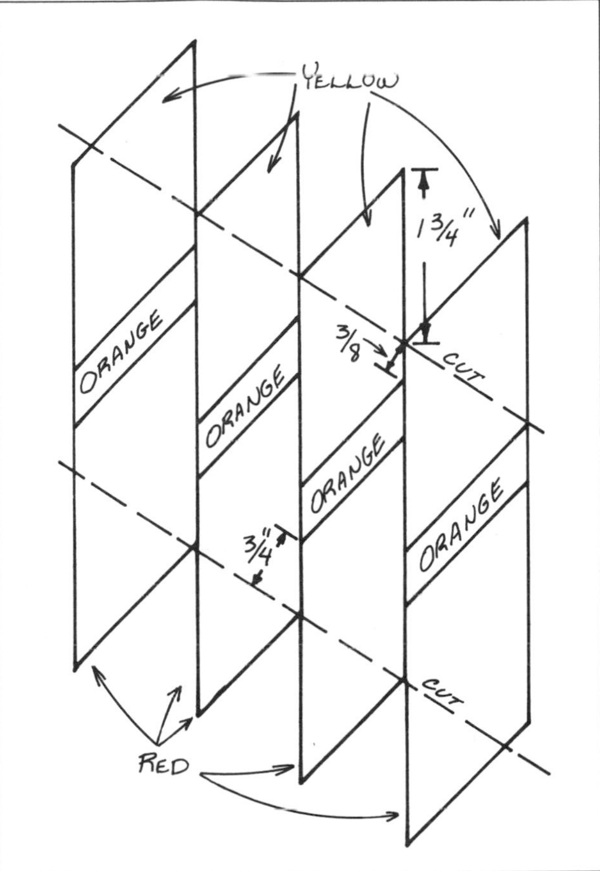

5. When all of the strips have been sewn together, mark a straight cutting line across the yellow sections, ⅜ inch above the aligned upper corners of the diagonal seams, as shown in **Figure S**. Mark a second cutting line across the red sections, ¾ inch below the aligned lower corners of the diagonal seams, and cut along each marked line.

6. Cut two ⅞-inch-wide orange borderstrips and stitch one to each long edge of the patchwork as you did the previous borders. Label the assembly Left Front D, and file.

7. The next tricolored assembly appears on the right jacket back. Placement is shown in **Figure BB**, labeled

Figure T

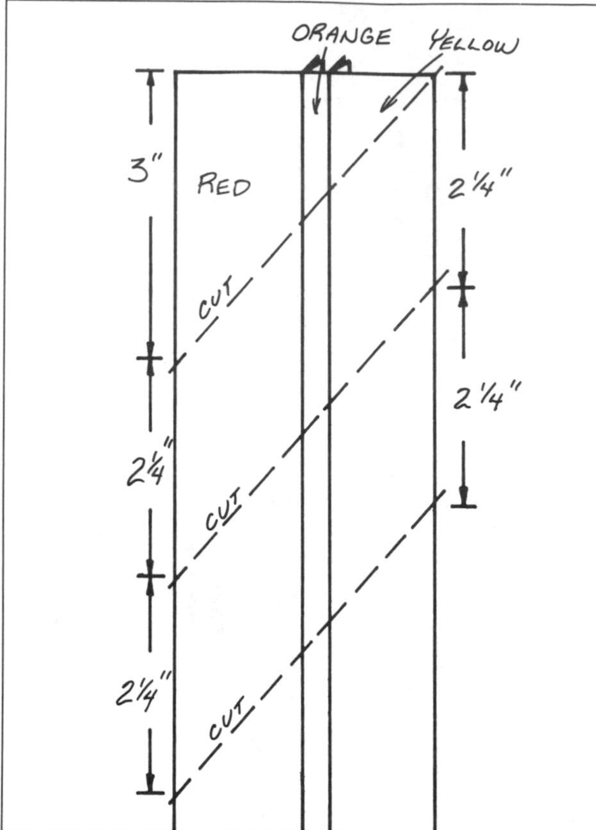

Figure U

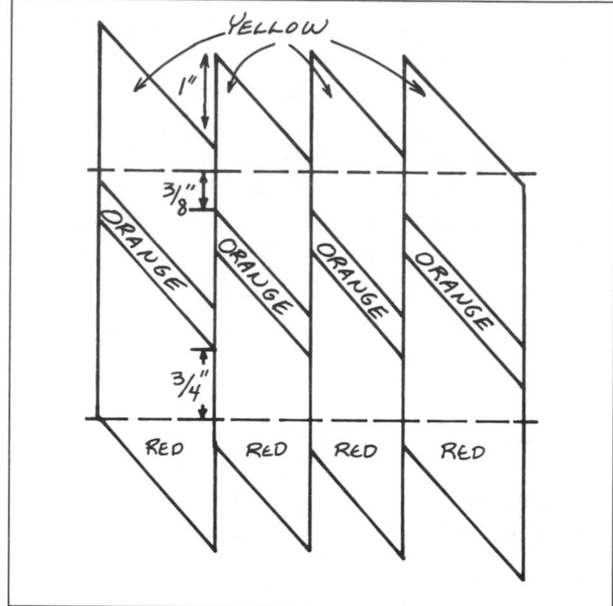

Patchwork Assembly D. For this assembly cut one straight red strip, 1⅝ x 32 inches; one orange, ¾ x 32 inches; and one yellow, 1⅜ x 32 inches. Stitch together the three strips side by side and even at both ends, placing the orange strip between the red and yellow ones.

8. This assembly is cut into tricolored strips as shown in **Figure T**. Measure along the free long edge of the yellow strip, beginning at one end, and mark points at 2¼-inch intervals all the way to the opposite end. Measure along the free long edge of the red strip, beginning at the same end, and mark a point at 3 inches. Measure along the same edge from the first marked point, and mark points at 2¼-inch intervals all the way to the opposite end. Cut across the assembly at an angle between each two successive points, as shown in **Figure T**. You should be able to get twelve complete tricolored strips from the assembly.

9. Stitch together the tricolored strips side by side, offsetting the ends by 1 inch as shown in **Figure U**. This placement should align the upper and lower ends of the diagonal seams, as shown. Make certain that all strips are turned the same way end for end, so the color arrangement remains constant throughout. When all of the strips have been sewn together, mark a straight cutting line across the yellow segments, ⅜ inch above the aligned upper ends of the diagonal seams, as shown. Mark a second cutting line across the red segments, ¾ inch below the aligned lower ends of the diagonal seams. Cut across the assembly along each marked line.

10. Cut two ⅞-inch-wide orange border strips and stitch one to each long edge of the patchwork. Label the assembly Right Back D, and file.

STRING-QUILTING

To make the outer jacket pieces you must string-quilt the patchwork assemblies, along with filler strips, to the muslin backing pieces. The filler strips will be cut as you work. We suggest that you review the sections on string-quilting and fan-quilting in Tips & Techniques before you begin.

Figure V

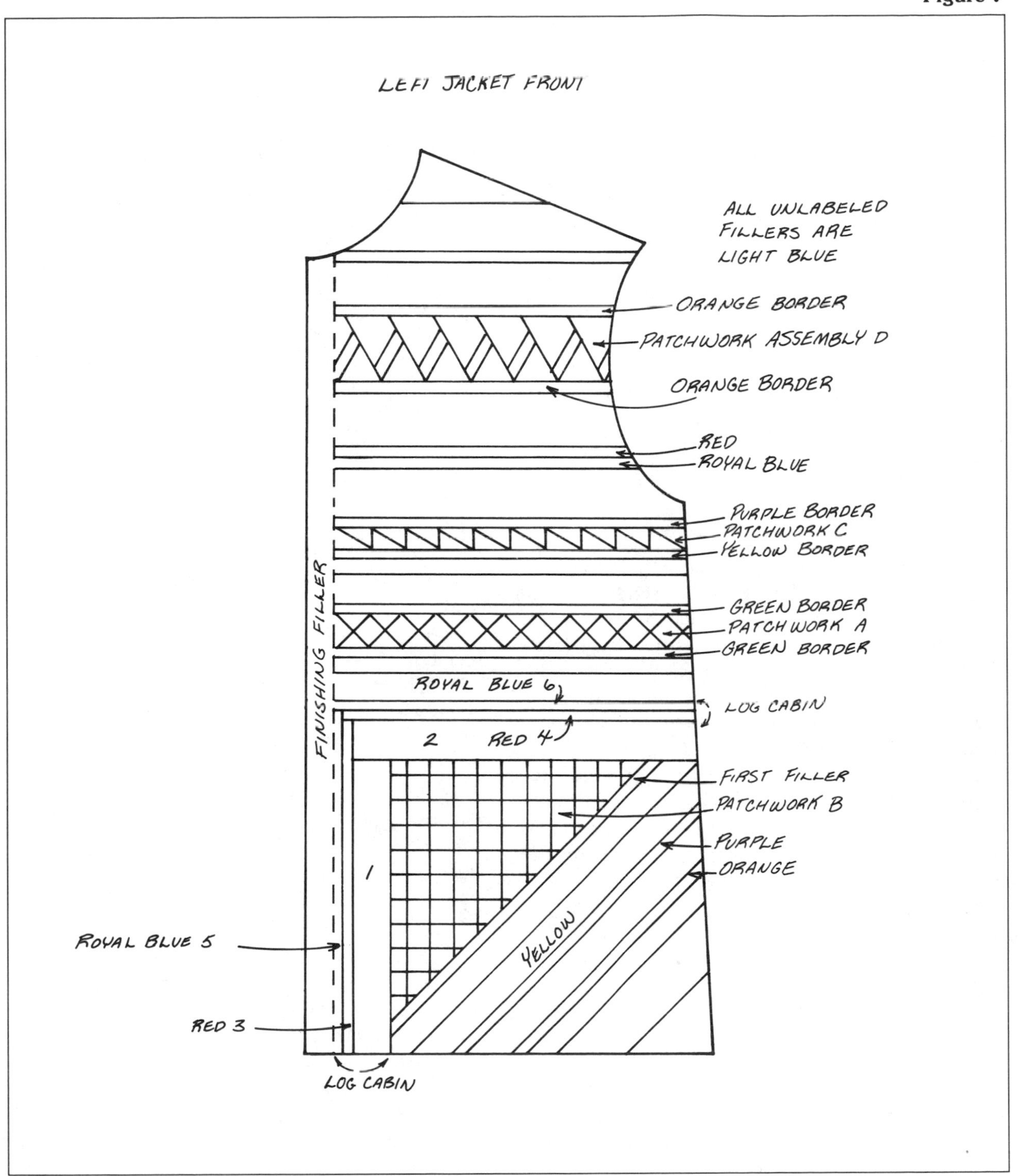

LEFT JACKET FRONT
ALL UNLABELED FILLERS ARE LIGHT BLUE
ORANGE BORDER
PATCHWORK ASSEMBLY D
ORANGE BORDER
RED
ROYAL BLUE
PURPLE BORDER
PATCHWORK C
YELLOW BORDER
GREEN BORDER
PATCHWORK A
GREEN BORDER
ROYAL BLUE 6
LOG CABIN
2
RED 4
FIRST FILLER
PATCHWORK B
PURPLE
ORANGE
FINISHING FILLER
1
YELLOW
ROYAL BLUE 5
RED 3
LOG CABIN

Figure W

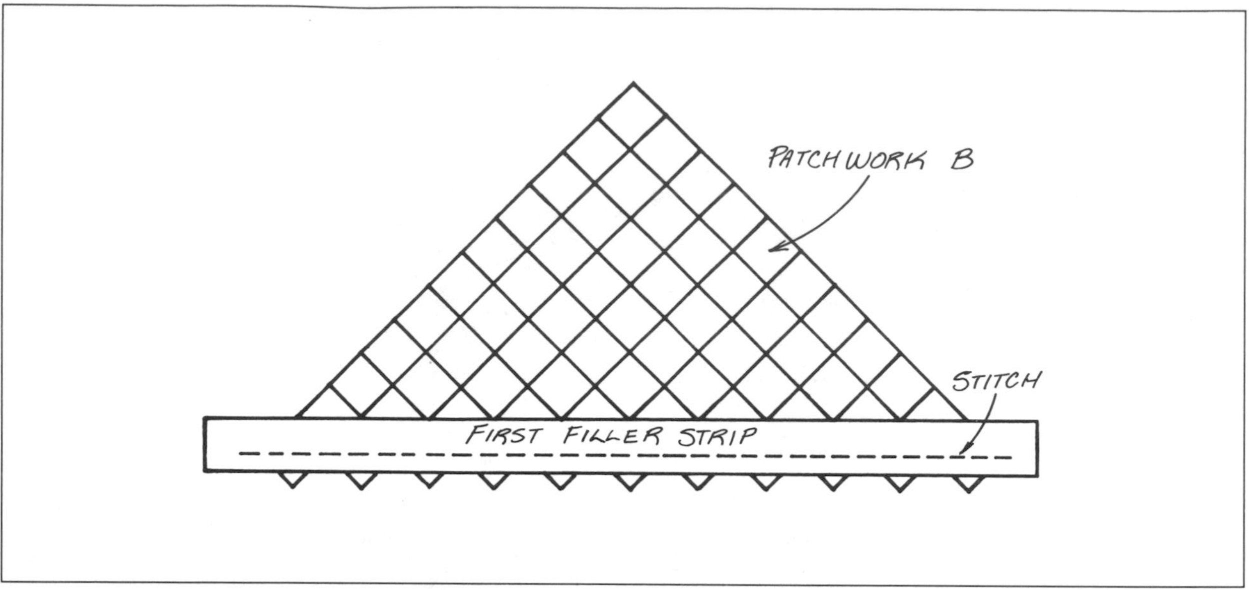

The Left Front

1. The left jacket front is shown fully assembled in **Figure V**. Place one of the muslin Jacket Front pieces on a flat surface, turning it as shown in **Figure V**. Cut away the seam allowance along the entire length of the center front. Pin the Left Front B patchwork assembly to the muslin piece where indicated; the zigzag edge of the patchwork should face the lower right-hand corner of the muslin backing piece.

2. The first series of filler strips will be string-quilted in place on the diagonal, beginning at the zigzag edge of the patchwork B assembly and working down toward the lower right-hand corner of the muslin piece. All of the filler strips are cut from the light blue primary jacket fabric, except for those specified on the diagram as another color. For the first filler, cut a strip of light blue fabric ⅞ inch wide and slightly longer than the zigzag edge of the patchwork assembly. Place the filler strip right side down on top of the patchwork, as shown in **Figure W**. The lower edge of the filler should be placed along the aligned inner corners of the zigzag patchwork edge, and the filler should extend equally beyond the patchwork at each end. Topstitch through all thicknesses (filler, patchwork, and muslin), ¼ inch from the long lower edge of the filler, as shown. Turn the filler strip downward over the topstitching, so that it is right side up and covers the zigzag edge of the patchwork. Press. An optional step at this point is to topstitch through the filler and muslin, ¼ inch from what is now the lower edge of the filler (see Tips & Techniques).

3. The next filler strip also is light blue. Cut a strip 1¾ inches wide and long enough to cover the next area. Place it right side down on top of the jacket front assembly, aligning the long lower edge with the lower edge of the first filler strip. Stitch the strip, turn it downward, and press gently.

4. The next filler strip is yellow, cut 1⅜ inches wide. String-quilt it in place as you did the others, turn it downward, and press.

5. Continue to cut and add filler strips in this manner until you reach the lower right-hand corner of the muslin backing piece. The remaining fillers used on this portion of the jacket were, in order: ⅞-inch-wide purple, 1¼-inch-wide light blue, ⅞-inch-wide orange, and three additional light blue strips of varying widths. When all fillers have been added, trim the ends even with the outer edges of the muslin backing piece.

6. The next six fillers form the log cabin assembly that borders the left and upper edges of the B patchwork

Figure X

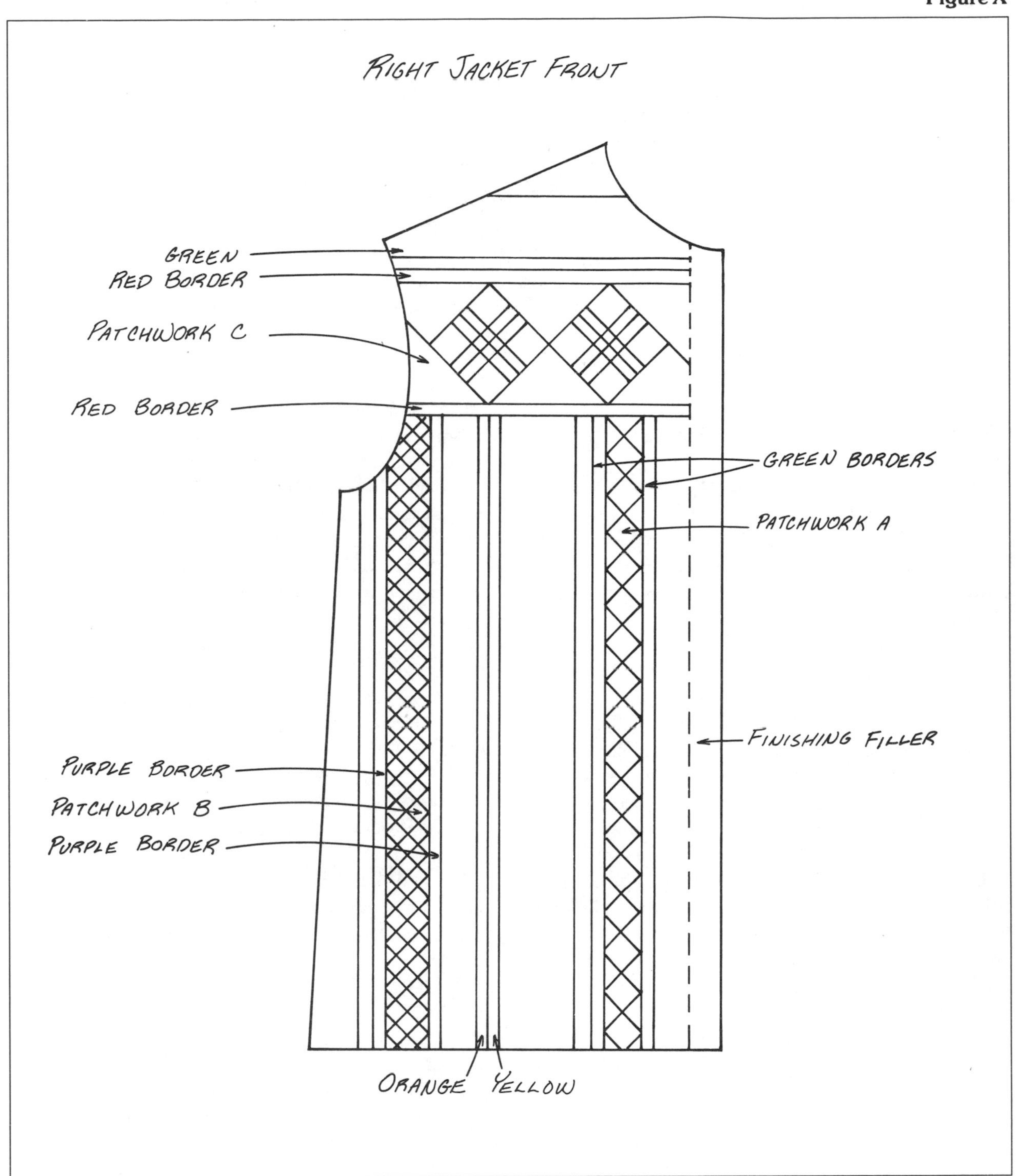
RIGHT JACKET FRONT
GREEN
RED BORDER
PATCHWORK C
RED BORDER
GREEN BORDERS
PATCHWORK A
FINISHING FILLER
PURPLE BORDER
PATCHWORK B
PURPLE BORDER
ORANGE
YELLOW

Figure Y

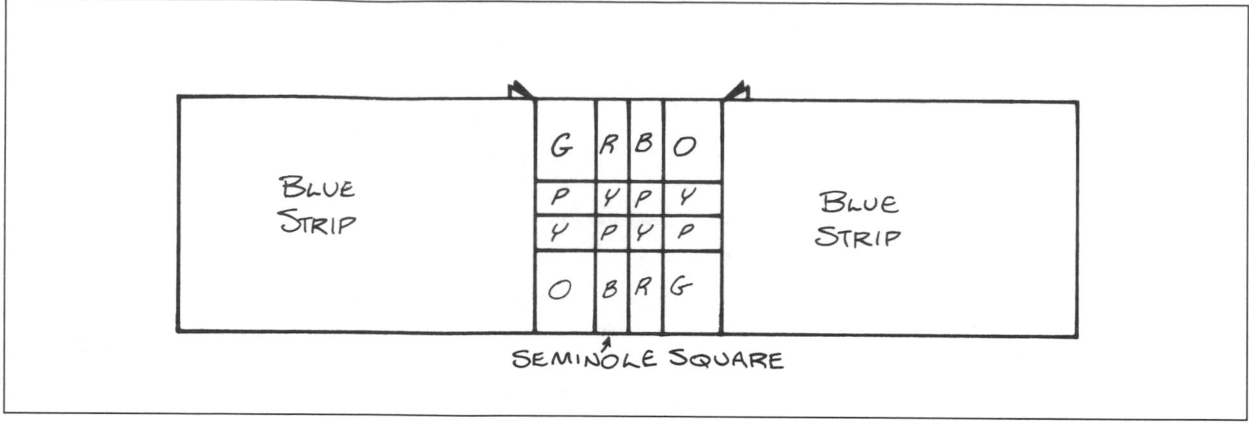

and lower diagonal fillers that already are in place. The log cabin fillers are numbered in **Figure V** to indicate the order in which they are added. For the log cabin fillers numbered 1 and 2, cut two light blue strips, each 2 inches wide and long enough to cover the areas indicated in **Figure V**. String-quilt the first filler along the left-hand edge of the patchwork and lower fillers, as shown; then add the second filler along the upper edge. The second filler should also cover the the upper end of the first log cabin filler. Cut two ⅞-inch-wide red strips for numbers 3 and 4; and two ⅞-inch-wide royal blue strips for numbers 5 and 6. String-quilt these strips to the assembly in the specified order. The space marked on the diagram as the "Finishing Filler" will be covered later with a long vertical strip that extends along the entire center edge of the jacket piece.

7. To finish the left jacket front, work upward from the top of the completed log cabin assembly to the top of the muslin backing piece, string-quilting filler strips and the specified patchwork assemblies as shown in **Figure V**. The fillers may be cut in whatever widths you like. As you can see, most of the fillers are the primary light blue jacket color, cut in varying widths. The red and royal blue fillers that fall between patchwork assemblies C and D are cut ⅞ inch wide. You will not have to add the patchwork border strips indicated on the diagram, as they already have been sewn to the patchwork assemblies. String-quilt each filler and patchwork assembly in turn, until the top is reached, and then trim the ends even with the muslin.

8. A light blue finishing filler strip runs vertically along the entire straight center front edge. It should be cut 2½ inches wide and slightly longer than the center front edge. Place the assembled left jacket front right side up on a flat surface, turning it as shown in **Figure V**. Place the finishing filler strip right side down on top of the jacket piece; the long left-hand edge of the filler should be placed ½ inch inside the center front jacket edge. Topstitch ½ inch from the left-hand edge of the filler, from top to bottom. Turn the filler strip outward over the topstitching and press. Turn the free long edge of the filler to the wrong side of the jacket piece, folding the filler along the center front edge of the jacket, and press. Trim the upper and lower ends of the filler to match the edges of the jacket piece, and then stitch across the filler near the upper and lower ends to secure the folded portion to the wrong side of the jacket.

The Right Front

1. Use the remaining muslin Jacket Front piece as the backing for the right jacket front. Placement of the patchwork assemblies and filler strips is shown in **Figure X**. Begin with the vertical fillers and assemblies that form the lower portion of the jacket piece, working from left to right across the muslin, and string-quilting each successive one in place. Again, all fillers are light blue except for those otherwise specified on the diagram, and the patchwork borders can be disregarded, as they already are attached to the patchwork assemblies. The light blue fillers are of varying widths, and the yellow

Figure Z

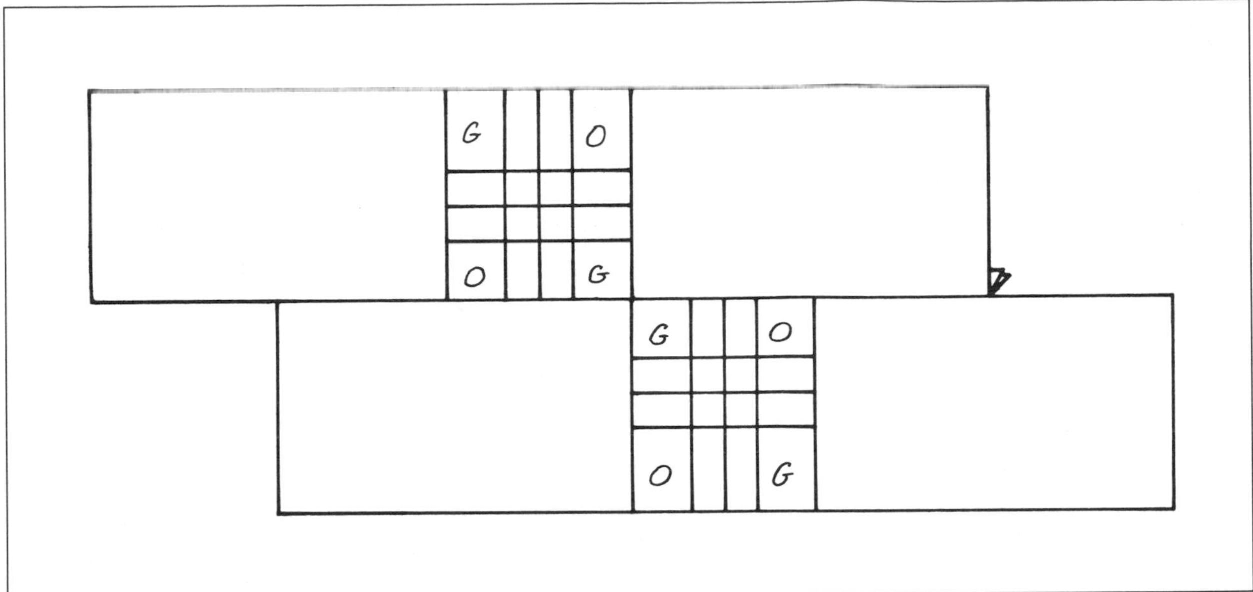

and orange fillers that fall between the B and C patchwork assemblies are cut ⅞ inch wide. The vertical dotted line on the diagram indicates placement of the finishing filler strip, which will be added after the horizontal upper pieces are attached.

2. The Seminole squares (patchwork assemblies C) must be finished before the upper horizontal work can be done. Cut two light blue strips, each 2½ x 4 inches. Stitch these pieces to opposite edges of one Right Front C Seminole square as shown in **Figure Y**, being careful to turn the square as shown. Cut two additional light blue strips of the same size as the first two and stitch them to the second Seminole square in the same manner, turning the square so that the second assembly is identical to the first one.

3. Stitch together the two assemblies from step 2 side by side, offsetting the ends so that the squares are corner-to-corner as shown in **Figure Z**. To complete the assembly, cut two additional light blue strips, each 3 x 8 inches. Stitch one of these strips to each outer edge of the assembly, as shown in **Figure AA**. Mark a straight cutting line across the assembly ⅜ inch above the aligned upper corners of the squares, and mark a second cutting line ⅜ inch below the aligned lower corners, as shown. Cut along each marked line.

4. Cut two ⅞-inch-wide red border strips, and stitch one to each long edge of the assembly as you did the previous border strips.

5. Refer back to **Figure X**, and complete the string-quilting of the right jacket front. Begin with the Seminole square assembly, string-quilting it in place so that the lower red border covers the upper ends of the vertical filler strips and patchwork assemblies that already are sewn to the muslin. Then add the remaining fillers as indicated in **Figure X**, working upward to the top of the muslin. The green filler immediately above the Seminole square assembly is cut ⅞ inch wide, and the remaining light blue fillers are of varying widths. When you have completed the string-quilting, trim the ends of the fillers and patchwork even with the edges of the muslin backing piece.

6. Cut and add the light blue finishing filler strip along the center front edge as you did for the left jacket front.

The Jacket Back

1. A diagram of the jacket back is provided in **Figure BB**. We'll begin with the right half. Pin the triangular checkerboard (patchwork assembly B) in place on the muslin backing piece, as you did for the left jacket front. String-quilt filler strips along the diagonal, working from

Figure AA

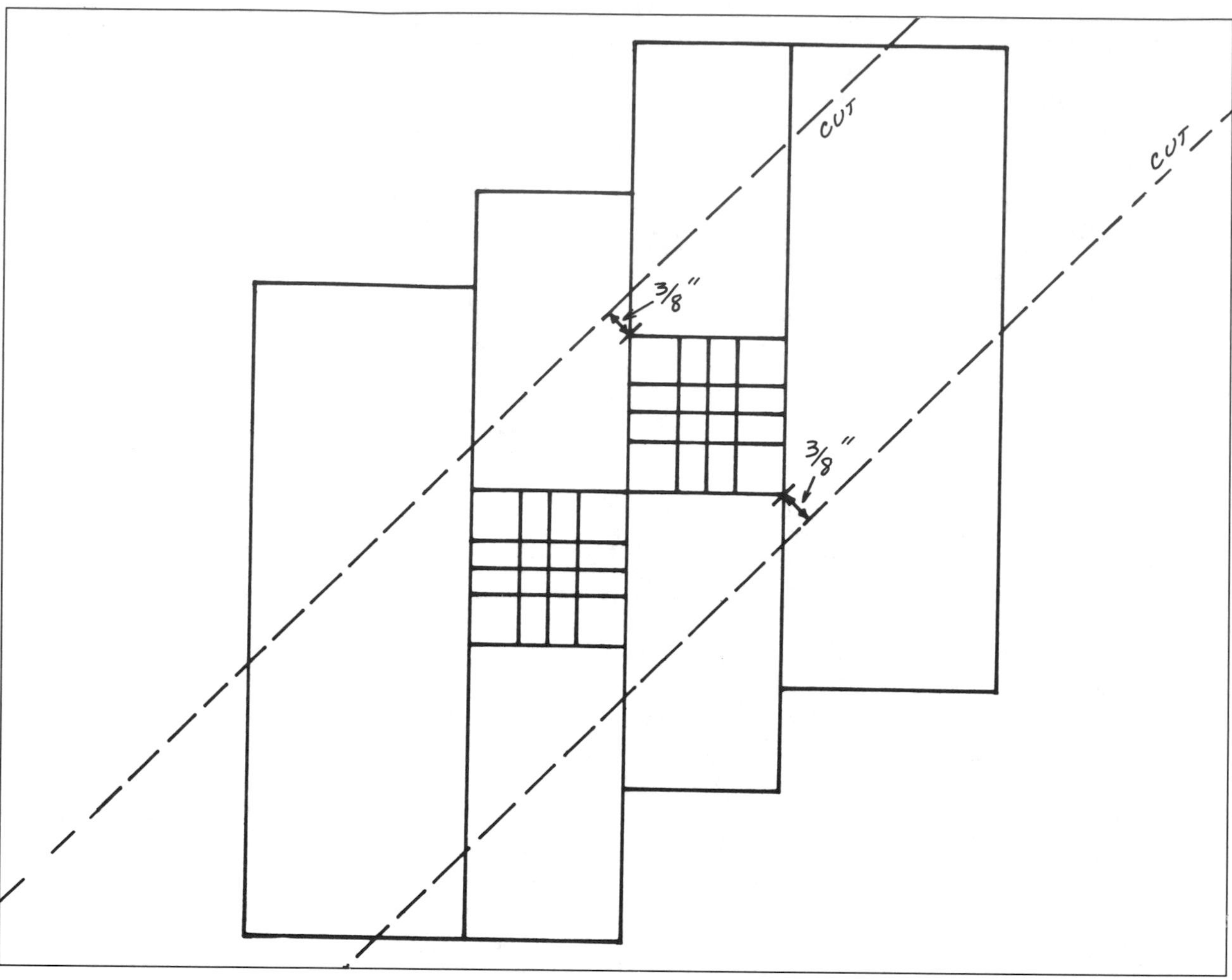

the zigzag edge of the patchwork assembly down to the lower right-hand corner of the muslin. The purple, royal blue, and orange fillers are cut 7/8 inch wide, and the light blue fillers are of varying widths. Trim the ends of the fillers even with the muslin backing piece.

2. The next eight fillers form a log cabin that borders the upper and left-hand edges of the checkerboard and lower diagonal filler strips. They are numbered in **Figure BB** to indicate the order in which they are attached. The log cabin fillers numbered 1 and 2 are light blue, cut 1¼ inches wide; the red and royal blue fillers numbered 3, 4, 5, and 6 are cut 7/8 inch wide; and the light blue fillers numbered 7 and 8 are cut 2¼ inches wide. String-quilt the log cabin fillers in place in the order indicated, and trim the ends even with the muslin.

3. To finish the right half of the jacket back, work upward from the top of the log cabin, string-quilting the specified patchwork assemblies and fillers to the muslin. As noted in **Figure BB**, most of the fillers are light blue, cut in varying widths. The yellow filler that falls between patchwork assemblies D and A is cut 1¼ inches wide, but the red and orange fillers near the top are cut 7/8 inch wide. When you have completed the right half of the jacket back, trim all fillers and patchwork even with the edges of the muslin backing piece.

4. Before you begin work on the left half of the jacket

Figure BB

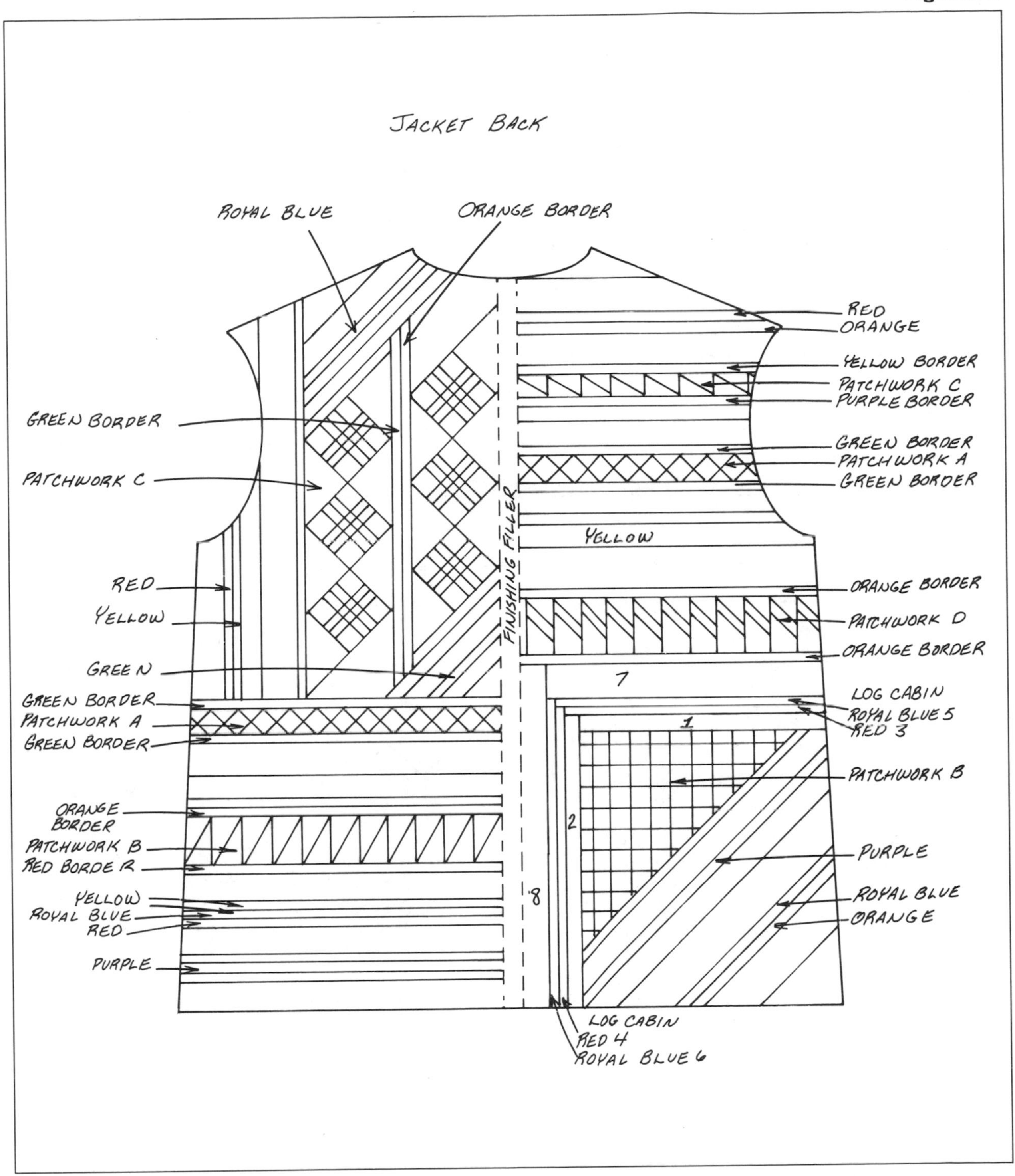
JACKET BACK
ROYAL BLUE
ORANGE BORDER
RED
ORANGE
YELLOW BORDER
PATCHWORK C
PURPLE BORDER
GREEN BORDER
PATCHWORK C
GREEN BORDER
PATCHWORK A
GREEN BORDER
YELLOW
FINISHING FILLER
RED
YELLOW
ORANGE BORDER
PATCHWORK D
ORANGE BORDER
GREEN
7
GREEN BORDER
PATCHWORK A
GREEN BORDER
LOG CABIN
ROYAL BLUE 5
RED 3
1
PATCHWORK B
ORANGE BORDER
2
PATCHWORK B
RED BORDER
PURPLE
YELLOW
ROYAL BLUE
RED
8
ROYAL BLUE
ORANGE
PURPLE
LOG CABIN
RED 4
ROYAL BLUE 6

Figure CC

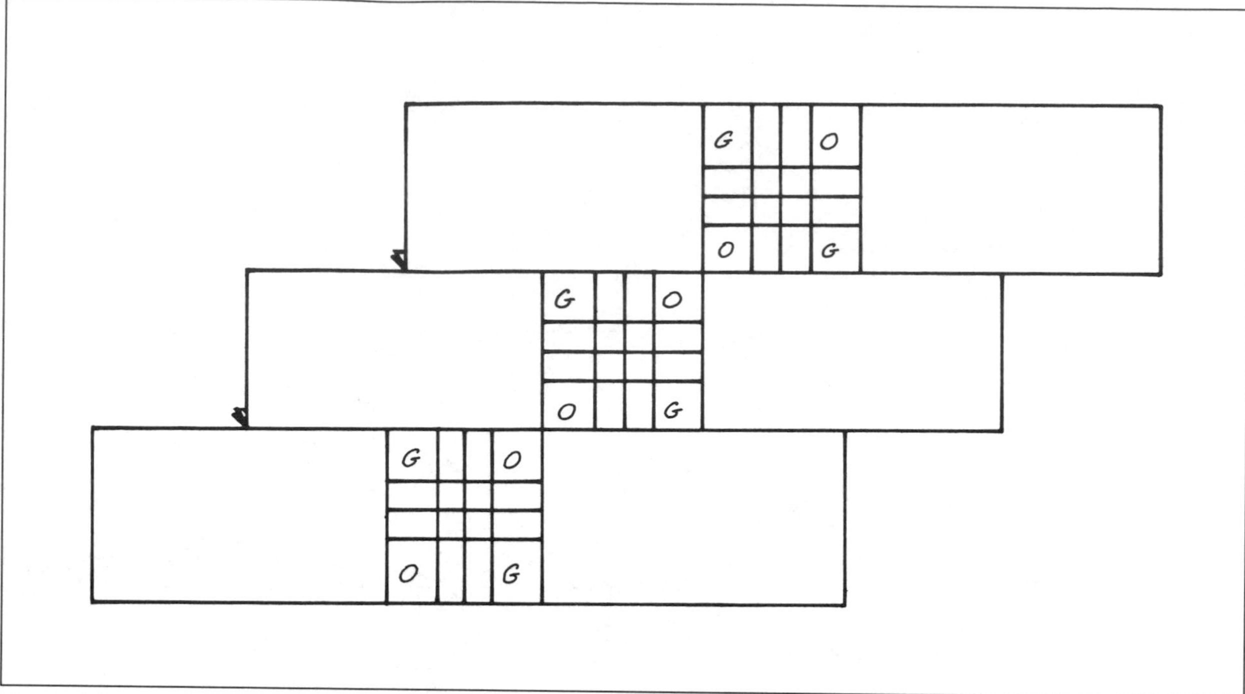

Figure DD

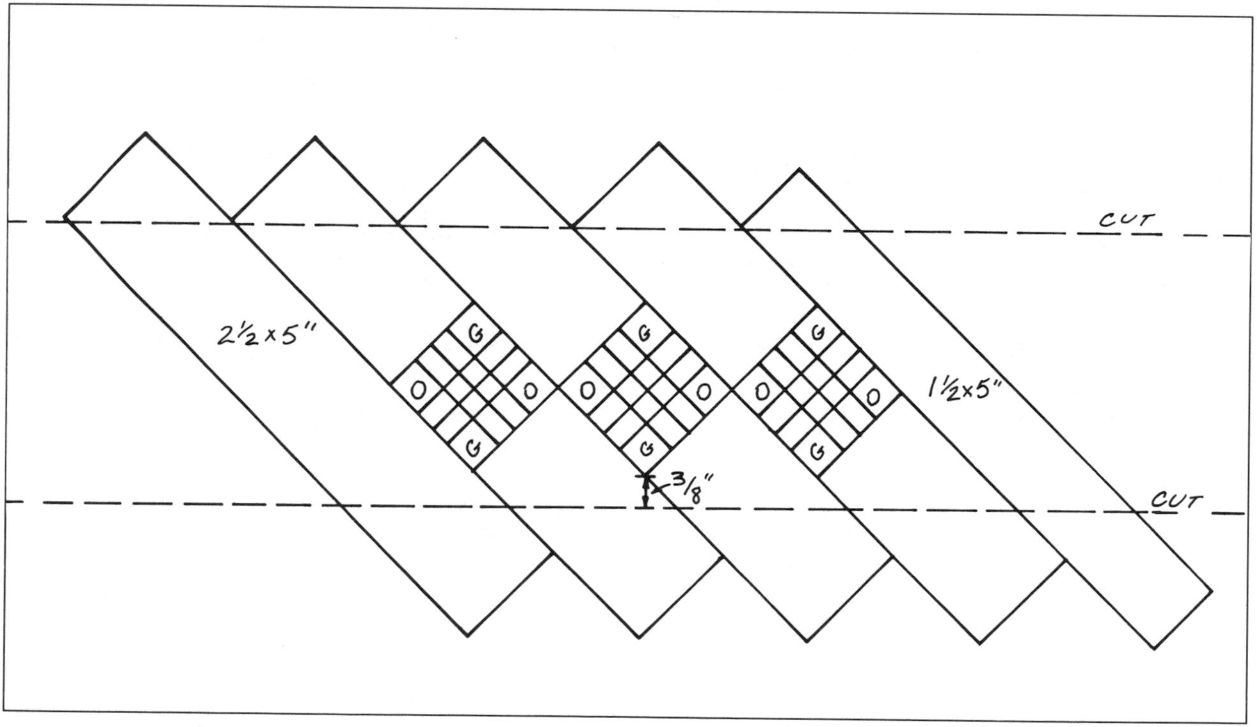

Figure EE

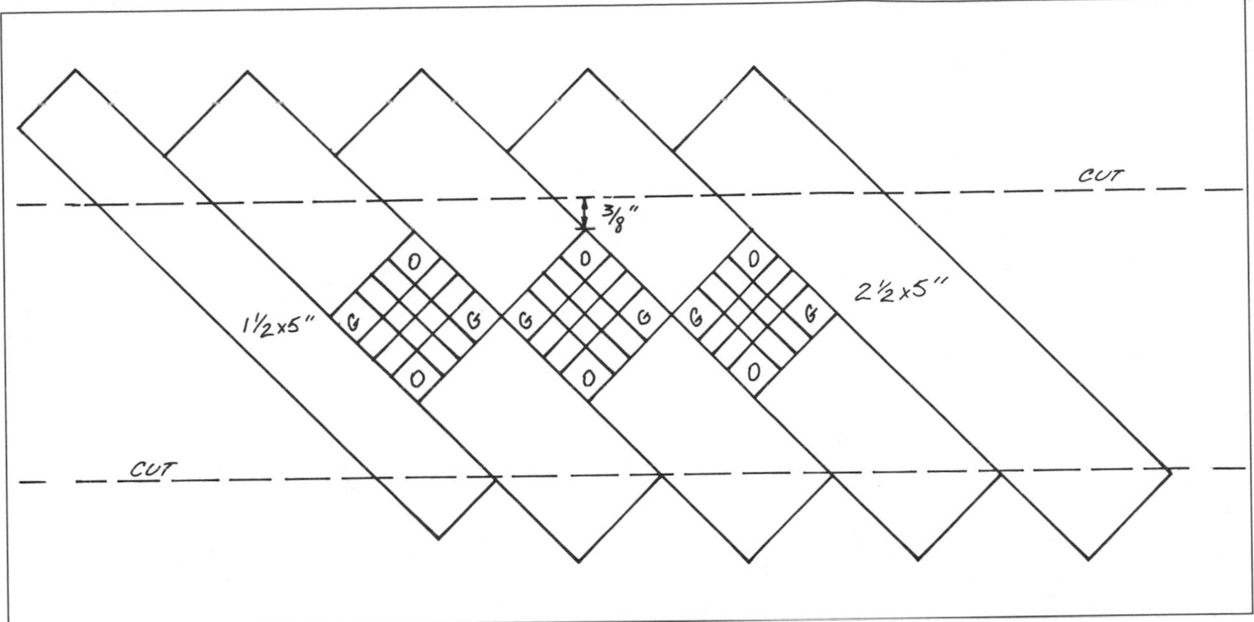

back, the six Seminole squares (Left Back C patchwork assemblies) must be finished as you did those for the right jacket front. To begin, cut six light blue strips, each 2½ x 4 inches. Choose from the six Left Back C Seminole squares the three that are identical to the ones on the right jacket front. Stitch a light blue strip to each of two opposing edges of one square, as you did before, turning the square so that the assembly is identical to the one shown in **Figure Y**. Repeat these procedures for each of the two remaining identical Seminole squares, turning each square so that all three assemblies are identical in color arrangement. Stitch together these three assemblies side by side, offsetting the ends so that the Seminole squares are corner-to-corner (**Figure CC**).

5. Cut two additional light blue pieces: one 1½ x 5 inches, and one 2½ x 5 inches. Stitch these pieces to the side edges of the Seminole square assembly as shown in **Figure DD**. Measure and mark a straight cutting line ⅜ inch from the aligned lower left-hand corners of the Seminole squares, as shown. Mark a second straight cutting line above the aligned upper right-hand corners, as close as possible to the upper ends of the assembled strips. Cut along each marked line.

6. Cut a ⅞-inch-wide orange border strip, the same length as the assembly from step 5. Place the strip and the patchwork assembly right sides together, aligning one long edge of the strip with the lower left-hand cutting line of the patchwork assembly. Stitch the seam ¼ inch from the aligned edges, turn the strip outward, and press. Do not stitch a border to the opposite edge of the patchwork.

7. Repeat the procedures in steps 4 and 5 to create a second Seminole square assembly, using the three remaining Left Back C Seminole squares and cutting additional light blue strips. The assembly should look like the one shown in **Figure EE** when you have finished the procedures in step 5; note the color arrangement within the squares, the placement of the outer light blue strips, and the placement of the cutting lines.

8. Cut a ⅞-inch-wide green border strip, the same length as the assembly from step 7. Place the border strip and the patchwork assembly right sides together, aligning one long edge of the strip with the upper right-hand cutting line indicated in **Figure EE**. Stitch the seam ¼ inch from the aligned edges, turn the border outward, and press.

9. The assemblies from steps 6 and 8 are now sewn

Figure FF

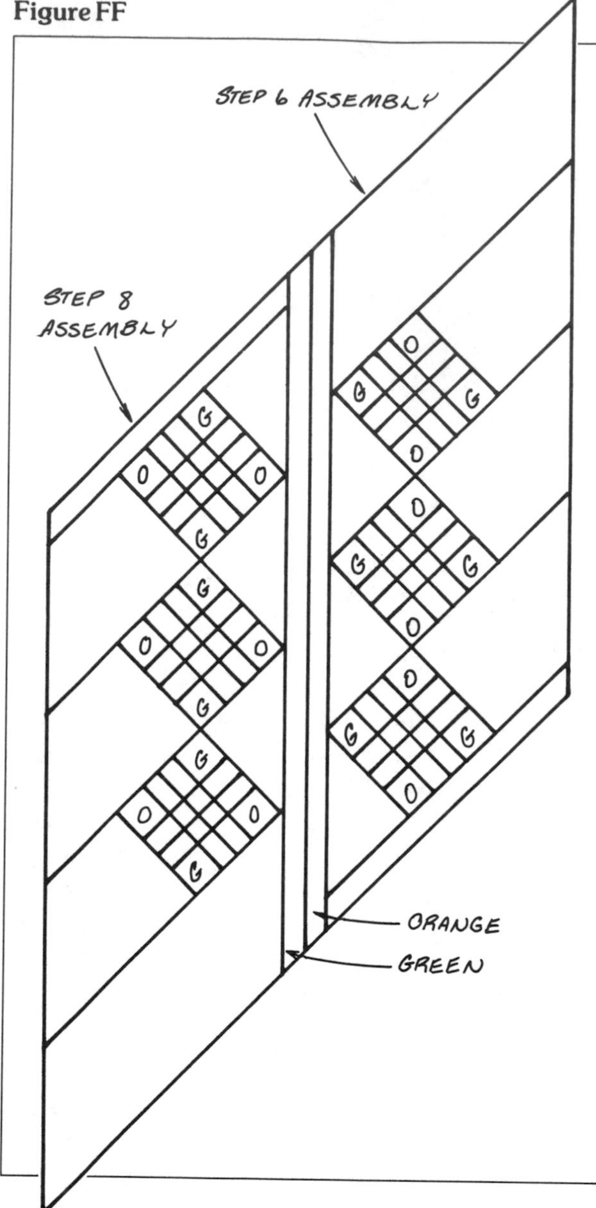

together side by side, offset as shown in **Figure FF**. As you can see, the right-hand corners of the Seminole squares in the step 8 assembly should be aligned with the corner-to-corner points in the step 6 assembly. To stitch the center seam, place the assemblies right sides together, aligning the free long edges of the two border strips. Adjust the vertical placement of the assemblies and stitch the seam ¼ inch from the aligned edges, so that the finished assembly looks like the one shown in **Figure FF**.

10. To finish the left half of the jacket back, refer to **Figure BB** and pin the Seminole square assembly in place on the muslin backing piece. Begin string-quilting filler strips in place, working on the diagonal from the lower edge of the Seminole square assembly downward to where the patchwork assembly A will be placed. The filler strips in this diagonal area are mostly light blue, cut in varying widths, with the exception of a single ⅞-inch-wide green strip noted on the diagram. When the lower diagonal area has been filled, proceed to the diagonal area above the upper angled edge of the Seminole square assembly. Cut and add light blue fillers of varying widths, and one ⅞-inch-wide royal blue filler where indicated.

11. The next area to be filled is the section of vertical filler strips to the left of the Seminole square assembly. Cut and string-quilt long light blue fillers, plus one red and one yellow filler, each ⅞ inch wide, as shown in **Figure BB**.

12. Now work downward from the bottom of the diagonal and vertical fillers to the lower edge of the muslin backing piece, string-quilting the patchwork B and C assemblies and remaining filler strips in place. As noted in **Figure BB**, most of the fillers are light blue, cut in varying widths, with the exception of one yellow, one royal blue, one red, and one purple filler, each cut ⅞ inch wide. When you have finished, trim the ends of all fillers and patchwork even with the outer edges of the muslin backing piece.

13. Cut a light blue finishing filler strip for the vertical center line of the jacket back; the finishing filler should be cut slightly longer than the muslin backing piece and ½ inch wider than the area to be covered. Press a ¼-inch seam allowance to the wrong side of the filler along one long edge only. Place the strip right side down over the right half of the assembled jacket back, aligning the unpressed long edge of the filler ¼ inch inside the right-hand edge of the area to be covered. Topstitch ¼ inch from the unpressed long edge. Turn the filler right side up over the line of topstitching, and blind stitch the pressed edge to the jacket back. Trim the upper and lower ends of the filler even with the edges of the muslin backing piece.

Figure GG

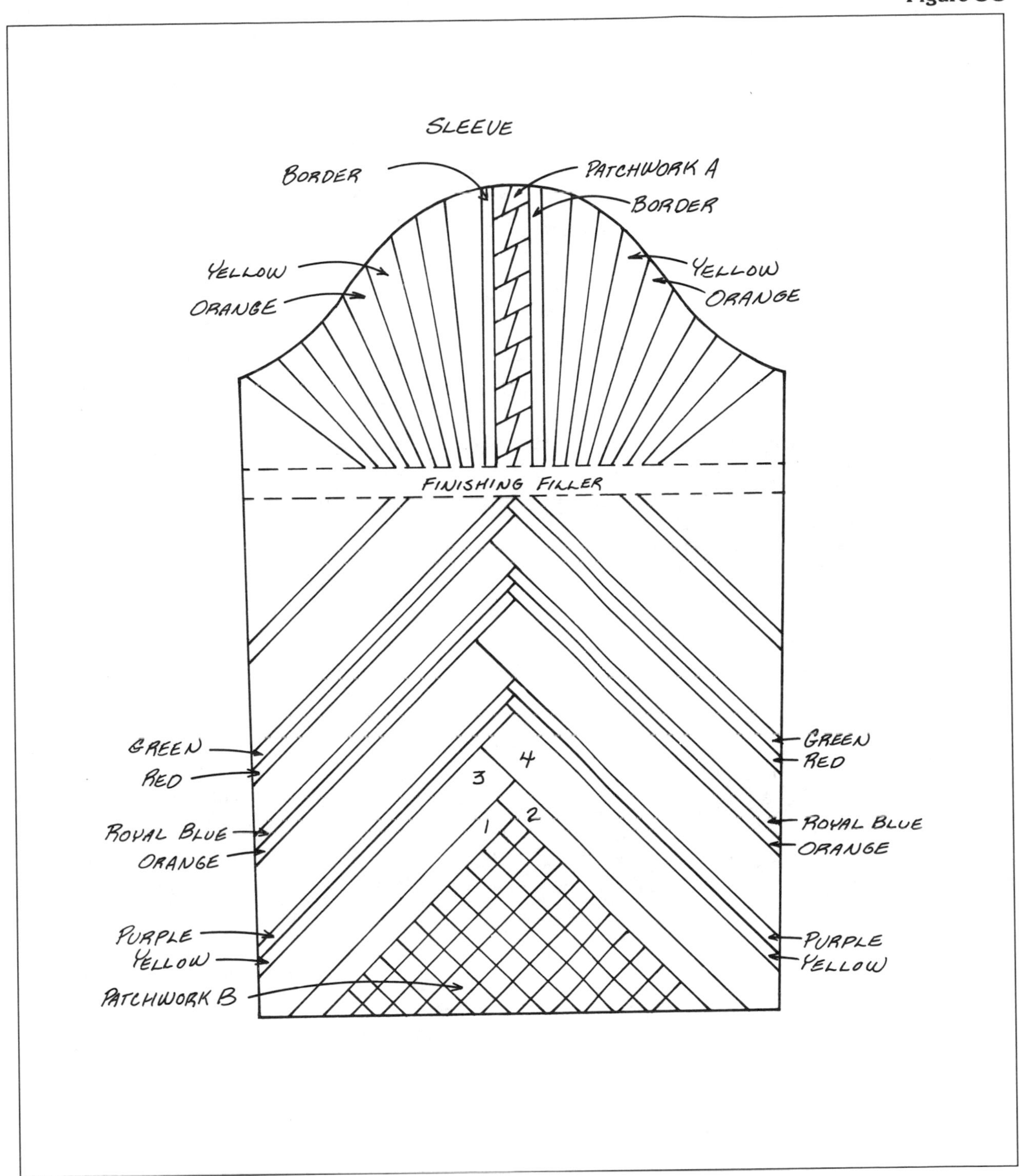

SLEEVE
BORDER
PATCHWORK A
BORDER
YELLOW
ORANGE
YELLOW
ORANGE
FINISHING FILLER
GREEN
RED
ROYAL BLUE
ORANGE
PURPLE
YELLOW
PATCHWORK B
GREEN
RED
ROYAL BLUE
ORANGE
PURPLE
YELLOW
1
2
3
4

The Sleeves

Both sleeves are identical, so we'll provide instructions for one sleeve only.

1. A diagram of the assembled outer sleeve piece is provided in **Figure GG**. Begin by pinning the patchwork assembly B to the muslin backing piece, so that the outer corners of the zigzag patchwork edge lie just inside the lower edge of the muslin piece. Cut and add the fillers that form the diagonal log cabin above the patchwork assembly, as shown, string-quilting each one in place. The light blue fillers were cut in varying widths, and those of all other colors were cut ⅞ inch wide. Note that the fillers are added in a standard log-cabin order: one along one edge of the patchwork, then a second along the other edge, then a third along the original edge, etc. The first four fillers are numbered in the diagram – simply continue to add the specified fillers, alternating sides with each succeeding filler, until you reach the area designated in **Figure GG** as the finishing filler. Trim the lower ends of the log cabin fillers even with the lower edge of the muslin.

2. Pin the patchwork assembly A in place on the muslin, placing it vertically along the center line of the sleeve as shown in **Figure GG**. The fillers on each side of this patchwork are fan-quilted in place, working downward from each side until the area reserved for the horizontal finishing filler is reached. The fillers are cut in varying widths; most are light blue with the exception of one yellow and one orange filler on each side of the patchwork. Refer to Tips & Techniques if you need help with specific instructions on fan-quilting. Basically, it is the same as string-quilting, but the lower end of each strip is moved toward the previous strip before the topstitching is done. When all of the fillers have been added, trim the upper ends even with the muslin backing piece.

3. Cut a light blue finishing filler strip ½ inch wider than the area to be covered. Press a ¼-inch seam allowance to the wrong side of the strip along one long edge only. Place the filler right side down on top of the lower portion of the sleeve, aligning the unpressed long edge with the upper ends of the log cabin fillers. Topstitch ¼ inch from the unpressed edge of the filler, and turn the filler right side up over the topstitching. Blind stitch the pressed edge of the filler to the upper portion of the sleeve.

Figure HH

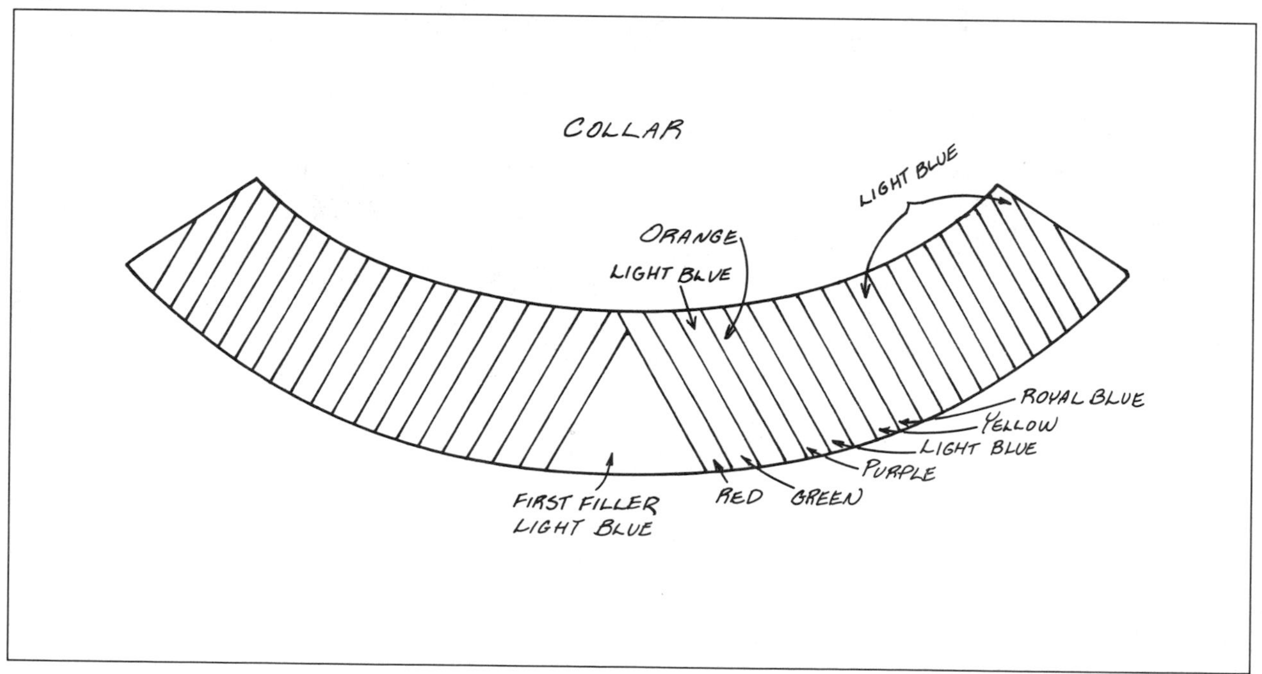

4. Cut a light blue Casing piece, 2 inches wide and the same length as the lower edge of the sleeve. Place the Casing piece right side down on top of the sleeve, aligning one long edge of the Casing with the lower edge of the sleeve. Stitch ¾ inch from the aligned edges, and then turn the Casing piece outward. The casing will be finished during the final jacket assembly.

5. Repeat the procedures in steps 1 through 4 to assemble a second, identical sleeve.

The Collar

The outer collar piece contains no pre-assembled patchwork, but consists of narrow string-quilted strips. A diagram is provided in **Figure HH**. Use the muslin Collar piece as a backing, and cut and add fillers as specified in **Figure HH**. The collar is symmetrical: the color progression is the same on both sides. The center back filler was cut 2½ inches wide, and all remaining fillers were cut ⅞ inch wide. When all of the fillers have been added, trim the ends even with the muslin backing piece.

ASSEMBLING THE JACKET

The patchwork jacket pieces are assembled to form the outer layer of the jacket, and the lining pieces are assembled separately to form the lining layer. In the final assembly, the outer and lining layers are joined, the zipper is added, and elastic is threaded through the sleeve casings.

The Outer Layer

1. Place one of the patchwork outer Jacket Front pieces right side up on a flat surface, and place one of the light blue Pocket pieces right side down on top, as shown in **Figure II**. (Pocket placement dots are indicated on the scale drawing of the Jacket Front pattern, **Figure A**.) Stitch ¼ inch from the aligned edges, as shown in **Figure II**. Turn the Pocket piece outward over the seam line and press.

2. Stitch a second Pocket piece to the remaining patchwork outer Jacket Front piece in the same manner, turn it outward, and press.

3. Stitch a third Pocket piece to one side edge of the patchwork outer Jacket Back piece in the same manner, and a fourth Pocket piece to the opposite side edge of the Jacket Back. Turn both Pocket pieces outward and press.

Figure II

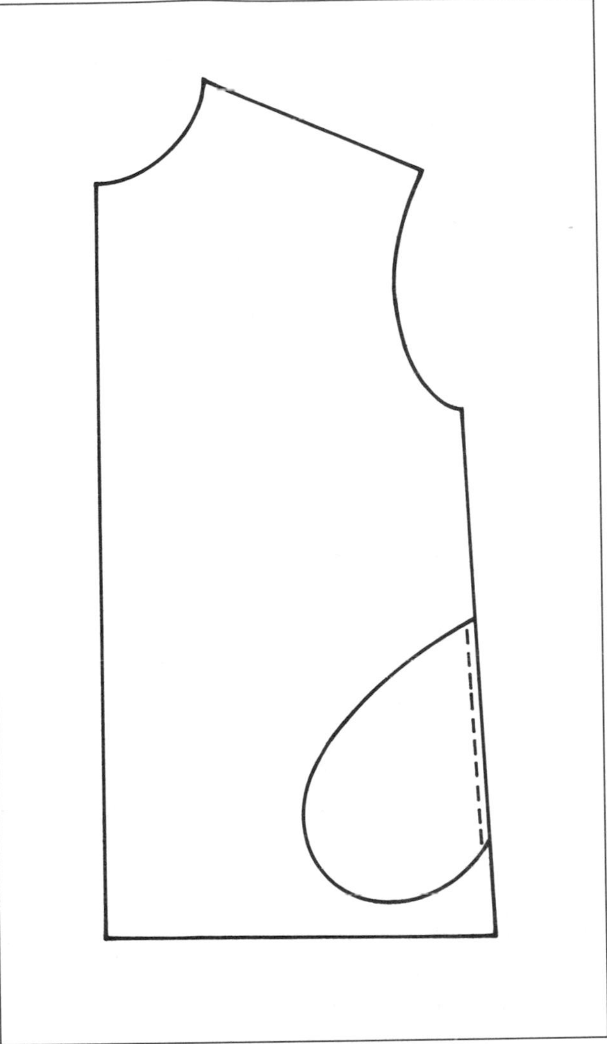

4. Place the patchwork Jacket Back piece right side up on a flat surface, and place the two Jacket Front pieces right sides down on top. Stitch the shoulder seam on each side, as shown in **Figure JJ**, and press the seams open.

5. Open out the jacket pieces and place the assembly right side up on a flat surface. Pin one of the patchwork Sleeve pieces to the jacket, placing right sides together and easing the curved upper edge of the Sleeve to fit

Figure JJ

the armhole edge on one side of the jacket. Stitch the armhole seam as shown in **Figure KK**. Clip the curve, turn the sleeve outward, and press the seam allowances toward the jacket.

6. Repeat the procedures in step 5 to attach the remaining patchwork Sleeve to the armhole edge on the opposite side of the jacket.

7. Fold the jacket right sides together along the shoulder seams. Stitch the underarm and side seam on each side as shown in **Figure LL**, from the lower edges of the sleeve casing up to the armhole seam and from the armhole seam down to the lower edges of the jacket front and back pieces. Note that each side seam should be left open between the upper and lower corners of the pocket. Press the seams open.

8. Stitch the two Pocket pieces together along the aligned long curved edges, on each side of the jacket. Turn the jacket right side out. The collar will be added later, during the final assembly.

The Lining Layer

1. The jacket lining is assembled in the same manner as the outer layer, but there are no pockets. Follow the procedures described for the outer layer to assemble the lining-fabric Jacket Front, Jacket Back, and Jacket Sleeve pieces.

2. Place the patchwork and lining-fabric Collar pieces right sides together and stitch a continuous seam across one end, along the long upper edges, and across the opposite end. Leave the long lower edge unstitched (**Figure MM**). Clip the curves and corners and turn the collar right sides out. Press the seam allowances to the

Figure KK

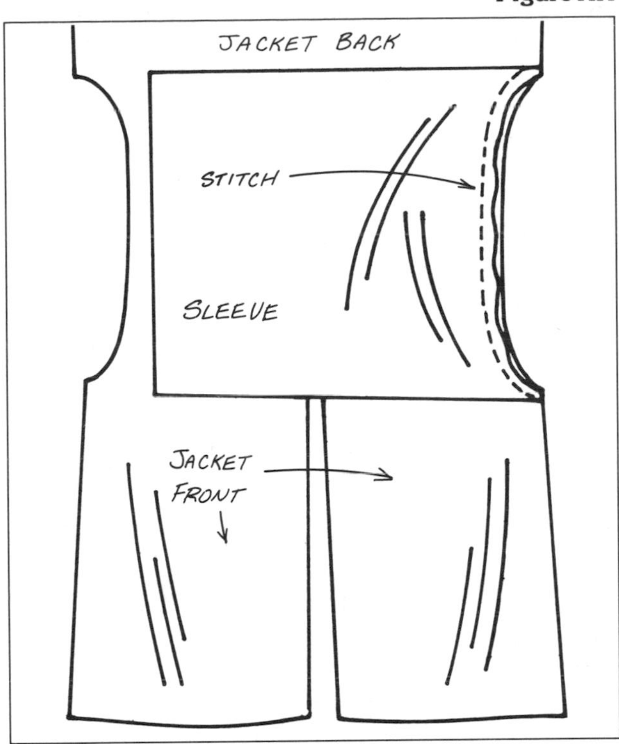

inside along the open edges of the lining and outer layers.

Final Assembly

1. Follow the manufacturer's instructions to install the zipper in the outer jacket assembly, leaving enough space between the lower end of the zipper and the unfinished lower edges of the jacket front sections so that a hem can be stitched later.

2. Press the seam allowance to the wrong side of the fabric along the center front edge of each lining-layer jacket front piece. Place the outer and lining jacket assemblies right sides together and stitch the seam along the aligned lower edges only. Press the seam open.

3. Turn the lower edge of each sleeve casing to the wrong side of the outer sleeve, and press. Press the seam allowance to the wrong side of the fabric around the lower end of each lining-layer sleeve. Place the lining and outer jacket assemblies wrong sides together, and tuck the lining-layer sleeves inside the outer-layer sleeves. Blind stitch the pressed lower edge of each lining-layer sleeve to the inside of the casing near the

Figure LL

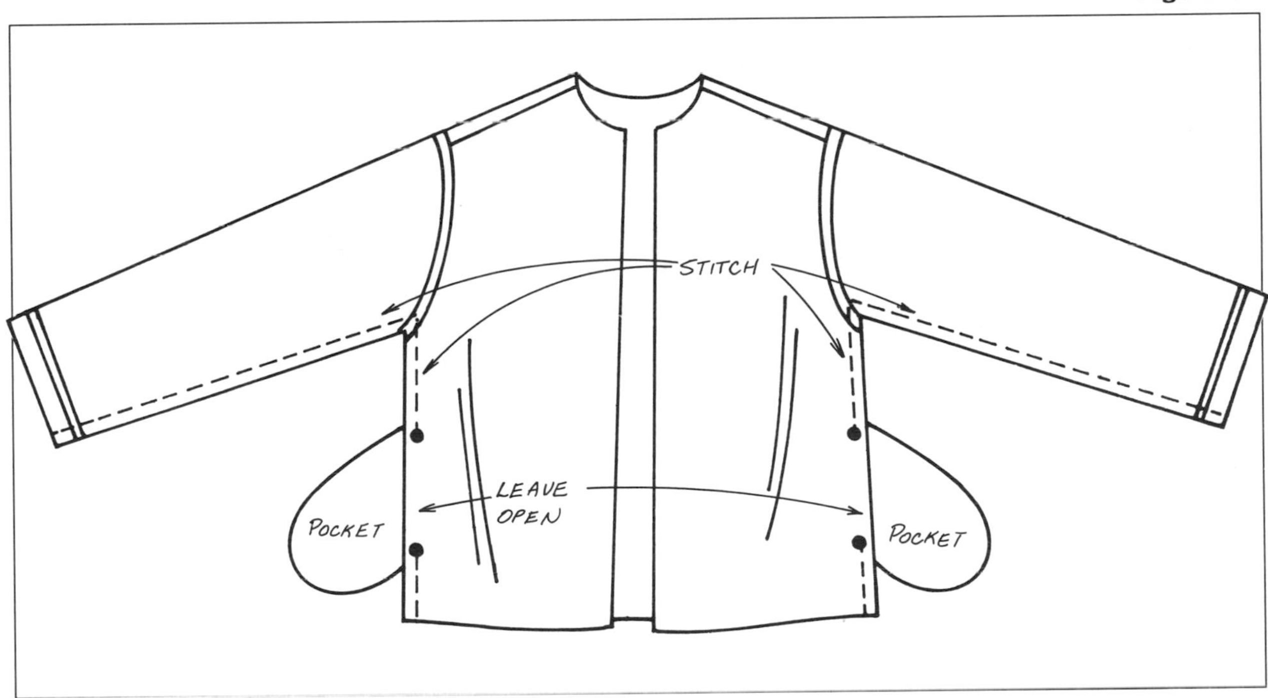

Figure MM

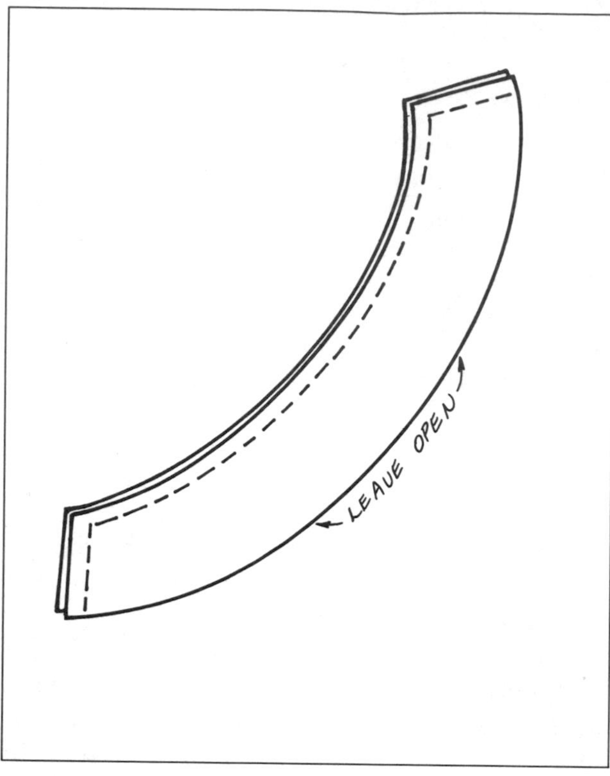

lower edge of the outer-layer sleeve. Topstitch through all thicknesses, close to the top of the casing on the right side of each outer sleeve.

4. Cut one length of elastic, about 2 inches longer than a measurement taken around your wrist. Slit open the underarm seam of one sleeve lining, between the end of the sleeve and the line of topstitching just above it. Thread the elastic through the slit and on around the sleeve. Stitch together the ends of the elastic, tuck them back inside the lining, and whipstitch together the slit-open edges of the lining seam. Repeat the procedures in this step to finish the end of the other sleeve.

5. To finish the center front edge of each jacket front, blind stitch the pressed lining edge to the wrong side of the zipper on the back of the corresponding outer jacket front piece.

6. Align the raw neckline edges of the lining and outer layers and baste them together close to the edges.

7. Insert the basted neckline edges of the outer and lining jacket layers between the layers of the assembled collar. Blind stitch the pressed lower edge of the outer collar layer to the right side of the outer jacket layer, and blind stitch the pressed lower edge of the lining collar layer to the right side of the lining jacket layer.

Tips & Techniques

Enlarging Scale Drawings

A typical scale drawing is shown in **Figure E**. Each small square on the scale drawing represents a 1-inch square on the full-size pattern. For the enlargement, you'll need a large sheet of paper containing a grid of 1-inch squares. (You can purchase dressmaker's pattern paper, which has the grid already on it.) To make the enlargement, simply reproduce the lines of the scale drawing onto the paper with the full-size grid, working one square at a time, as shown in **Figure A**. Be aware that some of the scale drawings in this book are scaled to 1 square = 2 inches; each small square on the drawing represents a 2 x 2-inch square on the larger pattern paper. A legend provided with each scale drawing specifies what scale was used.

Figure A

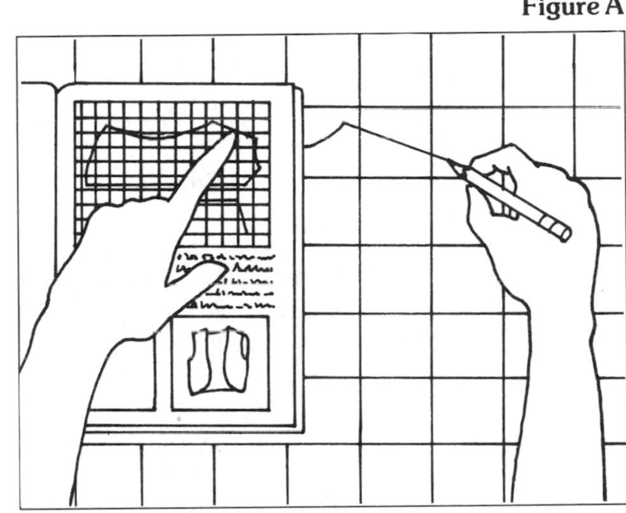

Terms

Seam Allowance – On all patterns, a solid line indicates the outer edge of the pattern piece, which also is the cutting line. A broken line inside the solid cutting line indicates the seam line. The area between the seam and cutting lines is called the seam allowance.

Clipping Corners and Curves – When a seam is curved or runs around a corner, the seam allowance must be clipped so that the fabric will lie flat when it is turned right side out. Curved seam allowances should be clipped as shown in **Figure B**: For an outside curve, make several short straight clips from the outer edge toward the seam line. For an inside curve, make V-shaped cutouts. For a corner seam, clip off the corner of the seam allowance. With any type of clip, take care that you do not cut the seam itself.

Materials

For each project in this book, we have provided a materials list that specifies the amounts, types, and colors of fabric used. You may, of course, use other fabrics. For projects that are one-size-fits-all, the materials

Figure B

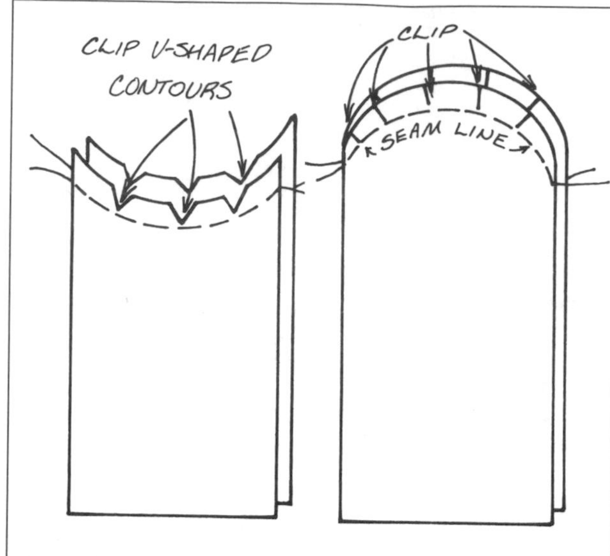

list may be taken at face value. For projects that must be altered to fit, you may need slightly more or less fabric than specified.

When choosing fabrics, keep in mind that the fiber content determines how the fabric will react to washing and wearing. If fabrics of various colors are called for in a single project, it's best to stick with the same type of fabric for all colors. All fabrics should be washed, dried, and pressed *before* you begin work.

Patterns

You may prefer to purchase commercial patterns rather than enlarge our scale drawings and then alter the full-size patterns to fit. Altering is not difficult. The first thing you'll need to do is to measure yourself, or the person who will be wearing the finished project.

When you have enlarged the scale drawings of all pattern pieces for a particular garment, compare the dimensions of the pattern *between* the seam lines to your measurements. If the pattern is too small around, you must widen both the front and back patterns. This can be done by cutting vertically between the shoulder edge and the lower edge, separating the sections enough to make up the extra width, and taping them to a backing piece of pattern paper. When you do this, be sure that the horizontal lines of the pattern match up across the gap. Keep in mind that when you widen a vest front pattern, for instance, the amount by which it is widened will be doubled in the finished garment, because there are two front pieces.

Shoulder, waist, hip, and bust alterations all can be done in this manner. To alter the length, simply cut across the patterns horizontally and separate or overlap the sections. Think about it logically, and you'll end up with a garment that fits perfectly. Be sure to consider which other pattern pieces will be affected by the alterations: If you lengthen a vest or jacket front pattern, you must lengthen the back pattern as well; if you widen a vest or jacket back pattern, recheck the shoulders and neckline for fit.

Most of the patterns that are symmetrical are provided as half patterns, with the center edge designated as "place on fold." When altering these patterns, keep in mind that the full-size fabric piece will be twice as large as the pattern. When cutting the fabric, fold the fabric into a double thickness and pin the pattern to it so that the "place on fold" edge is aligned along the fold of fabric; do not cut along the fold. Whenever you must cut two separate fabric pieces from a single pattern, double the fabric and cut both at once, so the pieces are mirror images of each other.

There are several vests in this book. We have provided scale drawings for Vest Front and Back patterns in **Figure C**. **Figure D** shows several ways in which the design of the Front can be varied.

In **Figure E** you'll find a scale drawing for the drop-waist dress sleeve pattern. The depth of the curve along the upper edge of the sleeve will determine how puffy the sleeves will be. For exaggerated puffiness, make the curve deeper. If you want the sleeve to have a tailored look (no puffiness), make the curve narrower and the same length as the armhole edge of the garment. The length of the lower sleeve edge determines how large the sleeve will be around the lower end.

Several of the projects in this book call for circular patterns, which are made using a compass. There are a couple of alternatives: You can trace around a circular object that is the right size, or use the string and pencil trick. Tie one end of a piece of string around a pencil. Measure along the string from the pencil, a distance

1 square = 1 inch

Figure C

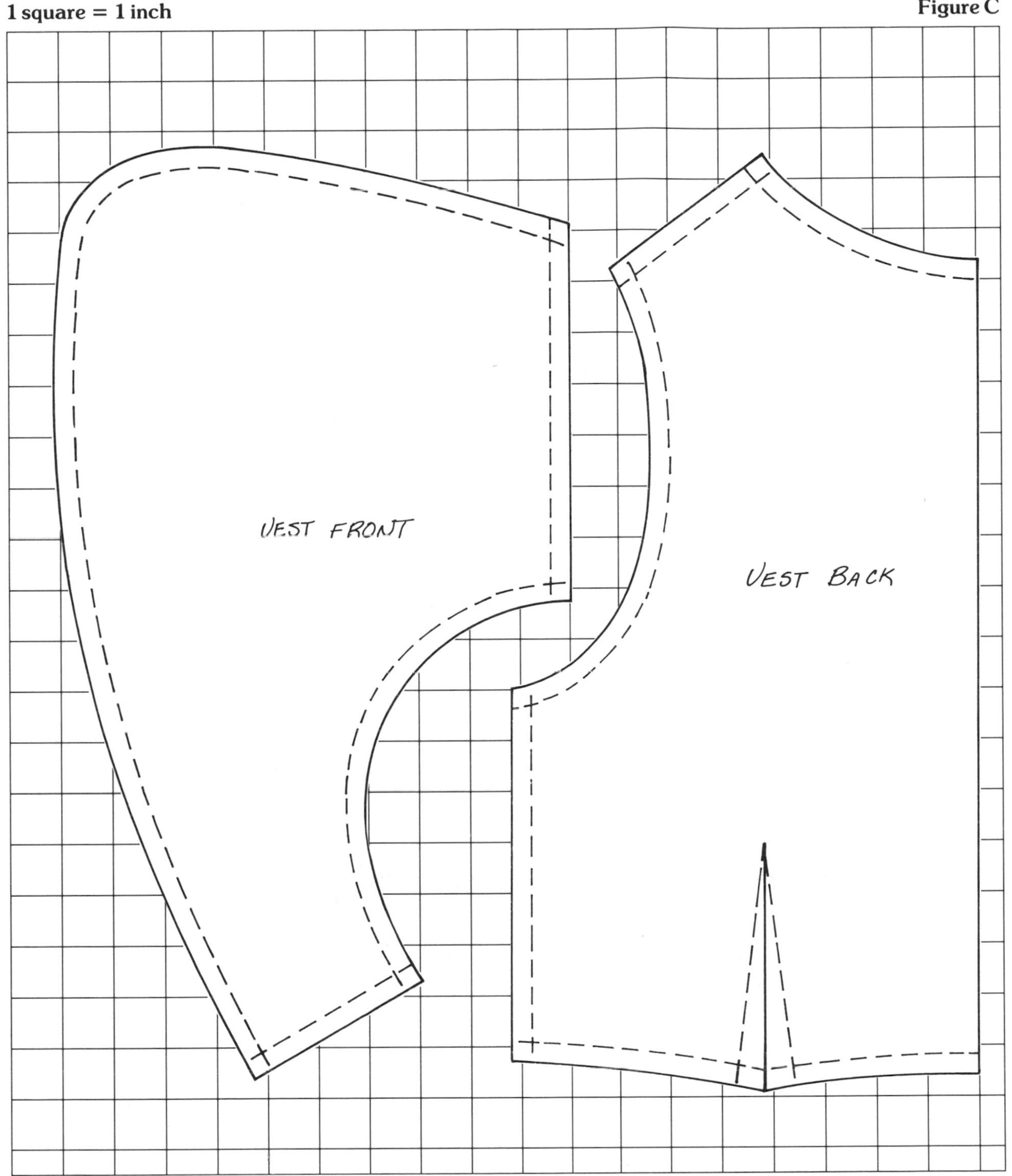

Figure D

Figure E 1 square = 1 inch

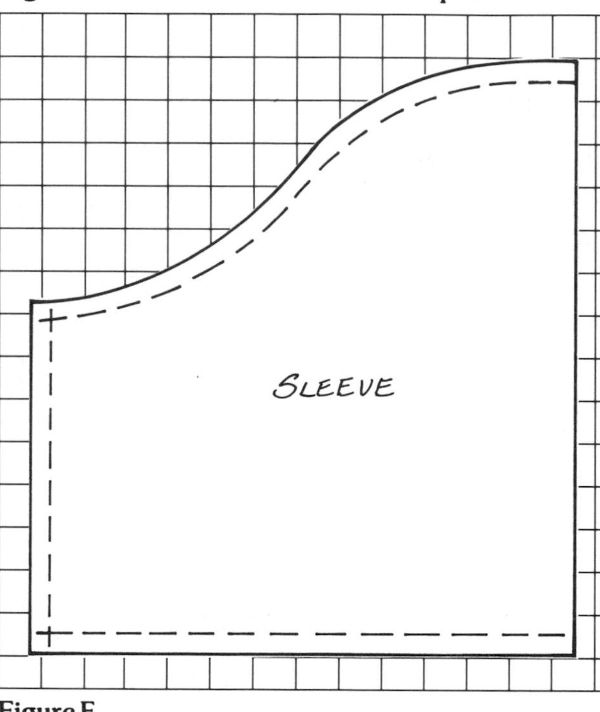

Figure F

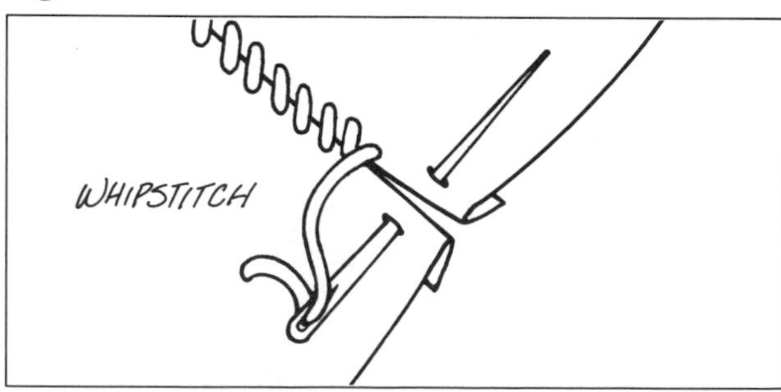

Figure G

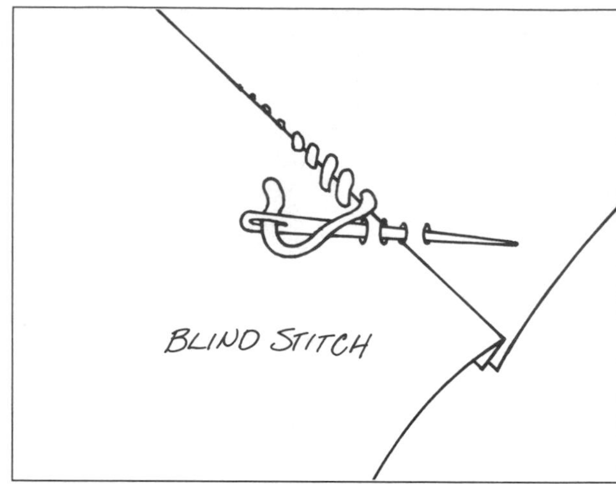

equal to the radius of the desired circle (half the diameter). Mark this point on the string. Secure the string to a piece of pattern paper by pinning through the marked point on the string, and then rotate the pencil around the secured point to draw the circular outline.

Machine Stitches

Topstitching is a final stitch done on the visible side of the fabric assembly or garment. Take care to make very straight lines of topstitching.

Basting may be done by hand or machine. For machine basting, set your stitch length selector to the longest stitch available. Most basting is simply a way to secure the fabric assembly temporarily, and normally is removed later, so use a thread color that contrasts with the fabric – you'll be able to see the basting easily when it comes time to remove it.

Zigzag stitching may be used to finish raw edges or to add decorative stitching lines. For appliques, use a closely spaced zigzag stitch.

Hand Stitches

Whipstitching joins two fabric pieces, catching an equal amount of fabric on each edge (**Figure F**). Each stitch is worked straight across, resulting in a diagonal stitch pattern on the visible side of the fabric.

Blind stitching (also called slipstitching) joins two fabric pieces so that the stitching is invisible on the right

Figure H

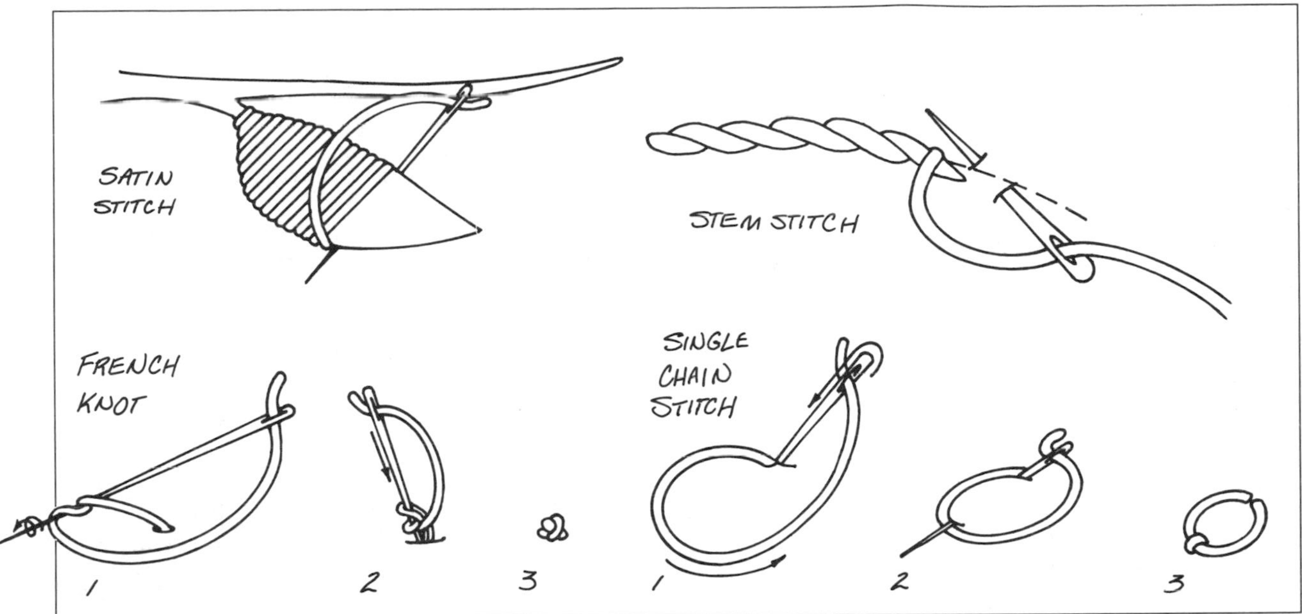

Figure I

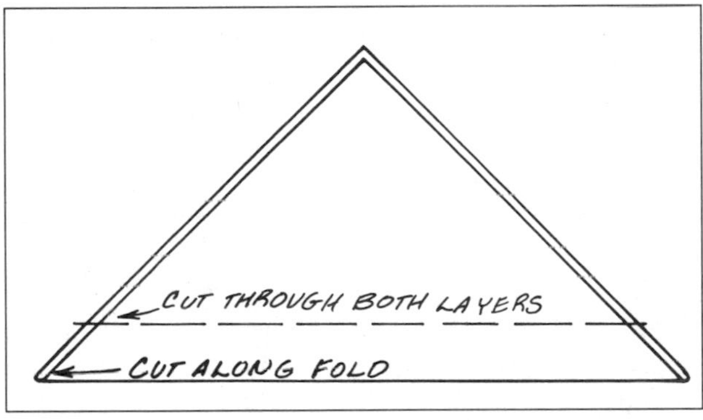

side of the assembly (**Figure G**). Insert the needle inside the folded edge of one fabric piece, and keep it inside the fold for the length of one stitch. Bring the needle out and take an invisible stitch inside the fold of the adjoining fabric piece.

Hand basting requires that you work a line of running stitches, each about ½ inch long, through the fabric assembly.

Embroidery Stitches

Cotton emboroidery thread is composed of six twisted strands, which can be separated. The fewer strands you use, the smaller the needle you need, the more stitches you will take, and the finer the finished work will look. Use an embroidery hoop to hold the fabric flat as you work.

Illustrations of several embroidery stitches are provided in **Figure H**. With a little practice even a beginner can produce stitches that are smooth and uniform. Press the completed embroidery on the wrong side of the fabric, using a steam iron.

Cutting

If you want your patchwork to look good, it's extremely important to cut the initial strips very straight. Use a rigid straightedge (not a flexible measuring tape) to draw the outlines before you cut. A slightly wavy edge will result in sloppy-looking patchwork.

Straight strips should be cut with the grain of the fabric. Bias strips are cut so that the grain runs diagonally. Use bias strips to bind curved edges and to make piping, because they are stretchy and will not pull and wrinkle the way straight-cut binding strips do. To cut bias strips, first cut a fabric square. Use a T-square to check that all corners of the square are precise 90-degree angles. Fold the square in half diagonally, and cut

Figure J

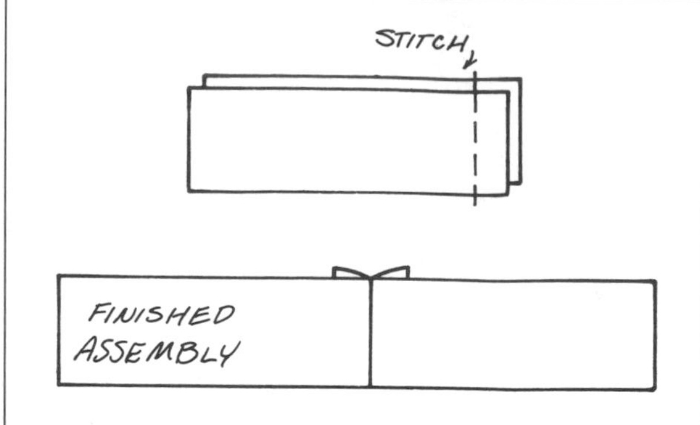

Figure K

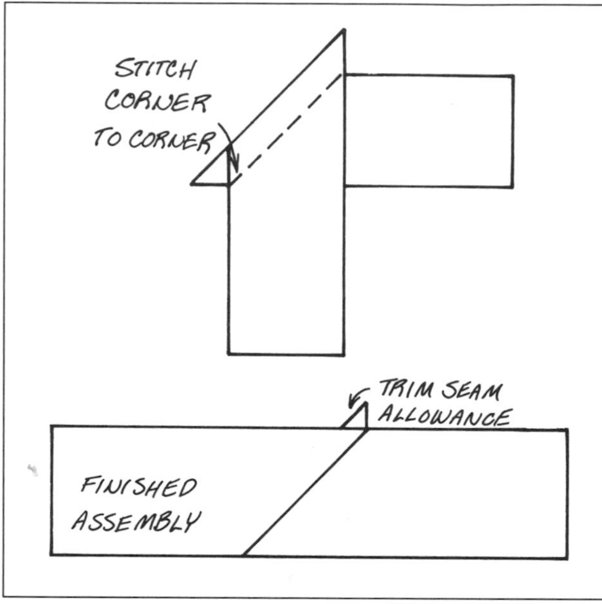

Figure L

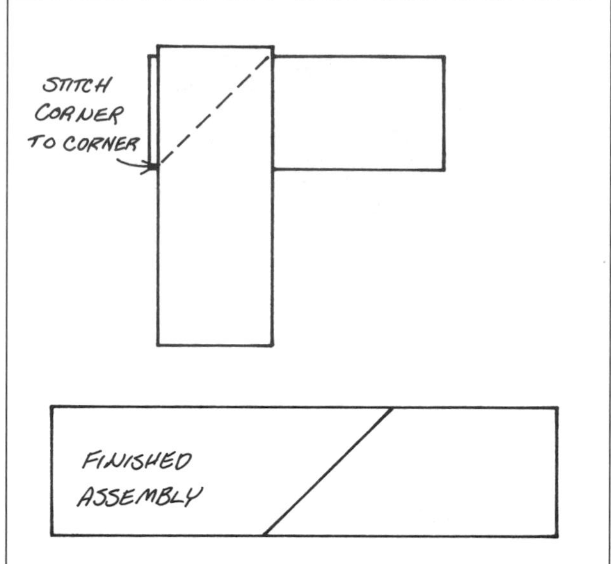

through both layers as shown in **Figure I**. The distance between the fold line and the second cutting line determines the width of the bias strip.

Piecing Strips

To make a long fabric strip, you may have to piece together several shorter strips end to end. To piece strips with square-cut ends, place two strips right sides together, align the ends, and stitch across the strips 1/4 or 1/2 inch from the aligned ends (**Figure J**). Press the seam allowances open, or press them both in the same direction. Open out the two strips, and continue to add additional strips in the same manner until the desired length is achieved.

To piece strips with angled ends, place two strips right sides together as shown in **Figure K**, adjusting the angled ends so that a straight seam stitched across them will begin and end at the corners formed by the overlapped ends. This creates an angled seam, as shown.

To piece square-cut strips and produce an angled seam, place the two strips right sides together at right angles, as shown in **Figure L**, and stitch from corner to corner.

Making Corded Piping

Piped seams and edges can provide additional color interest. To make your own, first measure the length of all seams and edges that you wish to pipe. For each seam and edge, cut and piece together bias strips to achieve the required length. Place one assembled bias strip wrong side up on a flat surface, and place a length of cord along the center of the strip. Fold the strip around the cord, aligning the two long edges of the strip, and then use a zipper foot attachment to stitch through both layers of fabric, as close as possible to the cord inside (**Figure M**).

Figure M

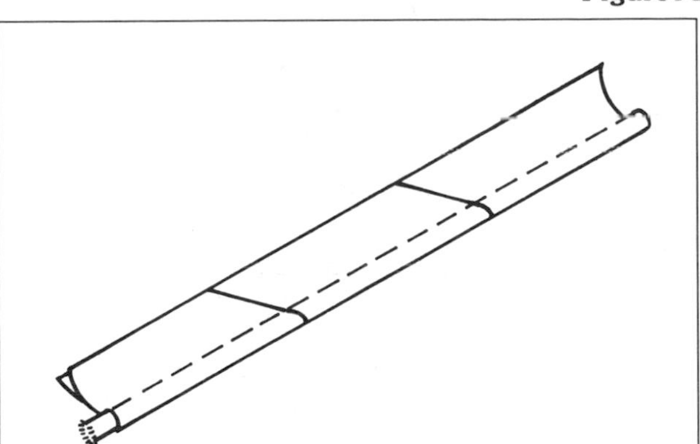

Gathering

Run two lines of basting stitches close to the edge to be gathered, leaving long tails of thread at both ends. Pull the tails of thread as you push the fabric toward the center. When the edge is gathered to the required length, tie off the threads at each end and adjust the gathers evenly along the edge.

Binding Raw Edges

If the fabric you are using is prone to ravel, you'll need to finish the edges of the seam allowances. The easiest way is to zigzag stitch over each raw edge. Another method requires binding tape, which can be purchased at a fabric store, or binding strips, which you can cut from fabric at home. To finish a seam allowance edge using binding tape, first press open one long edge of the tape. Place the tape right side down along the seam allowance (with the body of the garment folded out of the way), adjusting it so that the pressed-open fold line is as close as possible to the seam line. Stitch through the tape and allowance along the fold line (**Figure N**). Turn the tape outward over the stitching line, and whipstitch the pressed edge to the wrong side of the garment, as shown. Binding strips are used in the same manner, but instead of pressing open one edge to begin, you must press under the other long edge to finish up.

There are some projects in this book that employ binding strips to encase raw edges that are not seam allowances. These binding strips will show on the finished garment. To encase a raw edge, the strips should be cut at least 2 inches wide and 1 inch longer than the edge. Place the strip and the fabric assembly right sides together, aligning one long edge of the strip with the edge to be bound. Stitch ½ inch from the aligned edges. Turn the strip outward over the stitching line, press the seam allowances toward the strip, and press a ½-inch allowance to the wrong side of the strip along the free long edge. Fold the strip in half lengthwise, wrong sides

Figure N

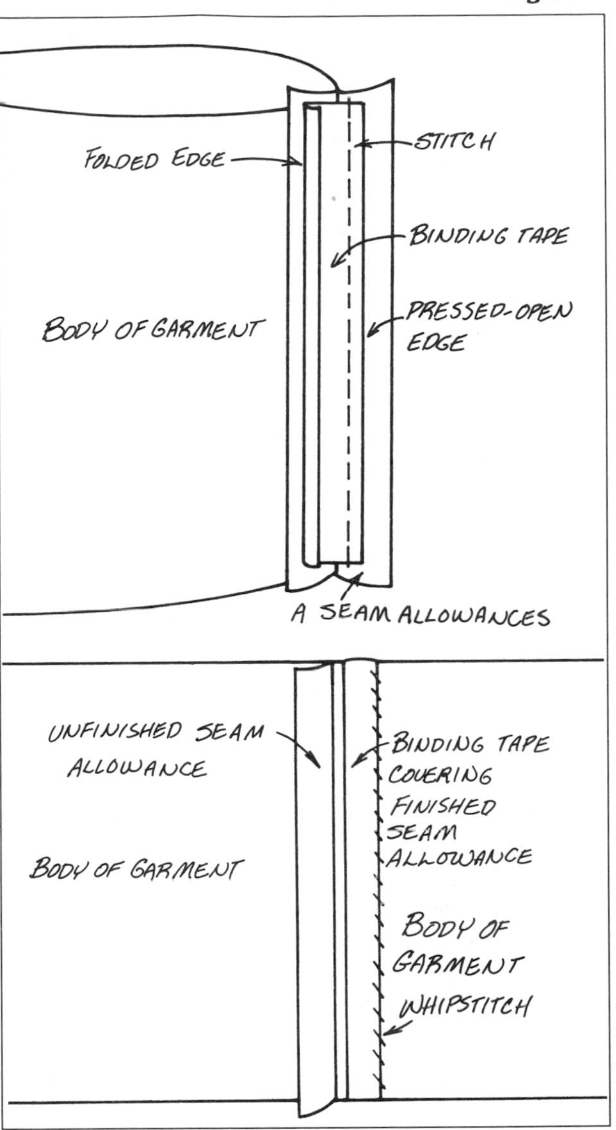

together, so that it encases the raw fabric edge, and whipstitch the pressed edge to the wrong side of the fabric assembly.

The ends of this type of binding may be finished in one of two ways: If they will be covered by another binding strip along an adjacent edge, or if they will be sewn into a seam, simply trim the ends of the binding strip even with the edges of the fabric assembly. If the ends will show, the strip should be sewn to the fabric assembly in a slightly different manner. Begin by placing the strip and fabric assembly right sides together. Stitch ½ inch from the aligned edges. Turn the strip outward and press a ½-inch allowance to the wrong side of the strip along the free long edge. Now fold the strip in half lengthwise, placing *right* sides together, and stitch across each end just outside the edge of the fabric assembly. Trim the end seam allowances and turn the strip right side out so that it encases the edge of the fabric assembly. Whipstitch the pressed edge of the strip to the wrong side of the fabric assembly.

Patchwork and Quilting

Many of the patchwork assemblies in this book are Seminole patchwork. Each individual project plan contains specific instructions. Some general information is presented here.

Most Seminole patchwork consists of variously colored fabric strips, which are first sewn together side by side. Place two strips right sides together and align one long edge of one strip with one long edge of the other. If the instructions specify that the ends should be offset, adjust them so that they are offset by the specified distance, as shown in **Figure O**. Stitch a normal seam (usually ¼ inch wide for patchwork) along the aligned long edges, as shown. Open out the two strips and press both of the seam allowances in one direction.

When you have sewn together the specified number of strips, cut across the assembly to create shorter strips, each consisting of all colors in the original assembly. The instructions will specify whether you should cut straight across the strips or at an angle. The shorter strips are then sewn together end to end in the same manner as you would piece single strips; or they are sewn together side by side, usually with ends offset, in the same manner as you would sew together single strips side by side.

Figure O

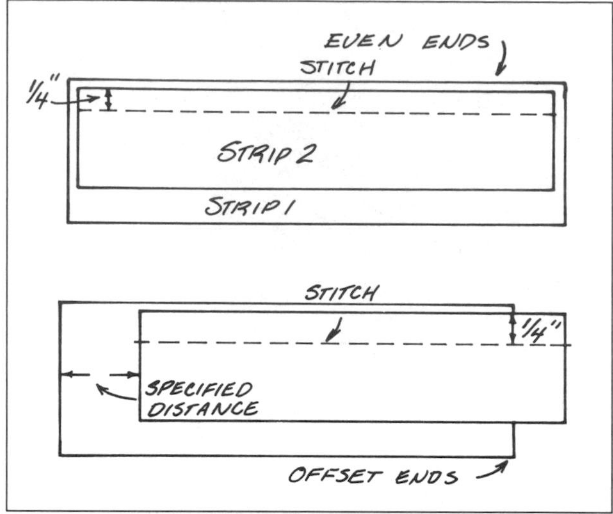

String-quilting is a method of assembling strips side by side. It can be done by sewing them together as specified above, or it can be done on a piece of backing fabric. The latter is recommended when you must sew together lots of narrow strips. There are two different methods for string-quilting on backing fabric.

Method 1 – Pin the first strip right side up on the backing fabric. Place the next strip right side down on top of the first one, aligning one long edge of the second strip with one long edge of the first, and stitch the seam ¼ inch from the aligned edges (diagram #1, **Figure P**). Turn the second strip right side up, folding it along the stitching line, and press (diagram #2, **Figure P**). Continue adding strips in this manner until all are in place.

Method 2 – Do you find it difficult to produce a perfectly straight stitching line? If so, use this method: Pin the first strip right side up on the backing fabric. Mark a straight stitching line ¼ inch from the long edge that will be joined to the second strip, and carefully stitch along the marked line. Place the second strip right side down on top, aligning the edges, and pin it in place from the wrong side of the backing fabric. Turn the assembly wrong side up, and use the existing line of stitches as a guide to stitch through all thicknesses. This will give you a perfectly straight seam. Remove the pins

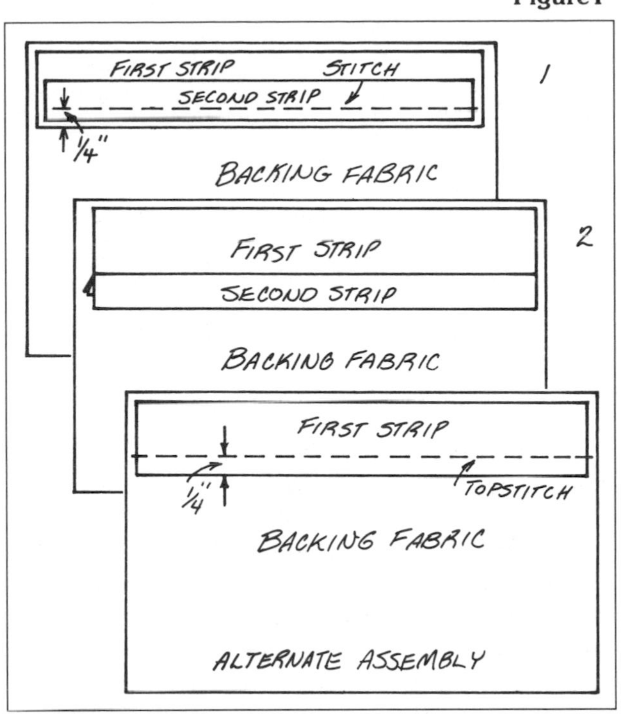

Figure P

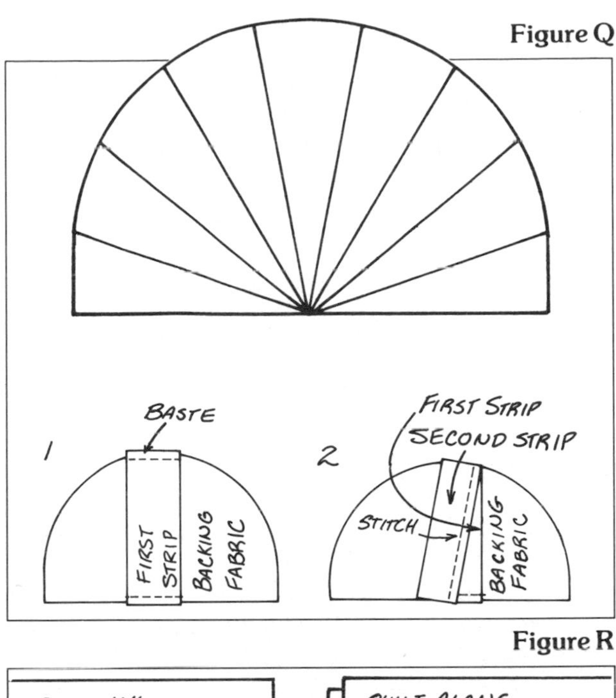

Figure Q

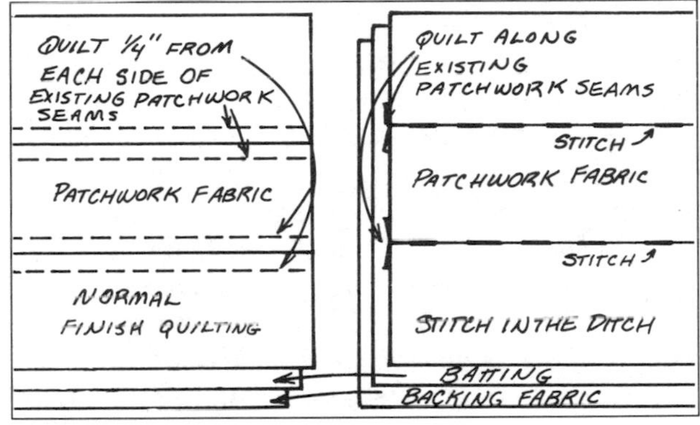

Figure R

and turn the assembly right side up. Turn the second strip right side up, folding it along the stitching line, and your assembly should look just like the one shown in diagram #2, **Figure P**. Continue to add strips in this manner, and all of your seam lines will be straight.

Fan-quilting is very much like string-quilting, but it produces a design like the one shown in **Figure Q**. Fan-quilting should be done on backing fabric.

Place the first strip right side up on the backing fabric as shown in diagram #1, **Figure Q**, and baste across each end. Place the second strip right side down on top, aligning the long right-hand edge of the second strip with the long right-hand edge of the first strip. Hold the upper right-hand corner of the second strip in place, and move the lower end to the left. Pin the second strip in place and stitch through all thicknesses, 1/4 inch from the right-hand edge of the second strip (diagram #2, **Figure Q**). Turn the second strip right side up, folding it along the stitching line, and press.

Continue to add strips in this manner, working from the second strip down to the bottom of the backing fabric; then repeat the same procedures to fill in the area to the left of the first strip. You can use the same pre-stitching technique as the one used for string-quilting, if you have trouble producing straight seams.

Finish quilting describes any method of quilting together the outer patchwork fabric, a batting layer, and a layer of backing fabric. It can be done by hand or machine, but either way, the stitches should be short. Hand quilting stitches should be about 1/8 inch long. Normal finish quilting involves stitching 1/8 or 1/4 inch from each side of each existing patchwork seam line. **"Stitch in the ditch"** finish quilting involves quilting directly along each existing patchwork seamline. Both are illustrated in **Figure R**.

About the Family...

The Family Workshop, a one-of-a-kind creative idea company, is located in Bixby, Oklahoma. The company specializes in the field of how-to, with subjects ranging from fabric crafts and woodworking to home improvement, photography, and computers.

The Family Workshop originated, quite literally, on the Baldwins' front porch. Ed and Stevie, long-time hobbyists and experts in the do-it-yourself field, began writing a newspaper column called "Makin' Things." Since 1977, the family has grown to include other craftspersons, woodworkers, artists, and editors, who have helped provide the public with do-it-yourself tips, pointers, and projects through television programs, syndicated columns, quarterly newsletters, and a series of books for a number of major publishing houses.

Ed and Stevie, nationally known and respected how-to newspaper columnists, appeared in over 100 segments of a TV series that provided viewers time- and money-saving ideas for making things at home.

This energetic couple also has done a number of product promotions for major companies in the do-it-yourself field, as well as appearing in various TV commercials. They have been featured in training films and demonstrations for several different organizations.

Since the birth of the company, the Baldwins and their staff have authored and produced more than a dozen how-to books. These publications include subjects such as family computers, furniture building, and making projects from fabric scraps. Impressively, nine of the books have been either main, featured alternate, or alternate selections for either the Better Homes & Gardens or Popular Science book clubs.

The Family Workshop currently produces three syndicated weekly newspaper columns. The original craft-oriented column, "Makin' Things," was first written and produced in 1975. Since that time, Ed and Stevie and their staff have created two additional columns: "The Woodwright," and "Kid's Stuff." The three columns appear weekly in publications with a combined readership of over 26 million. "Classified Crafts," their most recent newspaper service, was started in 1983. The Family Workshop's newspaper features run in more than 500 daily and weekly newspapers across the country, with more than 750 appearances per week.